Evaluating and Treating
Adult Children of
Alcoholics

EVALUATING AND TREATING ADULT CHILDREN OF ALCOHOLICS

VOLUME ONE: EVALUATION

Timmen L. Cermak, M.D.

Edited by Pamela Espeland

A Johnson Institute Book
Professional Series
Minneapolis

A JOHNSON INSTITUTE PROFESSIONAL SERIES BOOK

Published by the Johnson Institute
7151 Metro Blvd., Suite 250
Minneapolis MN 55439-2122
(612) 944-0511

Library of Congress Cataloging-in-Publication Data

Cermak, Timmen L.
    Evaluating and treating adult children of alcoholics /
Timmen L. Cermak.
        p. cm. — (Professional series)
    Includes bibliographical references and indexes.
    Contents: v. 1. Evaluation — v. 2. Treatment.
    ISBN 0-935908-64-1 (v. 1) : $21.95 — ISBN 0-935908-66-8 (v. 2) : $21.95
        1. Adult children of alcoholics—Mental health.   2. Psychotherapy.
I. Title.   II. Series: Professional series (Minneapolis, Minn.)
RC569.5.A29C47   1990
616.86′1—dc20   90-5057
                                                                    CIP

ISBN 0-935908-64-1

PRINTED IN THE UNITED STATES OF AMERICA

10   9   8   7   6   5   4   3   2   1

For
Mary, Elizabeth, and Katherine

CONTENTS

ACKNOWLEDGMENTS

It is impossible to acknowledge all the people who have been my teachers. There are those whom I have met, those whom I have heard speak, and those whom I have only read. There are those who considered themselves my teachers, and those who considered themselves my peers, students, clients, friends, relatives, and probably even my enemies. There are certainly those to whom I have already expressed appreciation, and those to whom I have not. To you all, I owe a debt of gratitude for teaching me most of what is written in this book. At the same time, I accept full responsibility for all that I have chosen to write, and for what I have still failed to understand.

There are many who have supported my writing of this book. Carole Remboldt, of the Johnson Institute, is a master at wading through the morass of my first manuscripts and discovering what value lies hidden within. Her endurance deserves to be recognized. Her editorial comments and pleas for clarity and simplicity have also contributed immensely to my work. The text was then masterfully edited by Pamela Espeland, who is largely responsible for whatever ease of reading may exist.

I am indebted to the staff at Genesis Psychotherapy and Training Center (San Francisco) who, by their refusal to accept anything simply because I said it, have continually pressed me to develop my thinking. Thank you, Mary Brand Cermak, M.F.C.C., Walter Beckman, Ph.D., Marcia Bradley, M.F.C.C., Roger Lake,

M.F.C.C., Debra Muse, Psy.D., Lisa Rood, L.C.S.W., and Jacques Rutzky, M.F.C.C. Administrative help at Genesis has always been professionally provided by Marilyn Meshak Herczog and Gloria Ruiz.

Without support on the homefront, little of value would happen professionally; and little professionally would be of value. To my wife and colleague, Mary, I express special appreciation. And to my daughters, Elizabeth and Katherine, I say, "Thanks for not understanding how any of this could be more important than getting down on the floor and playing."

EDITOR'S NOTE ON LANGUAGE AND ABBREVIATIONS

The term "alcohol and other drugs" is used throughout this book to emphasize that alcohol *is* a drug, just like cocaine, marijuana, valium, uppers, downers, or any other mind-altering drug. Too often, people talk about "alcohol or drugs" or "alcohol and drugs" as if alcohol were somehow different from drugs and in a category by itself. The consequences of addiction are essentially the same for all these mind-altering drugs, and the need to find ways to prevent or intervene with their use is equally as urgent.

The term "chemical dependence" is used because it covers addiction to all these mind-altering drugs, and because it's short and simple.

Also for reasons of brevity and simplicity, these abbreviations are used:

- "AA" refers to Alcoholics Anonymous.
- "ACA" refers specifically to adult children of alcoholics, those beyond the teen years.
- "Adolescent COA" refers to COAs in their teen years.
- "CD" refers to chemical dependence.
- "COA" (children of alcoholics) refers to all offspring of alcoholics, of any age. It is the most general category.
- "FAS" refers to Fetal Alcohol Syndrome.
- "NA" refers to Narcotics Anonymous.
- "NACoA" refers to the National Association for Children of Alcoholics.

- "PT" refers to psychotherapy.
- "PTSD" refers to Post-Traumatic Stress Disorder.
- "Young COA" refers to COAs from birth to adolescence.

VOLUME ONE:
EVALUATION

INTRODUCTION

Suddenly, it seems, everyone is interested in children of alcoholics (COAs). To those of us who have worked to bring this population into the public eye, this represents a mixed blessing. On the one hand, it's gratifying to see the public recognize what has long been under everyone's nose, yet completely overlooked by all but a few. On the other, such an explosion of interest in the subject does have a downside.

Since the 1980s, when public awareness of COAs first sparked and caught hold with breathtaking speed, many elements of faddishness have been mixed in with the very substantial events occurring within the chemical dependence (CD) field, the general mental health field, and the self-help programs at the grassroots level. It has become increasingly difficult to sort the meaningful information from the less meaningful and even misleading.

Evaluating and Treating Adult Children of Alcoholics has been motivated by the need for a clear, integrated approach to understanding and helping over 28 million Americans[1]—men and women whose lives have been deeply affected by a parent's chemical dependence. It is based on twelve years of firsthand experience treating COAs. In that time, I have learned that treating clients who have grown up in alcoholic homes is both challenging and professionally satisfying, and that working to understand the nature and origins of adult problems rooted in

3

childhood experiences is intellectually rewarding. Few populations provide a better opportunity to explore the many ways in which "the child is father of the man."

The movement to focus attention on persons who grew up with alcoholic parents is not entirely new. During England's early 18th century Gin Epidemic, artists such as William Hogarth recorded the havoc parental drunkenness created within families. His famous "Gin Lane" shows an infant falling from a drunken woman's arms to its death. Other paintings from the same era picture facial deformities in children which we now realize result from Fetal Alcohol Syndrome (FAS).

Later, in the United States, much of the Temperance Movement's emotional intensity came from those who spoke out on behalf of "the children of inebriates," and it was known that COAs were more likely to come in contact with the juvenile justice system. Around the turn of the century, Massachusetts passed the first bill in the United States to mandate health education in public schools, with its primary purpose being to teach about alcoholism. And a popular best seller of the period, *Ten Nights in a Barroom*, told of how a child came to murder his alcoholic father.

Why did this early interest founder and become unfashionable? Perhaps because Prohibition was pronounced a failure and repealed. Whatever the reasons, it has been a long, slow process for COAs to come back into the spotlight.

A critical part of this process has been our society's gradual acceptance that child abuse (physical, emotional, and sexual) is not just an ugly rumor but an everyday reality. In the 1960s, when a few voices first described battered children, they were met with pervasive denial. Over the next two decades, this denial was effectively dismantled, and today we have child protection services in nearly every community—safety nets to catch the most overtly abused children.

Those of us now championing the rights of COAs stand on the shoulders of these early child-abuse pioneers. Without their successes, I doubt that COAs would have been accepted so quickly as a distinct population with special problems.

There are two main reasons for today's widespread interest in COAs: the growth of self-help programs for adult children of alcoholics (ACAs), based on the original Alcoholics Anonymous (AA) framework, and the development of an autonomous CD field. In the United States, major advances in treating alcoholics occurred in spite of (or because of) the benign neglect of the medical establishment. Although AA and the many programs it has spawned arose with the help of a physician, it drew its inspiration and energy from the general public. And it was only when the treatment of alcoholism and other drug addictions budded off from traditional psychiatric practice that effective treatment became generally available.

Chemical dependence workers were freed from decades of theoretical traditions which were not producing results with alcoholics. The CD field became intensely pragmatic, guided by empirical experience rather than theoretical principles. It aligned closely with AA, both because of AA's effectiveness and because increasing numbers of CD workers were themselves recovering alcoholics.

The founders of AA (1935) were aware from the outset that an individual's alcoholism affects his or her spouse and children. This awareness helped give rise to Al-Anon (1951) for spouses and Alateen (1957) for teenage children. But it did not affect treatment programs until the 1960s, when family systems theorists entered the picture. During the 1970s, the concept of alcoholism as a "family disease" led to the establishment of family education programs in treatment centers throughout the country. In most cases, these were directed toward spouses; rarely was age-appropriate education or treatment provided for young COAs. But the scene was being set for today's events. It soon became impossible for workers within the CD field to open the issue of family treatment without sensing the plight of youngsters locked within unhealthy family environments.

It is tempting to criticize the general mental health field, especially those individuals most directly involved with studying child development, for having kept silent about the obviously debilitating effects of growing up in an alcoholic home. By focusing on this small group of researchers and clinicians, however, we miss the point that society as a whole has been and still is ambivalent about the use of alcohol, turning a blind eye to the damage it does to our neighbors, entertainers, athletes, and coworkers, not to mention our families and ourselves. This ambivalence stems in part from the fact that most people who drink do not appear to be adversely affected, and is reinforced by fear that efforts to raise awareness of the dangers involved with alcohol abuse run the risk of being denigrated as neo-prohibitionist.

Within the CD field today, the problems of COAs (both young and adult) have become mainstream. COAs are being taken very seriously, if for no other reason than that they represent the largest identifiable pool of tomorrow's alcoholics and other drug addicts. Roughly fifty percent of all people being treated for chemical dependence are themselves children of alcoholics. Clearly COAs and alcoholics are populations with extensive overlap; there is no room for an "us versus them" approach. The CD field is committed to serving COAs. All it needs are enough resources and expertise.

Individual therapists within the general mental health field also seem to be discovering the value of focusing attention on COAs. Their professional organizations and academic hierarchy, however, still tend to dismiss COA issues as pop psychology. The subject is intensely popular on the grassroots level, and publications for and about COAs are largely directed toward the lay public and are commercial best sellers—evidence, in the professionals' view, that this is a phenomenon produced by effective marketing and public gullibility. Meanwhile, practicing clinicians are becoming increasingly aware that they have been treating ACAs without knowing it. In many cases, a majority of a therapist's caseload turns out to be ACAs. As more clients self-identify with the issues, fewer therapists can afford to remain uninformed.

How should therapists be trained to treat ACAs? At the moment, neither the CD field nor the general mental health field provides optimal training. The emergence of COAs as an identifiable population demands that these two fields no longer remain separate. It is time to insist on expertise within both fields. The crossover of therapists and curriculum will benefit everyone, even as it challenges CD and mental health workers intellectually and in terms of traditional turf issues.

For over a decade, I have had the opportunity to work with alcoholics and adults who grew up in alcoholic homes. My psychiatric training, and my training within the CD field, have both been called on in full. The more I learn from my psychotherapy clients about how difficult childhood experiences translate into adult problems, the more this enhances my grasp of psychodynamics, child development, and the disease of chemical dependence. My intellectual capacities are insufficient to fathom within my lifetime all the lessons to be learned from exploring the basic human truths that COAs' lives lay bare. This book summarizes my understanding at this point in time. I hope that it will benefit other clinicians, and stimulate interest in academicians and researchers who have not yet been introduced to the topic.

There is a popular saying in the medical field: "If you understood everything about alcoholism, you would know the whole of medicine." A parallel axiom applies to COAs: "If you understood everything about the children of alcoholics, you would know the whole of psychology." Both of these sayings gain their truth from the widely diverse symptoms seen in both alcoholics and COAs, as well as the pervasiveness with which each affects a person's life. With an estimated 28 million COAs of all ages, this population is bound to be heterogeneous. Childhood with an alcoholic parent affects different people in different ways, but the fact that it *does* affect them is inevitable. We all beg, borrow, and steal much of who we are from our early environment. The language we speak, the accent we speak in, our manners, mannerisms, values, myths, and expectations all come from (or are in reaction to) the extended family we grew up in. When that family is affected by chemical dependence, this becomes the backdrop against which we live our lives. Sometimes the effects are negative, sometimes they are positive, most often they are neither—they simply are part of our history. Without knowing that history, we cannot know ourselves.

The faddish nature of treating COAs comes in part from the tendency of therapists to regard the label as a diagnosis. This book outlines the framework we have developed at Genesis Psychotherapy and Training Center for fully evaluating ACA clients and developing individualized treatment plans. The Genesis framework takes advantage of what we believe is of value in the label, but keeps us from falling into simplistic thinking. A full *psychological evaluation of all ACA clients is necessary.* It is important for therapists to stop forgetting this in their haste to respond to the needs of COAs, their impulse to dip into a ready market to fill their practice, or their unwillingness or inability to deal with unresolved personal issues that blind them to the complexities of working with this population.

It is time for increased professional rigor in our approach to treating COAs. Speaking for myself, I know that I must treat each individual client as a new story. My expertise in psychiatry and chemical dependence has attuned my ear to a few common refrains in that story, but that doesn't mean I can stop listening. The day I stop listening is the day I add to the wounds my clients bring me for healing.

Finally, it should be self-evident that the subject matter at hand is far too vast to be covered in a single work. Because we are at an early stage in our understanding of COAs, I ask the reader to tolerate the folly of my trying to cover as much as I do.

Timmen L. Cermak
September 1990

1

THE IMPORTANCE OF EVALUATION AND DIAGNOSIS

There are many ways to heal mental disorders. The process of psychotherapy, with its essential components of accurate evaluation and diagnosis, is one of the more powerful approaches. When evaluation and diagnosis are done properly, they become an integral part of treatment by individualizing the approach to a client's specific needs. When they are ignored, therapeutic efforts may dissolve into disorderly guesswork. Even when the guesswork is correct—as it often can be, with highly intuitive therapists—the craft of psychotherapy cannot be effectively taught without a diagnostic framework for organizing one's perceptions and treatment plans.

PROS AND CONS OF DIAGNOSIS

Not everyone agrees that diagnosis is important to therapy. Some therapists have received inadequate training in this area; others have become sloppy or overwhelmed by the task. And at least three groups traditionally have an aversion to diagnosis: social activists, members of the CD community, and those associated with the human potential movement and transpersonal psychology.

Starting in the 1960s, social activists correctly pointed out that diagnostic labels can have negative consequences when used punitively or with cultural bias. A few even claimed that such labels can create mental illness. While these arguments caution us against the potential misuse of diagnosis, they overlook the critical role diagnosis plays in helping us to recognize patterns of human behavior, especially those that provide us with clues about future behavior (prognosis). Such patterns do exist. Diagnostic systems give us the tools we need to see them, interpret them, and communicate what we know about them.

Some members of the CD community cite the frequent misdiagnosis of alcoholism as a reason not to use psychiatric diagnoses. They have a legitimate complaint. Countless alcoholics have undergone treatment for depression and even schizophrenia, sometimes for decades, while their primary disease has gone unattended to. Once the drinking stopped, so did the depressive symptoms or bizarre behavior. Therapists without training in chemical dependence often are unaware that it's absurd to try to establish a meaningful psychiatric diagnosis for any individual who is actively alcoholic or in the first few months of sobriety. But this doesn't mean that diagnosis itself is at fault.

Many schools associated with the human potential movement and transpersonal psychology believe that clients should be allowed to set their own treatment agendas. They further maintain that therapists should work toward relationships that are more peer-oriented than hierarchical, and take a here-and-now stance. All this may become more difficult once diagnostic conclusions have been reached, but it doesn't make the diagnostic process less necessary. The reality is that every therapist operates with a best guess, consciously held or not, about what is troubling or blocking a client. Diagnosis brings this best guess into awareness, sharpening and clarifying it. In the absence of diagnosis, it still affects the therapy through the therapist's unconscious behavior.

THE GENESIS MODEL: SIX AXES
FOR EVALUATING ACAs

While diagnosis usually requires more than a single encounter with a client, evaluation begins with the first interview—or before, with the first telephone contact. Anything that gives you an initial impression of a client should enter in, even including a period of "telephone tag." (Do the client's messages begin sounding more irritable, desperate, apologetic? Or do the requests for you to return the call remain consistent in quality?)

Evaluation helps you decide which therapeutic approaches are most likely to help the client. Before you can make this decision, you need a clear idea of what you think is causing the client's problems. This will come from what you bring to the therapeutic setting, as well as what the client brings. A thorough evaluation rests upon being aware of the internal set with which you approach the client—your own attitudes toward alcoholics and ACAs, the theoretical framework that guides your work, your identity as a therapist, the ways you market yourself—since these affect how you will see the client's problems.

At Genesis, we use six specific categories for evaluating ACAs, in addition to the standard demographic and historical data needed for any psychotherapy client. (Mental status exams are added when a need is indicated, and do not differ from standard procedures for conducting psychological evaluations.) Any case presentation is expected to speak directly to each of these six categories, or the evaluation is considered incomplete.

Readers familiar with Theodore Millon's framework for understanding the nature and causes of personality disorders, described in *Disorders of Personality: DSM-III, Axis II*,[1] may recognize the parallel between our first four evaluation axes, described below, and Millon's assertion that the origin of personality disorders lies in a combination of these factors:

- Temperament (i.e., Biology)
- Pathologic Learning, from
  —events that create intense anxiety
  —emotionally neutral models of behavior that reinforce coping strategies that are deleterious when generalized to settings for which they are unsuitable
  —insufficient experiences requisite to learning adaptive behaviors.

The parallel is intentional and reflects our belief that a family environment disrupted by chemical dependence is fertile ground for the development of personality disorders.

Corresponding to Millon's "temperament" is our axis of biology/genetics, which focuses on the propensity toward alcoholism inherited by 25% of COAs. His "events that create intense anxiety" we have renamed "the wound." His "emotionally neutral models of behavior" are represented by our concept of "poor woundcare," or co-dependence. "Insufficient experiences requisite to learning adaptive behaviors" is our fourth axis, "underlearning."

Biology/Genetics

Is alcoholism really a disease? For many people, this is still an open question, although the CD field generally tries to close debate on it. There has been little dispassionate exploration of the specific ways in which alcoholism conforms to our current concept of disease. What we *do* know is that alcoholism contains an inheritable component.

The mere fact that a client has an alcoholic parent is enough to justify a full alcohol and drug history. It is the therapist's responsibility to be aware of the COA's increased risk for chemical dependence; to be able to recognize early, often subtle problem signs; and to explore this issue with clients in a way that teaches at the same time it gathers information.

The Wound

Children in alcoholic families experience an extraordinarily high level of stress. Sometimes the causes are overt, such as physical abuse, and can be easily pointed to years later. At other times they are covert, such as the daily tension of living in a family that energetically avoids acknowledging the anger and sadness everyone feels. Either way, stress can leave its mark—perhaps as a layer of defensive armor that becomes a lifelong character trait, or as anxiety that comes when the level of stress overwhelms one's defenses.

The best studied example of what happens when one is overwhelmed by stress involves veterans of armed combat. Historically referred to as "soldier's heart," "shell shock," "combat fatigue," and "war neurosis," this condition is now called Post-Traumatic Stress Disorder (PTSD). Full-blown PTSD exists in some ACAs, but not in the majority. However, some elements of PTSD are found in enough ACAs that it is necessary to evaluate the degree to which each individual client is suffering from stress-induced phenomena that originated in childhood. The conclusions of this evaluation are extremely important in developing effective treatment plans.

Poor Woundcare

The scar left by any wound depends as much on the care given the wound as on the depth of the wound itself. Consider two children who both get exactly the same cut. The first child's cut is immediately washed and disinfected, while the second child's cut is neglected. After a week, the first child's wound is knitting together nicely, with little scarring likely. But the edges of the second child's wound are swollen and infected, with the probability of a permanent scar.

The same holds true for psychological wounds. For example, sexual or physical abuse has a very real traumatic effect on a child, but the extent of emotional scarring depends as much on whether the child suffers in silence while the family denies that the abuse occurs. The lack of an adult to listen to and validate the child's feelings can do as much damage as the abuse itself. The quality of woundcare is critical.

COAs grow up denying the stresses of their dysfunctional families. Directly and indirectly, they are told not to talk about them, and to rise above them as a sign of virtue and maturity. Denial becomes a coping strategy that only makes things worse. People in denial stay in harmful environments long past the point where their health is adversely affected.

The term "co-dependence" arose within the CD field to describe the pattern of ineffective coping strategies seen in alcoholic families—strategies which contribute to very poor wound-care. Today co-dependence has expanded to refer both to the kinds of interactions which govern alcoholic family systems, and to the way family members see themselves and interact with others outside the family.

Although the CD field does not usually deal with character diagnoses, the concept of co-dependence clearly has much in common with many traditional personality disorders. Like them, co-dependence is a pervasive, underlying stance toward the self and others which is expressed in every attitude and action. While co-dependence is not restricted to alcoholic families (it exists throughout the range of family dysfunctions), it somehow achieves its quintessential form in this setting. The co-dependent's psychological stance is virtually indistinguishable from that of an alcoholic during active stages of addiction.

It is important to understand that co-dependence constitutes far more than dysfunctional coping strategies. It is an entire character structure, of which these strategies are simply overt expressions. Every ACA must be assessed for the intensity and rigidity of co-dependent personality traits. This assessment is the topic of Chapter 4.

Underlearning

Abnormal behavior can result from excessive levels of stress, or from dysfunctional coping strategies. It can also result from insufficient exposure to normal behavior—what we call underlearning. When one grows up without mature adult role models and healthy family dynamics, there are things one never learns.

ACAs commonly complain that they "don't know what's normal." This can be a form of resistance to exploration and change, or it can be a sign of underlearning. The therapeutic approach should differ depending on which is being encountered, resistance or underlearning. This assessment is the topic of Chapter 5.

Deficits from underlearning are found at the cognitive, emotional, and identity levels. At the cognitive level, a client's knowledge base may contain random "empty categories"—gaps in what he knows about the world which most people his age would have filled naturally in the course of growing up in our society. At the emotional level, a client's experiential base may be incomplete; certain feelings generally shared throughout our culture may never be shared in highly chaotic families. At the identity level, developmental tasks necessary for maturation may never have been encountered, leading to an impoverished sense of self.

Once a client is exposed to models of healthy behavior and self-image, cognitive and emotional deficits can be reversed, often remarkably quickly. Identity deficits usually require more intensive psychotherapy to correct.

Dual Diagnosis

The system of diagnosis set forth by DSM-III-R[2] makes it clear that mental disorders can stem from more than one source. For therapists, this translates into two important caveats: First, *ACA and COA are labels, not diagnoses*. Second, diagnoses directly related to the experience of growing up in an alcoholic family do not preclude concurrent diagnoses with no special reference to being a COA.

COAs can also be schizophrenic, manic depressive, or actively borderline, for example. This is just one reason why therapists who treat ACAs must call on all of their insight and skill. For some clients, dealing with "ACA issues" only makes things worse. The therapist can't assume that resolving these issues is a universal cure-all. Not everyone will benefit from exploring their experience within an alcoholic home and how it continues to affect their present lives. And almost no one will achieve perfect harmony only by facing these issues.

When I emphasize that ACA and COA are labels, not diagnoses, I mean that they should be used as tools when appropriate, but that the entire context of a person's life must be evaluated before one can determine this appropriateness. There is no excuse for exposing well-compensated schizophrenics or active borderlines to intense, unstructured, cathartic experiences just because they also happen to be COAs. Therapists have a responsibility to formulate their treatment plans on the basis of thorough evaluations and accurate diagnosis. At Genesis, we safeguard against oversimplification by including dual diagnosis as one of the six axes in our evaluation framework.

Stage of Recovery

There are many distinctions between chemical dependence (CD) and psychotherapy (PT) treatment models. One of the most important involves the concept of recovery.

The CD model focuses on recovery; PT models focus on disease. Psychotherapists tend to see recovery as the ebbing of symptoms; CD workers view it as an orderly addition of healthy skills and perspectives. Of course, CD workers are concerned with treating one disease—alcoholism—as opposed to the broad range of mental disorders psychotherapists address. In the CD model, recovery proceeds in recognizable stages, allowing therapists to continually evaluate whether clients are making enough of the right kind of progress to avoid falling back into their disease.

This emphasis on the emergence and protection of health places the CD field closer to the human potential movement than many psychotherapists. It should not be surprising that many of the same negative attitudes exist toward them both. It has often been said, for example, that the CD field, like the human potential movement, lacks rigor, consists of more fluff and opinion than research and theory, and comes closer to a "philosophy of life" than a scientific approach. This fails to recognize the value their developmental approach to health does possess for specific clients.

As the CD field expanded its interests beyond the identified patient to include the spouse, then the whole family, and now offspring of all ages, its concept of recovery has remained remarkably intact and valuable. Many, if not most, ACAs seek therapy after first being introduced to the recovery concept by the CD field.

When a therapist is incapable of assessing a client's stage of recovery, two things happen: First, treatment plans are insufficiently individualized to meet the client's specific needs and take advantage of his or her specific capabilities. Second, events contributing to healing (e.g., acknowledging powerlessness) which can be explained within the CD recovery framework may be "invisible" to the therapist, who loses important tools for helping the client. These are the reasons why, at Genesis, we include an evaluation of the stage of recovery for every client seeking psychotherapy.

CONCLUSION

The fact that the "ACA syndrome" is also found in people from homes which were dysfunctional for reasons other than chemical dependence—emotional, physical, or sexual abuse; a parent's psychiatric illness, chronic physical illness, or disability; religious extremism; or terrorizing experiences such as the Holocaust—often creates considerable confusion. Many clients who never had an alcoholic parent still see themselves as "ACAs" and complain that their sense of isolation is increased by feeling excluded from the "ACA movement." Meanwhile several leaders in the COA field have gradually been generalizing their area of concern to include all "children of trauma."

Alcoholic families are a subset within the larger population of dysfunctional families. There are, however, at least three reasons why COAs have gained status as a separate population. First, they are self-identifying in record numbers. Second, their connection with the CD field has given them access to the guidance, structure, and coalescing effect of Twelve Step self-help programs. And third, their previous "invisibility" has created an intense bond among them, especially now that they are no longer invisible.

There are at least three more reasons on the professional level why COAs are seen as a distinct group. First, their emergence from within the already separate CD field has kept them from being absorbed into other groups from dysfunctional families, most of which come out of the general mental health field. Second, despite the many ways in which COAs overlap with survivors of other trauma, there are a few areas of uniqueness— notably the biology/genetics issue, and to a lesser extent, co-dependence issues. Third, it is easier to conceptualize how childhood experiences lead to adult problems by considering ACAs than by looking at the full range of dysfunctional families. Alcoholism narrows down the variables; although alcoholic families have many differences, they also have many things in common. Understanding ACAs gives us a window for studying the childhood origins of adult psychological problems.

When therapists learn that a client was physically or sexually abused as a child, they automatically take this very seriously. They immediately assume that surface symptoms indicate undercurrents flowing through the very foundations of the client's identity. I believe that this point of view applies equally well to adults who were raised by chemically dependent parents, and that their childhood experiences were just as influential. That is why, at Genesis, we have developed evaluation axes that are consistent with the known causes of character disorders. And that is why we insist that a full psychological evaluation be performed on every ACA client.

Once it is known that a client has an alcoholic parent, data should automatically be collected in the six areas of biology/ genetics, the wound, poor woundcare, underlearning, dual diagnosis, and the stage of recovery. Only after this evaluation is complete can the treatment plan be sufficiently individualized to maximize therapeutic effectiveness. This thorough evaluation is the responsibility of all professional therapists.

2

AXIS I:
PERSPECTIVES ON ALCOHOLISM
NECESSARY FOR EVALUATING
ACAs

Before looking at how children cope with alcoholic parents, we must have a clear idea of what it is they are having to cope with. Many fine books have already been written about the disease of alcoholism. This chapter focuses specifically on information that helps us to understand those aspects of alcoholism which most affect the alcoholic's offspring: genetics, alterations in the alcoholic parent's personality, alterations in the family, and recovery.

THE DISEASE CONCEPT

An understanding of alcoholism begins with the question of whether it is seen as a disease or as the result of willful misconduct. Therapists treating COAs must be clear about how they answer this question, since it has such profound implications for how they view each client's parent. It is best for this question to be answered thoughtfully, rather than by blind acceptance of a dogmatic "party line" or by reactionary and emotional rejection of legitimate research findings.

Despite years of debate, the disease concept of alcoholism is a curious phenomenon. On the one hand, the American Medical Association in 1956 declared that alcoholism is a true disease. On the other, no one ever talks about the "disease concept of cancer." The debate is still being waged over whether the disease of alcoholism is merely a concept (albeit one that has great value in the treatment of alcoholics), or whether it is in fact an entity.

I suspect that this debate would be resolved if people's emotions were not so tied up in the topic. Each side strives not only to establish the legitimacy of its own argument, but also seems hellbent on discrediting opposing arguments (and often the opponents themselves). Where matters of health are concerned, we humans tend to think somewhat irrationally. It's hard to be objective when our own mortality is at stake.

Disagreements often hinge on whether excessive drinking is "voluntary" or "involuntary" behavior—a point illustrated by recent arguments in Congress and the Supreme Court on whether alcoholism should be considered "willful misconduct." Perhaps the best way to reach a working agreement is to grant the truths both sides contain, then tolerate the paradox which results.

Obviously it's foolish to deny that alcohol consumption is in part voluntary. No one forces alcohol down anyone's throat. Furthermore, there are some people who consume alcohol in a deliberate effort to kill themselves (although I suspect their numbers are quite small). It is their chosen route for suicide.

But excessive drinking also clearly has an involuntary component: in the development of addiction, with its changes in brain function and personality, and in the inheritability of alcoholism. Once a person's brain function and personality are altered, however subtly, by chronic alcohol intake, the question of voluntary versus involuntary behavior gives way to questions of impaired capacity to make healthy decisions, which are clearly more appropriately seen in terms of disease rather than morality.

The brain dysfunctions which occur with active and chronic alcoholism are important to ACAs for two reasons. First, understanding them helps to make sense of the environment in which ACAs spent their early childhood. Second, ACAs addicted to alcohol will have to come to terms with the same brain dysfunctions in themselves. But it is the inheritability of alcoholism which presents the most persuasive data in favor of the disease concept, and which is of obvious importance to children of alcoholics.

GENETICS

The Inheritability of Alcoholism

All humans have a genetic propensity toward alcohol addiction. The biochemical makeup of our species reacts to alcohol in specific ways. Whenever we ingest sufficient quantities, our livers become more effective at burning it up, and our brain cells become modified enough that they react (sometimes violently) to its sudden withdrawal. None of these things take place in reaction to lemonade, carrots, penicillin, or the vast bulk of other things we consume.

Is this genetic propensity toward alcoholism inherited? Do certain families contain genetically transmitted characteristics which lead to more alcoholism within those families? There is a formal procedure for approaching and answering questions like these which has been used to study everything from eye color to diabetes and schizophrenia. It has also been applied to the question of alcoholism.

Family tree studies[1] clearly indicate that alcoholism clusters within families, and is not randomly distributed among the population. The evidence is as good as, or better than, that for schizophrenia, which few people doubt is largely hereditary. However, it is not proof of genetic transmission. It is only consistent with a genetic basis. The question of whether families "teach" children to become alcoholic by modeling alcoholic behavior also needs to be addressed.

Family studies further show that an individual family member's risk of becoming alcoholic depends on how many alcoholics are in the family, and how close their relationship is. The greater the number, and the closer the relationship, the higher the risk.

Studies of fraternal and identical twins point to the probability of genetic transmission.[2] Fraternal twins have no more genetic material in common than any two siblings born at different times. When one fraternal twin is alcoholic, studies find that 30% of their twinmates are also alcoholic. Identical twins have twice as much genetic material in common as fraternal twins. When one identical twin is alcoholic, studies find that 60% of the twinmates are as well.[3] While this doesn't yet prove genetic transmission, it becomes harder to blame the doubled incidence of alcoholism in identical twins on the "special treatment" they received, as opposed to fraternal twins. Still, it can be argued that identical twins are programmed by their social environment to be alike in as many ways as possible.

Adoption studies provide the most compelling data.[4] When male children of alcoholic fathers are adopted at birth into families without active alcoholism, they continue to run four times the rate of alcoholism as children of nonalcoholic fathers—sometimes up to nine times, when the birth father's alcoholism is accompanied by significant social dysfunction and sociopathy. The control group against which these sons of alcoholics were compared includes sons of nonalcoholics, also adopted at birth, who show no increase over the general public's rate of alcoholism (7% in the Scandinavian country where this study was performed). Adoption *per se* does not increase the likelihood of alcoholism.

Other aspects of these studies hold more than passing interest. When a small but statistically significant group of sons of alcoholics were inadvertently adopted into families where the adoptive father was eventually diagnosed as alcoholic, the sons suffered no additional increase in their rate of alcoholism. The researchers also took a look at brothers of the studied sons of alcoholics who were not adopted. Presumably they were subject to the same genetic influences, as well as growing up in an alcoholic home; again, their rate of alcoholism was four times that of the control group.

In other words, no matter how the data were analyzed, genetic factors were demonstrated to have an effect, while environmental factors could not be demonstrated to play a role. Studies of daughters of alcoholics remain more sketchy but point to similar findings.

The simplest explanation for these data, which have been confirmed and replicated often enough to be taken seriously, is that genetic material capable of promoting alcoholism is passed from generation to generation. No learning within the alcoholic family or interpersonal experience with the alcoholic is necessary for this predisposition toward alcoholism to exist.

Hereditary influences on alcoholism have been demonstrated in nonhuman species as well.[5] Strains of mice have been bred which "voluntarily" drink alcohol to the point of addiction. Experiments like these have also revealed huge variations in sensitivity to alcohol ingestion, with behavioral differences paralleled by differences in the brain's reaction to alcohol. The fact that these animal models exist greatly undermines the possibility that different degrees of potential for alcoholism among humans can always be explained by different learning experiences and environments.

Establishing the fact that genetic transmission creates a propensity toward alcoholism is not the final word in the disease concept debate. Opponents might argue that what is transmitted is a deficit of intelligence or character, and that this deficit is the foundation for a lot of foolish behavior, including alcoholism. Proponents still must demonstrate precisely what is inherited, if some people inherit more of it than others, or if the entire COA population is at the same increased risk. This brings us to the question of "markers."

The Search for Markers
of Alcoholism

Can certain personality traits be identified as markers to predict the probability of alcoholism? A vast body of research into the "alcoholic personality" once explored this possibility. Two problems eventually led people to abandon this approach. First, research which establishes statistical probabilities for large groups of people is irrelevant to individuals, who either do (100%) or do not (0%) develop alcoholism. Second, the effort to describe "pre-alcoholic personality structures" went bust.

Studies which look at personality before alcoholism occurs (as opposed to looking retrospectively, after alcoholism has begun) show that personality disorder is more likely the result of alcoholism than its cause. With what we now know about the subtleties of personality characteristics, we are still unable to pinpoint any which are clearly the precursors of alcoholism. (Some theorists, including the author, are exploring whether the personality traits associated with co-dependence might include easy entry into chemical abuse. We must take care not to simply reintroduce the concept of an alcoholic personality in an altered form.)

To date, there are no reliable personality markers for alcoholism. Nor are there any clinically significant biological markers, although tantalizing clues seem to be mounting on the horizon, and researchers assume that it's only a matter of time.

Some of the most substantial work in this area is being done by Marc Schuckit,[6] who has compared sons of alcoholics and sons of nonalcoholics across a wide range of variables: psychological testing (including MMPIs, Eysenck, and locus of control), metabolism (absorption and degradation rates, as well as peak blood alcohol levels after ingestion of standard amounts of alcohol), feelings of intoxication, cognitive and motor performance, and hormonal response to alcohol ingestion (cortisol and prolactin). All of these studies were done before and after ingesting different amounts of alcohol—either a placebo dose (to control for differences on the basis of expectation), low dose, or high dose (producing approximately legal levels of intoxication). Each subject was tested in all three conditions, and neither subject nor tester were aware of the dose of alcohol being used (i.e., double blind conditions).

Differences were found between COAs and the control group in both the low dose and high dose conditions. Sons of alcoholics had less of a response to the alcohol challenge situation along three dimensions: subjective response, motor control, and hormonal response. In the placebo condition, there were no significant differences between the groups. Schuckit's research shows that, for whatever reason, sons of alcoholics feel less intoxicated, experience less effect on their muscle control, and secrete less cortisol and prolactin in response to ingesting alcohol. Preliminary data suggest that COAs may separate into two subgroups, with one third accounting for most of the positive results described above. This would support the conclusion that not all COAs receive the same inherited tendency toward alcoholism; some are at higher risk than others.

Interesting research is also being done in the area of brain wave differences between sons of alcoholics and sons of nonalcoholics. These differences are found in a technically complex measurement involving computer recording and averaging of brain waves following a novel stimulus (such as one high-pitched tone embedded in several low-pitched tones), known as the P300 event related potential.[7] The P300 occurs approximately 300 milliseconds after such a stimulus, when the brain's electrical activity has a small positive wave (thus the label "P300"). Whenever a subject is told to expect these infrequent novel tones, and to count them, the P300 wave increases.

Because the P300 wave is markedly shorter in height in chronic alcoholics than in nonalcoholics, researchers wanted to know whether a deficit in the wave is apparent *before* an alcoholic begins his or her drinking career. In other words, is this shorter wave caused by chronic alcoholism, or is it a marker? What better way to explore this question than to test the sons of alcoholic fathers? When this research was undertaken, it was found that sons of alcoholics *do* have a decreased P300, although it is midway between the intensity found in normal controls and chronic alcoholics.

What does this mean? Nobody knows yet. Before drawing conclusions, we need to answer the same question facing Schuckit's work: are all sons of alcoholics equally affected? Plus there is the confounding problem of how exquisitely sensitive the P300 wave is to expectations. (In fact, the wave is more sensitive to expectancy contingencies than to any other variable.) This greatly confuses the issue of whether researchers are dealing with an inherited versus a learned phenomenon. It is quite possible that living within a stressful and arbitrary environment conditions a person's basic response to novelty, which seems less novel the more chaos one routinely experiences. Further research is necessary, and warranted.

Finally, direct studies of DNA from alcoholics have begun to report exciting results. Although still needing verification, Noble and Blum[8] report direct genetic distinctions between alcoholics and nonalcoholics. Analyzing DNA from brain tissue, they found that the presence of a specific variety of dopamine receptor correctly classified 77% of alcoholics, and its absence classified 72% of nonalcoholics. Efforts are already underway to develop techniques for genetic analysis from simple blood samples, which will allow this research to be correlated with the findings outlined above, as well as with clinical data.

We still have a lot to learn about markers for alcoholism and genetically inherited differences in COAs, but the prospects for achieving meaningful breakthroughs have never been brighter. Further exploration of current findings deserves the full support of our scientific community. With help from rapidly developing technology, answers to the question of what is passed genetically from alcoholic parent to alcoholic child seems closer than ever.

What we will do with these answers poses another series of questions. Once reliable markers have been identified, it will be possible to test people—physiologically, biochemically, or genetically—for the propensity toward alcoholism. This will give rise to difficult public policy issues. The tradeoff between stigmatizing an individual and being able to target prevention efforts where they are most needed will have to be weighed carefully, both as public health policy and civil rights issues.

For example, would an insurance company have the right to demand testing for the marker before issuing automobile insurance to a sixteen year old, and the right to refuse coverage to anyone who tested positive? On the other hand, could we as a society afford to ignore the impact mass testing and intensified prevention efforts could have in curtailing the devastation of alcoholism? Questions like these will have no easy answers.

Even the most optimistic scenario creates its own problems. Imagine for a moment that a foolproof marker is discovered and widespread prevention efforts become almost universally successful. After a period of time, we will lose a sense of the natural history of alcoholism. People will begin to doubt that it exists, and the "myth of alcoholism" will gain greater credence. We can expect that alcoholism will remain an emotionally loaded topic long after any of us is around to discuss it.

THE DISEASE PROCESS: HOW ALCOHOLISM AFFECTS THE INDIVIDUAL

How Alcoholism Affects the Brain

The effects of alcohol on the body, from liver disease to heart failure, kidney failure, and muscle weakness, have been catalogued repeatedly. The brain is part of the body, and must function properly for the human mind to be clear. The effects of chronic alcoholism on the nervous system, from peripheral nerve damage to dementia and memory loss, have also been catalogued in many places. Three of these effects have special meaning for COAs.

Blackouts

Although the disruption of brain mechanisms underlying blackouts still needs clarification, there is little doubt that they stem from physical, rather than psychological, events.[9]

A blackout is not a loss of consciousness. Rather, it is a period of time (ranging from seconds to days) during which the immediate content of a person's mind does not get stored in long term memory. Events can be recalled for approximately three minutes; after five minutes, absolutely no memory for them remains. It's like taking pictures with an empty camera. Everything seems normal until the next morning, when it is discovered that no memories—no pictures—remain from the day before.

Blackouts are important for two reasons. First, many COAs report having had a blackout the first time they drank alcohol. Second, many COAs have lived with a parent who experienced memory losses.

The first reason provides dramatic evidence that blackouts are not dose-related. They are an idiosyncratic way that certain people's brains respond to alcohol. In informal surveys I have made, virtually everyone who experienced blackouts upon initial contact with alcohol was a COA, as were over 90% of those who reported having blackouts during the first year of their drinking. If these findings were validated by proper research, this would strengthen the argument that heredity plays an important role in the high rate of alcoholism in COAs. From a clinical standpoint, blackouts in ACAs must be taken as presumptive evidence for a genetic propensity to addiction.

Parental memory losses are incomprehensible to young children, especially when the parents themselves haven't the faintest clue what is happening. The natural reaction among children is to question their own perceptions ("Did I really hear my father say he was going to kill me last night? This morning he is treating me like he loves me"), or to assume that the parent's forgetfulness is motivated by lack of concern for the child's feelings.

It is impossible for an ACA to accurately reconstruct the history of his or her childhood without understanding the impersonal nature of blackouts. By "impersonal nature," I mean that they are simply a symptom of the disease, like liver failure. No one ever had liver failure because he did not love his child. No one ever had a blackout because she lacked concern for others. But this is how many COAs experience their parents' blackouts.

Mood Swings

The effects of intoxication extend far beyond the time when alcohol is in the bloodstream. Although these effects may be subtle, they keep a person from operating at peak potential, both physically and emotionally. A motorcycle racer once told me that his lap times did not return to their consistent superior level for two weeks following a one night binge. From the standpoint of many children of alcoholics, it is the subtle, long-term effects drinking has on their parents' emotions which has the greatest impact.

Even moderate drinking leads to increased mood swings. In one study,[10] two groups of women were taught to rate the intensity of their mood swings throughout the day. One group totally abstained from alcohol, while the other group had up to two drinks a day, three days a week. When mood ratings were compared *for those days that no one drank*, the drinkers had significantly higher highs and lower lows. As we try to understand the experience of growing up with an alcoholic, mood swings must be factored in.

Frontal Lobe Deficits

Of all the effects alcohol has on the human brain, those on the frontal lobes may be the most subtle and least understood. The frontal lobes are the seat of very high level cognitive functions, including the ability to abstract, make judgments, and shift sets (i.e., abandon one perspective for viewing a problem and adopt a different one from which new solutions become possible). These functions are extremely important for effective problem solving.

In testing the mental functions of alcoholics early in recovery, it is common to find that neither memory capacity nor general intelligence have declined, but frontal lobe tests are abnormal. For example, Trails A and B is a simple "connect the dots" test. First the dots are labeled "1, 2, 3 . . ." Next they are labeled "A, B, C . . ." After it has been shown that the alcoholic can perform each of these without any trouble, the combined test is given. The dots must now be connected in the following order: "1, A, 2, B, 3, C . . ." In other words, the client must shift sets from numbers to letters and back again after connecting each dot.

Most people take a little bit longer to complete this portion of the test. But alcoholics with frontal lobe damage are not only much slower, they make a lot of mistakes.

The Stroop test is another, even more Machiavellian means of testing frontal lobe function. First the client is asked to read a column of words. The four words used are all colors (e.g., "red, blue . . ."). Then the client is asked to name the color of a column of x's, each of which is printed in different colors. These two preliminary tests document that verbal skills are intact and there is no color blindness. Finally, the client is asked to read a series of words, each of which is the name of a color, but printed in a noncorresponding color. In other words, the word "red" might be printed in blue ink. The test of the frontal lobes is whether the client can maintain one set (reading the verbal message) in the face of a competing set (the actual color the word is printed in).

No one performs the final portion of the Stroop easily, or even flawlessly. Any amount of frontal lobe dysfunction is quickly revealed. Many alcoholics in early recovery who seem perfectly intact in other cognitive ways perform miserably on the Stroop.

It is important to pay attention to frontal lobe deficits, a neurophysiological phenomenon, because they are often indistinguishable from denial, a psychological phenomenon. We typically view alcoholics as being in denial when they seem unwilling to shift sets from believing that alcohol is the solution to their problems to seeing that it is more the cause. We should pause for a moment and ask how people can make such a dramatic change in their perception of the world. It is not their elbow that does it. It is their brain, more specifically their frontal lobes. When the frontal lobes are partially decommissioned, the ability to see through denial decreases, and at some point slides over into the inability to see things in a new light.

The alcoholic in denial with frontal lobe damage is like a blind man who can't see how to get to the eye clinic, or a man with a broken ankle who can't walk to the emergency room. The very tool needed to get help is the tool that is broken.

And this is the person the COA lives with and grows up around. This is mommy or daddy. This is the person all the childhood battles around discipline, independence, and growing up are fought with.

It can be useful for ACAs to learn how cunning, baffling, and powerful the effects of alcohol on the brain really are. Then it no longer makes sense to say that their parents "should have been able to see" the damage they were doing with their drinking. Once ACAs accept that their parents may have been incapable of this, they can start drawing a more realistic picture of the past. That picture may contain a parent who was even more overtaken by alcohol than the ACA ever suspected. But everyone's healing begins from a point of honesty. We must continually pursue what was real.

How Alcoholism Affects
the Alcoholic

The Alcoholic's Personality and Behavior

The classic description of chemically dependent behavior is Jellinek's framework for the progressive nature of alcoholism.[11] Jellinek catalogued over 40 specific symptoms of alcoholism and placed them along a continuum, from normal to alcoholic drinking. Phase I (pre-alcoholic) is characterized by drinking to relax. Phase II (early alcoholic) begins with blackouts, and includes sneaking drinks, preoccupation with alcohol, defensiveness, and guilt. Phase III (addiction) is marked by physiological dependence, loss of control, and mounting relationship and financial problems. And Phase IV (chronic alcoholism) is characterized by major damage to a variety of organs (liver, heart, brain), delirium tremens, and death.

According to Jellinek, as the disease progresses, behavior invariably spirals downward through the development of tolerance and physical dependence to the loss of control. At the same time, the drinker's denial gradually deepens and becomes more rigid. Eventually denial becomes a way of life, with its own internal momentum; it is no longer invoked solely to protect one's drinking or other drug use. It begins to keep secrets in every part of the alcoholic's life.

People who have not personally experienced denial, or witnessed it in others, seldom understand how powerful and how bold it can be. Alcoholics can deny almost anything, from the existence of obvious problems (e.g., the imminent breakup of a marriage or loss of a job), to denial of their own feelings, and of the drinking behavior itself. It's quite a shock to turn the corner into the kitchen, see someone take a gulp from a wine bottle, and have him deny what you saw by saying, "I was just checking to find out if too much cork got into the bottle to serve it to our guests."

Other researchers have described progressive addiction in terms of "ego deficits," "character pathology," and "field dependence." Each of these descriptions comes out of its own theoretical framework and focuses on different facets of the same behavior Jellinek observed. (I suspect that this behavior has changed less over time than our descriptions of it.)

- The *ego psychology* perspective highlights the "impulsivity, inability to delay gratification, low affect tolerance, a propensity toward panic-level anxiety and prolonged depression, and an unclear, confused sense of identity"[12] common to active alcoholics.

- The *character pathology*[13] perspective emphasizes a hierarchy of defenses, each of which is normal for a specific age, through which all humans progress as they gradually mature from childhood to adolescence and adulthood. As alcoholics become increasingly addicted, they rely more and more heavily on adolescent defenses such as projection, passive-aggressive behavior, acting out, and nonpsychotic denial of reality.

- The *field dependence* perspective accentuates the alcoholic's extreme susceptibility to social influence. Field dependence is a cognitive style, a way of structuring one's experiential world, in which events are experienced globally and diffusely, with the surrounding field (social environment) determining how they are organized.[14] Alcoholics have consistently been found to be field dependent. In other words, the primary determinant of how alcoholics think, feel, and act is peer pressure.

These and other descriptions of alcoholic behaviors are important to COAs. They are like pictures that help to explain what they have seen and heard their parents do. But it is even more important for COAs to understand the *experience* of being actively addicted. The ACA's identity was formed in intimate relationship with a parent who was lost in this experience.

The Alcoholic's Experience

The "Big Book" of Alcoholics Anonymous (AA) is a gold mine when it comes to revealing the internal life of the alcoholic. In self descriptions written by people in recovery, for example, we are given such vital insights as this:

> Selfishness—self-centeredness! That, we think, is the root of our troubles. Driven by a hundred forms of fear, self-delusion, self-seeking, and self-pity, we step on the toes of our fellows and they retaliate. Sometimes they hurt us, seemingly without provocation, but we invariably find that at some time in the past we have made decisions based on self which later placed us in a position to be hurt...[The] alcoholic is an extreme example of self-will run riot.[15]

Before recovery gives a person perspective on these characteristics, the experience of being alcoholic is similar to that of slowly being taken hostage by a seemingly benevolent dictator who is turning mean hearted in his old age. At first there is no sense that anything is going wrong. In fact, life is made a bit easier by the largesse of your benefactor. Eventually, as you find you have bought into the status quo more than you realized, feelings of resentment, bitterness, fear, and low self-esteem creep in and begin to rule your life. Finally it becomes a matter of personal survival. You don't know who you are anymore. Well-meaning advice from others only adds to the pressure to change what seems like a hopeless situation. The very experience of being held hostage, while simultaneously denying that a hostage crisis exists, begins to have such a psychological impact that it becomes the central theme of your life. There is little room left for others and their concerns. There is little energy left to be an effective parent or spouse.

Gregory Bateson[16] describes the entire life experience of an alcoholic as resting on beliefs which are internally flawed. The alcoholic is hostage to an illusion—what Bateson calls "the myth of self-power." The alcoholic constructs her experience around the myth that she has (or ought to have) more control over the world than is humanly possible. Whenever alcoholics fail to control their world, they assume it is their fault for not having tried hard enough—their willpower must have been inadequate. So they try harder to make "trying harder" a successful strategy. But blackouts, to give just one example, occur for physiological reasons and have nothing to do with willpower. Attempts to control them are doomed.

Alcoholics develop a disastrous pride—"an obsessive acceptance of a challenge, a repudiation of the proposition 'I cannot.'"[17] Self-esteem hinges on accomplishing the impossible by sheer force of will. This "myth of willpower" results from the alcoholic's deep separation from himself. He is left to identify *either* with that part of himself which is exercising willpower, *or* the part which is "failing" and out of control.

Typically, alcoholics choose the former and avoid taking responsibility for the latter. Either they deny that they have lost control, or they blame others for their failures of willpower. *The one thing alcoholics must see in order to change their behavior is that their beliefs about willpower are flawed.* Paradoxically, their basic problem solving strategy contains the very flaw they need to gain perspective on. They misinterpret the universal limitations of human willpower as evidence of personal inadequacy. There is no way that children in such a household can avoid having their own developing concepts of self-control and willpower shaped by this perception and the dysfunctional behaviors it leads to.

Traditional psychoanalytic theory, with its emphasis on the internal conflict of drives, has provided little effective understanding of the alcoholic. But more recent work in self psychology has revealed useful information about the alcoholic's separation from the self. Heinz Kohut[18] saw addicts as having deficits in their sense of self which are characteristic of pathological narcissism. Taking Kohut's theories further, Jerome Levin[19] outlines at least four kinds of self-pathology in alcoholics: "(1) they are self-destructive; (2) they lack certain components of the self that mediate self-care and maintain self-esteem; (3) they are overly self-involved; and (4) their very sense of being, their self-concepts or representations, are fragile and in jeopardy." This self-psychology perspective (which is explored in depth in Chapter 4) leads Levin to pointedly observe: "It is probably no accident that a *self*-help group [referring to AA] is the best known and one of the most successful therapies for the treatment of alcoholism."[20]

Narcissism is the name we give to personality disorders characterized by extreme self-centeredness. While narcissism does not necessarily precede addiction to alcohol or other drugs, it is almost always a consequence of the physical and psychological impact of chronic intoxication. The subjective experience of narcissism is often one of bouncing back and forth between the two incompatible feelings of grandiosity and depression. In describing narcissism, Freud spoke of "his majesty, the baby,"[21] while AA speaks of "the Great I Am and Poor Me"[22] and describes alcoholics as being "ego-maniacs with inferiority complexes."

In between these two incompatible feelings held by the alcoholic parent stands the child. As the child's own personality attempts to mature, it is in constant contact with a parent whose sense of self is poorly developed, fragmented, and internally at odds. The parent's life cannot be healed and made whole as long as alcohol remains its central focus. The child is left to fit in wherever possible.

THE DISEASE PROCESS:
HOW ALCOHOLISM
AFFECTS THE FAMILY

Family Roles

A lot of attention has been paid lately to the identification of specific roles which typically emerge in chemically dependent families. These have helped many ACAs better understand their life experience.

Sharon Wegscheider-Cruse[23] describes children in alcoholic homes as becoming Heroes, Scapegoats, Lost Children, and Mascots. If there is a nondrinking parent, he or she often takes on the role of the Enabler.

- *Heroes* react to the chaos of their home by trying to rise above it, control it, and contain it; to mediate conflicts; and to exert superhuman efforts to make up for their parents' deficiencies. Beneath these behaviors are feelings of guilt, inadequacy, and a sense of responsibility for the family's failings.
- *Scapegoats* react just the opposite. They deliberately misbehave to draw attention to themselves, or to exact some revenge for the pain their family is causing them. By giving the family something to focus on besides the alcoholism, scapegoats serve an important function. On a feeling level, they are responding mostly to their own hurt and anger.
- *Lost Children* make themselves as inconspicuous as possible, shrinking back from the family's dysfunction and fading into the woodwork. Because Lost Children are so successful at never being the center of the family's attention, few people are truly aware of how lonely they really are.
- *Mascots* seek attention by clowning, being cute, and distracting the family's focus from its problems. Their most common underlying emotion is fear.
- *Enablers* try to soften the impact of a family member's alcoholism, both on the family as a whole and on the alcoholic. As the alcoholic gradually neglects his responsibilities, the enabler steps in and shoulders them. The underlying feelings are usually anger, resentment, and an increasing sense of powerlessness—no amount of sacrifice can stop the alcoholic's disease. It can only hide the consequences of the drinking, thereby enabling it to continue.

In a similar vein, Claudia Black[24] describes children in alcoholic families as taking on the roles of the Responsible One, the Adjuster, the Placater, and the Acting-Out Child.

- *The Responsible Child* maintains order, often sacrificing her normal childhood to become a little adult—a pseudo-parent.
- *Adjusters* are reactors and chameleons, often with no solid sense of their own identity. They make little effort to initiate change, but rather respond to whatever chaos others create.

- *Placaters* are mediators, capable of advising warring parties, fixing problems, and keeping everyone's tension and pain at a minimum.
- *Acting-out Children* correspond to Wegscheider-Cruse's Scapegoats; they manifest and give focus to the family's tension and dysfunction.

Concrete, evocative labels like these have proved very important for many ACAs. They raise peoples' awareness of the patterns which are rigidly followed in alcoholic families. They give people a way to see these patterns and begin to understand the realities of life in an alcoholic home. They also help ACAs to accurately connect their childhood experiences with their adult selves.

The roles Wegscheider-Cruse and Black describe exist in nearly every family to some degree. The important points to remember are: (1) the more dysfunctional a family has become, the more these roles are called into play and imposed on children to meet the *family's* needs; and (2) the more dysfunctional a family has become, the more rigidly these roles have to be adhered to, especially during moments of increased stress. Healthier families, in contrast, permit children to explore different roles in their search for their identities—roles which best express their own internal needs, not the needs of the family.

Characteristics of Healthy Families, and Their Disruption by Parental Alcoholism

Before looking more closely at how alcoholism inserts itself into the family system and distorts normal development, it is useful to compare the characteristics of relatively healthy, functional families with the disruptions parental alcoholism can cause. The table on page 38 summarizes these comparisons and is followed by more detailed descriptions of the healthy family characteristics.[25]

- *Safety* for children means that grownups will meet their basic needs (for food, clothing, and shelter); will provide

Characteristics of Healthy Families	Disruptions Caused by Parental Alcoholism
Safety	Emotional unavailability of parent
	Parental loss of control
	Failure to protect children from hazards
	Direct physical/sexual/emotional abuse
Open Communication	Secrets kept to keep the peace
	Facade of normality maintained
	Feelings hidden
	Children made into confidants
Self-Care	"Scarcity" economy
	Alcoholic's needs come first
	Other people's problems are more important than one's own
Individualized Roles	Family's needs dictate roles
	Roles become rigid, especially during times of stress
Continuity	Chaos
	Arbitrariness
	Dissolution of the family
Respect for Privacy	Parents become intrusive
	Secrets are confused with privacy
	No respect for individual differences
Focused Attention Schedule	Determined by the alcoholic's, not by the child's, needs
Quality	Restricted range of emotions
	Alcohol-affected emotions never reach resolution

proper restraints and limitations to prevent accidental injury; will ensure that basic health care is available; will contain their own hostile and aggressive impulses; and will be emotionally available, particularly when the child is overwhelmed.

Alcoholism in a parent gradually erodes, and can eventually destroy, a child's sense of safety. There is nothing scarier to a child than the experience of a parent being out of control.[26] Since the disease of alcoholism is defined by a loss of control, it almost invariably imports an undercurrent of terror into the lives of the alcoholic's children.

- *Open communication* means that healthy families assume they will function best if all members are encouraged to be assertive, and if differing viewpoints are honestly expressed. At the same time, honesty is tempered by respect for the children's need for safety. Parents consider the children's level of comprehension and avoid forcing them to deal with emotionally charged material before they are ready. The need for open communication is not abused by turning children into confidants for the parents' fears.

  Alcoholics discourage open discussion of feelings or facts which jeopardize their drinking. The family is encouraged to invest more energy in maintaining a facade of normality than in confronting its problems. Further, when people become intoxicated, their sense of propriety regarding parent-child distinctions is often lost. Children may be confided in to a degree that terrifies them while giving them the sense of an inappropriately "special" relationship with the parent.

- *Self-care* in functional families means that everyone is encouraged and praised for taking good care of themselves. It is assumed that each family member is responsible for determining what he or she needs to stay healthy and keep growing. There is a fundamental trust that an endless supply of happiness is available.

  The alcoholic family's central belief is in a scarcity economy, where everything worth anything is in short supply.

Whenever any family member momentarily separates to recharge her own emotional batteries, the rest of the family feels betrayed. They close ranks and pressure the "deviant" to return to her assigned role and stabilize the family system.

- *Individualized roles* are clearer and more flexible in healthy families than in unhealthy ones. Each child's role is determined as much by his own unique strengths and needs as it is by the needs of the family. Parents help their children develop roles that truly reflect their personalities by staying clear about their own roles as parents.

  Although children often fight against the boundaries their parents set for them, this resistance is an important part of their growing up. For parents to set boundaries that are effective and meaningful, they must permit children to struggle against the restraints, and they must be flexible enough to change the restraints as a child becomes capable of assuming greater responsibility.

  The blurring of boundaries between parent and child in many alcoholic families is profoundly upsetting to children because it thrusts them prematurely out into the world. In order to stabilize the family system, children must play specific roles regardless of whether these roles are consistent with their personalities.

  The more the family is threatened, the more pressure children feel not to deviate from roles which add even marginal stability to the family. Unfortunately, the child who grows up rigidly identified with a single role often becomes stuck in that role as an adult.

- *Continuity,* derived from the consistent repetition of daily routines, from formal and informal rituals, and from the extended family and its history, is one of the most valuable gifts healthy families give to their youngsters. It serves as a touchstone in an otherwise wildly changing world, and it provides a sense of belonging to something of greater scope and significance than any individual family member can create on her own.

Alcoholics lack continuity at the core level, often experiencing huge personality changes in reaction to their blood alcohol level (and not in response to external events, which would at least be a bit more comprehensible to a child). Feelings change arbitrarily. Ground rules are constantly shifting. Even membership in the family can fluctuate without apparent reason, as step-parents may come and go without warning. Chaos is often present or lurking just around the corner.

In such an environment, a child has no experience with the connecting threads which tie intimate relationships together from moment to moment. Instead, he learns to expect erratic behavior from others, and becomes resigned to reacting to it as well as he can.

* *Respect for privacy* occurs within healthy families as a result of an underlying acceptance of the difference and separateness of each individual. There is a basic assumption that an individual's health and growth are not at odds with the needs of the family as a whole. Families gain strength by allowing each member the privacy she needs to develop her own talents and take care of herself.

Chronic alcoholism almost invariably destroys respect for privacy. Intoxicated parents either withdraw into themselves and leave children emotionally alone (which is not the same experience as having your privacy respected), or they become aggressively self centered and lose their ability to see the separateness between themselves and their children. They become intrusive; or, as the saying goes, "Alcoholics don't have relationships; they take hostages."

In the early stages of writing *A Time To Heal*, I used the working title "Childhood Held Hostage." Although I ultimately abandoned the working title because it focused more attention on the problem than the solution, it did express an important element of the experience of having an alcoholic parent.

A child's status as a child is frequently dishonored in alcoholic homes as the intoxicated parent barges into the bathroom, into the child's play, into the child's bed, and into the child's emotional life as though the child had nothing better to do than be present for the alcoholic's needs. When children are assumed to exist only to meet their parents' needs, they are assumed to have no separate individuality and no need for privacy. The child who can respond to this invasion in the most "adult" way (i.e., with understanding and empathy for the parent) is the least likely to provoke the parent into more outrageous behavior.

- *Focused attention* is a concept I developed to summarize many of the characteristics healthy families share, and to help explain the critical disruptions which occur in parent/child relationships in alcoholic homes.

    Children don't need constant attention in order to develop. In fact, constant attention is counterproductive because it eventually violates a child's need for privacy. What children need—and what high-functioning families give them enough of—is focused attention.

    This concept has two components: schedule and quality.
    —*Schedule* refers both to the frequency and timing of the attention a parent gives a child. Healthy families tend to follow a child-centered schedule. Children get attention in concert with *their* needs for food, comforting, reassurance, sharing of pleasure, or hygiene. The parents live by the children's schedule.

    When alcoholism causes a parent to become increasingly narcissistic, the attention-giving schedule becomes parent-centered. Child care is no longer tied to the child's needs, but is determined instead by a parent's alcoholism. For example, an alcoholic parent might check on a child during the night only after her own blood alcohol level has fallen enough to wake her. A sober parent will be awakened by the child who cries out during a nightmare, and immediately get up to check on the child.

    When children are cared for according to someone else's timing, they learn to control their needs rather than communicate them. The difference between a child-centered schedule and a parent-centered schedule is the difference between a universe that can be trusted and one that can't.

—*Quality* refers to the degree of emotional presence parents invest in the attention they focus on their child. Does the parent bring the full range of human emotional responsiveness to the interaction, or is he only partially available emotionally? Interactions with emotionally present parents are what teach children the nuances of their own emotional life. They are also what teach them the predictable ebb-and-flow of human interaction, since specific responses tend to follow similar events (e.g., when a child feels sad, parents are usually empathetic).

Alcoholic parents, almost by definition, cannot bring the full range of human emotions to bear in interactions with their children. When they are not intoxicated, they are preoccupied with getting their next drink. And once they get their next drink, the effects of alcohol on the brain restrict the range of available emotions and modify the dynamics of emotions which are available. Since children have nothing to compare their parents' behavior with, they assume that however they behave is normal. This can cripple a child's concept of intimate relationships.

Daniel Stern's descriptions of what he calls "affect attunement" add to our understanding of focused attention. They are discussed in Chapter 4.

Family Systems Theory

Recognizing the characteristics of healthy families, and the disruptions caused by parental alcoholism, gives us a framework for evaluating families and family histories that can increase our sensitivity to clinical data. This framework is further developed by the work of Peter Steinglass *et al.*[27] on how parental alcoholism affects family systems.

Steinglass defines an "alcoholic family" as one in which alcoholism has "become a central organizing principle around which family life is structured . . . an inseparable component of the fabric of family life."[28] He has studied three aspects of alcoholic family behavior: problem-solving strategies, daily routines, and family rituals.

Problem-Solving Strategies in the Alcoholic Family

Steinglass has found that alcoholic families interact in different ways, depending on whether the alcoholic is sober or intoxicated. The entire family system, and the roles individuals occupy within it, can cycle between two complementary states, each with its own behaviors, feelings, and problem solving strategies. In a sense, the internal "split" within the alcoholic's personality is externalized as the dynamic for the entire family system.

During sobriety, for example, anger may not be allowed. During intoxication, on the other hand, people might feel free to express their anger. Or, during sobriety, the alcoholic may dictate how family problems will be solved. But, as the alcoholic begins drinking and retreats into passivity, everyone can compete for the chance to suggest solutions to family difficulties. While different families develop their own unique sober and intoxicated styles, this cycling between two different states is very common in alcoholic families.

In a fascinating study of family interactions, Steinglass developed a card-sorting task which he used to test two groups of families: those where the alcoholic was in the first month of sobriety, and those where the alcoholic was still actively drinking (but not intoxicated at the time of testing). Family members were positioned at individual desks so they could hear one another but not see one another. Each family member was given a stack of cards and told to sort the cards however he wanted to. The cards could be sorted in three different ways: by the shape of the figure on the card (circle, square, etc.), by the color of the shapes, or by the number of shapes on each card.

For the first trial, families were told to sort the cards, but without speaking to one another. The way each member sorted the cards was noted and the cards were mixed. For the second trial, the families were allowed to speak to one another while they sorted the cards. For the third trial, they were again told not to speak.

During the first trial, people randomly chose their own sorting methods. During the second trial, when they were permitted to talk, both groups of families tended to develop a "family line"—one particular method for solving the problem of sorting the cards. The third trial yielded the most interesting results: In families with a newly sober alcoholic, people stayed with the "family line" developed during the second sorting. But in families with a drinking alcoholic, people went back to exploring their own individual problem-solving styles.[29]

Newly sober families are filled with uncertainty. They feel as if they are "walking on eggshells." Will the alcoholic stay sober? For how long? Even though the alcoholic may not be actively drinking, family members may still be actively co-dependent. They feel responsible for making sure that the alcoholic stays sober—and responsible if she doesn't. Also, they have lived in chaos for so long that it feels "normal" to them. On the one hand, they know that sobriety is good; on the other, it threatens the family's status quo. The alcoholic isn't the only one who must learn a new way to live.

The family tries to decrease its uncertainty by conforming—in the case of the card-sorting experiment, by approaching problems along a "family line." Should the family encounter a problem it can't solve, the only other option is for the alcoholic to "slip" back into active drinking, which releases family members to return to their own individual problem-solving strategies. This dynamic helps to clarify the unwitting pressure families in stress can exert on newly sober alcoholics to return to drinking.

Daily Routines in the Alcoholic Family

The surest sign of an alcoholic family is the invasion of daily routines by alcoholism. As the alcoholic begins to modify these routines in order to accommodate his alcoholism—never going to entertainment events where liquor is not sold, carrying breath fresheners, eating lunch at a bar every day in order to drink, and so on—all other family members make similar accommodations.

In a complex set of real-time observations in home environments, Steinglass *et al.* recorded the behavior of alcoholic families in detail. They noted, for example, the location of each person in the family, the distance between family members, and the number of their direct interactions. Behavior patterns emerged which closely correlated with the drinking patterns that existed in these families (stable wet, binge, and stable dry). The temperament, activity level, and regulation of distance among family members had taken on characteristic patterns as a result of the alcoholic's behavior.

For COAs, a parent's drinking is a pervasive, moment-by-moment influence that has invaded the very fabric of home life. Whether anyone is intoxicated at the moment or not is irrelevant to the underlying reality that the family system is continuously being altered by the presence of alcoholism as a central organizing principle, even for daily routines. For example, dinnertime might be scheduled later and later in the evening as a father begins staying longer at a bar on the way home from work. Or a family may buy a VCR, rather than go to the movies, so the parents can drink freely during the show.

Family Rituals in the Alcoholic Family

Steven Wolin and Linda Bennett have contributed to Steinglass's framework by documenting the ways alcohol disrupts family rituals.

Holidays, birthdays, and vacations "reinforce the shared beliefs and common heritage of those who take part in them."[30] They create continuity with the past and a sense of belonging to a wider universe than just the nuclear family. Their symbolic nature helps them serve a critical role as "conservers and transmitters of the family's core identity,"[31] bringing this identity into self-awareness.

The more thoroughly alcoholic a family has become, the more its rituals are invaded and disrupted by the alcoholism. In order to maintain important rituals, families must often choose to exclude the alcoholic.

Studying the rituals in a client's family history can give the therapist important clues about the extent to which alcoholism controlled the client's family system. This in turn can help the therapist see beneath the client's denial.

Concluding Remarks

An understanding of family systems theory inevitably leads to a single conclusion: Parental alcoholism, whether overt or subtle, has a significant impact on a child's family environment. When we combine this conclusion with an understanding of child development, we have no choice but to take seriously the fate of COAs. If we ignore this fate, or minimize the impact of a COA's experience with a chemically dependent parent, we ignore the very essence of psychological theory, family systems theory, and child development theories.

Both the evidence (research and clinical) and our underlying theoretical beliefs dictate this conclusion. Failure to recognize this fact may indicate either ignorance or denial, or both.

THE RECOVERY PROCESS

When the American hostages in Iran were released, they became ex-hostages. They did not return to freedom as though nothing unusual had ever happened to them. The terrifying experience of losing control of their fate will affect, both positively and negatively, how they feel about themselves and the world for the rest of their lives. Precisely the same is true for people who are ex-hostages to alcohol.

Thanks to Alcoholics Anonymous (AA) and chemical dependence treatment centers, many children now experience their parents' recovery from the disease of alcoholism. While this is undoubtedly the most fortunate outcome one could desire, *it must never be mistaken for the end of the problem as far as the children are concerned.*

Metaphorically, recovery means that the hurricane threatening one's life has stopped blowing, which is good. But will the survivors acknowledge that the hurricane ever happened, or will they try to force its memory into the distant past before all the feelings it generated have been aired and integrated? Will the adults be able to relate to their children's fears, or will they suppress them by subtle inattention and forge ahead into rebuilding the future?

Children do not have the same sense of the future as adults. The idea of "rebuilding the future" means little or nothing to them. The fact remains that the hurricane came, and it was terrifying. It changed each child's sense of what the world can do to him, and it left scars. The sun may be shining today, but the damage done yesterday cannot heal with time alone. Just as with the alcoholic, recovery will take an active process of healing.

Even in those fortunate cases where the alcoholic parent enters into truly deep recovery and returns to being emotionally available for the child, there are no guarantees that the child's wounds will heal. The AA "Big Book" graphically describes the plight of many members of alcoholic families, especially the children, even after the alcoholic has entered recovery:

> Drinking isolates most homes from the outside world . . . Cessation of drinking is but the first step away from a highly strained, abnormal condition . . . The entire family is, to some extent, ill. Let families realize, as they start their journey, that all will not be fair weather. Each in his turn may be footsore and may straggle. There will be alluring shortcuts and by-paths down which they may wander and lose their way . . .
>
> Now and then the family will be plagued by spectres from the past . . . The first impulse will be to bury these skeletons in a dark closet and padlock the door. The family may be possessed by the idea that future happiness can be based only upon forgetfulness of the past. We think that such a view is self-centered and in direct conflict with the new way of living . . .
>
> The alcoholic may find it hard to re-establish friendly relations with his children. Their young minds were impressionable while he was drinking. Without saying so, they may cordially hate him for what he has done to them and to their mother. The children are sometimes dominated by a pathetic hardness and cynicism.[32]

COAs can be left behind by a recovering parent who can't cope with their "hardness and cynicism," the scars of their fear, or their co-dependent belief in the myth of willpower. In some cases, children remain more cut off from their feelings, disturbed in their relationships with others, and locked in a struggle to keep their world (internal and external) under control than their healthier parent. Recovering alcoholics who see this happening are powerless to heal their children. In one of the final ironies of recovery, the roles have been reversed.

Situations like these illustrate how absolute the separation is between a parent's recovery and that of the child. Once the damage has been done—once a family has become alcoholic—every member of that family must undertake her own recovery. No one can do this for anyone else. The more family members enter into recovery, the more this becomes the new family norm, and the more support there is for everyone. But each person must find his own reasons for undertaking the work of his own recovery.

Stages of Recovery

Alcoholism is a profound experience. It is also extremely treacherous. Those who survive it have seen aspects of themselves which most people never encounter. They have also had the opportunity to discover how to give in to, and nurture, the process of internal healing—in order to survive. By practicing the principles of recovery in their daily lives, sober alcoholics can grow and mature in ways that were totally unknown to them before they became prisoners to their chemical dependence.

The recovery process in chemical dependents serves as a blueprint for many of the changes ACAs must make if they hope to leave their alcoholic families behind and find a fuller, more gratifying way of life. In brief, recovery has as much to offer other family members as it does the alcoholic, and the dynamics of the recovery process are nearly identical.

Stephanie Brown's[33] outline for recovery from alcoholism goes beyond the traditional Jellinek curve, which portrays chemical dependence as a progressive downward journey into denial and disease, while recovery is portrayed as the mirror image—a progressive return to health. Brown describes the predictable stages people pass through as they recover from addiction by gradually integrating their experience of how the disease affected them.

1. *The Drinking Stage* is characterized by the belief that control is possible. The loss of control, and the damage this has created, is dealt with primarily through denial and externalization.

2. *The Transition Stage* involves the two issues addressed in the First Step of Alcoholics Anonymous: "We admitted we were powerless over alcohol and that our lives had become unmanageable." The individual accepts the label of "alcoholic" and acknowledges that efforts to control drinking have been largely unsuccessful. The focus during the Transition Stage is on behaviors necessary to maintain abstinence.

3. *Early Recovery Stage* is a time to explore the wider implications of being an alcoholic and accepting human limitations. Before early recovery, alcoholics see the world as a mountain to be conquered by direct assault (drinking stage). After accepting that it can't be licked this way (transition stage), they "begin to take their direction *from* [italics mine] the mountain, moving backwards, forwards, and sideways, steadily gaining ground"[34] (early recovery stage).

   This is a time when the recovering person's distorted relationship to willpower is being reworked in many areas, not just those which involve drinking or other drug use. The focus moves during early recovery from behavioral steps needed to maintain abstinence to more general interactions with the environment, with special emphasis on interpersonal interactions.

4. *Ongoing Recovery Stage*, which follows the positive achievements of sobriety and more realistic and effective relationships with others, is a time of growing self acceptance. One's sense of self is further developed and fine tuned. For many, a spiritual focus emerges as a person moves "away from a self-centered view of the world to one which places the individual in relation to a larger universe."[35]

Jerome Levin[36] summarizes these four stages when he writes: "Psychological treatment aims to replace addiction with relationship and to use this emotional bond to promote integration and growth."

There is a negatively spiraling dynamic in alcoholics which must be broken before recovery can occur. This dynamic begins with a developmental arrest, or a regression during the drinking stage, in the experience of self. Addiction becomes a dysfunctional effort to repair this disturbance, and secondarily disrupts the interpersonal relations which could begin healing the deficit in self. The process of recovery unwinds the spiral through its focus on sobriety and dependence on others for support. As such dependence is antithetical to narcissism, recovery gradually builds a more mature foundation for the self.

Understanding the dynamic of recovery is useful in treating ACAs because children of alcoholics go through similar stages. This should come as no great surprise. Most of what ACAs know about willpower was learned at the knee of their alcoholic and co-dependent parents. Adults who experience gaps in their sense of self almost always pass these on to their children. This implies that ACAs not only have the same distorted relationship to willpower as active chemical dependents, but also possess similar deficits in their experience of self. It is little wonder that the recovery process is the same for both.

3

AXIS II:
THE WOUND:
POST-TRAUMATIC STRESS
DISORDER

At Genesis Psychotherapy and Training Center, "the wound" refers to the damage done by excessive stress—an everyday reality for children growing up in alcoholic homes. Stress is always present in relationships distorted by alcoholism. Sometimes it comes directly from the uproar of a parent's uncontrolled behavior. Other times it's a byproduct of denial; the family refuses to admit that it has a problem, or that the problem is important. Although stress is much more obvious in some families than in others, most ACAs experienced a high level during childhood. The effects of this wound often last well into adulthood, if not for life.

The diagnosis of Post-Traumatic Stress Disorder (PTSD) is useful for understanding how this wound occurs and how best to approach it in therapy. This chapter explores PTSD as a model for *one aspect* of what we see in COAs. The model offers a unifying framework for what often seem, on the surface, to be contradictory characteristics. It provides a new perspective on how stressful it must be to grow up in an alcoholic home, even a "nice home where things weren't all that bad."

The following case histories illustrate the apparently contradictory characteristics frequently seen in ACAs. To protect my clients' privacy, each is a composite portrait of several people I have seen in therapy.

CASE HISTORY:
THE NUMB DOCTOR

Deborah was born in Connecticut, where her father was a successful professor of biochemistry at a small liberal arts college. Her mother came from a lower socioeconomic class and had been abandoned at an early age by a severely alcoholic father.

Deborah's home life was highly structured and emotionally sterile. Father was devoted to his career and assumed that his wife would take charge of all family activities. He would arrive home at seven, have two martinis before dinner, and retire to his study for the rest of the evening. Deborah worshipped her father and longed for his attention. Because she never saw her parents argue, she accepted her family's intense belief that they were a model of mature, rational behavior. A brother six years Deborah's junior rounded out the perfect family.

Only two things marred the family's image, and no one outside the family ever saw either one. Mother's deep dependence on father was complicated by periodic depressions, during which Deborah quietly took over most of her mother's family functions. The first depression came after the birth of the younger brother and a move to San Diego, where Deborah's father obtained a more prestigious faculty appointment. He responded to his wife's depression with disgust, becoming even more emotionally remote and chiding her with platitudes about "strength of will."

The second blot on the family's self-image occurred during Deborah's early teen years, when her father's drinking suddenly escalated following the deaths of his mother and father. He was soon diagnosed as having a peptic ulcer and advised to stop drinking as part of his dietary treatment. Deborah's father immediately decided that it was irrational to drink, and he abstained for the rest of his life. He never entered a treatment or recovery program. In the years to come, his relationship with his wife became more distant and acrimonious because he expected her to end her depressions in the same way he had ended his drinking.

Although Deborah could remember few specific childhood events, she did recall, during therapy, that she had experienced panic attacks starting when she was about eight years old. They usually took place during the night, and she rarely told anyone about them. Once, when she was ten, a babysitter called her parents home from a restaurant because Deborah suddenly panicked at their absence. Her parents said little about this event; they simply went out less often.

Deborah always managed to do well in school, where she was highly motivated by praise from teachers. She often looked down on her classmates for acting younger than she. For years she looked forward to going away to college, and eventually she won a scholarship to a respected women's college in the East, where she continued to see her peers as immature. She threw herself into academic studies and discovered a special talent in biochemistry. She seldom dated and usually didn't enjoy it. Her best friend was a gay theater major. The two formed a bond out of being misunderstood outsiders. When graduation neared, Deborah's father began making plans for her to enter a graduate school of biochemistry. Instead, Deborah "found herself applying to medical schools" to study pediatrics.

The first two years of medical school were good times for Deborah. Except for worrying about her brother, whose grades and behavior were getting worse, she felt independent from her family. She lived with a boyfriend for more than a year until both entered the clinical years of medical school.

Direct patient contact was very stressful for Deborah. She became deeply upset when patients were in pain. Death haunted her. She quickly abandoned the idea of pediatrics, unable to tolerate children's vulnerability to suffering. During this time of emotional turmoil, Deborah leaned more heavily on her boyfriend for support, but shied away from intimacy. Their sexual activity plummeted to nothing. She began needing constant reassurance from him of her worth. Their arguments became fierce and frequent. When he left her, Deborah felt devastated and plunged into depression.

A kindly radiologist, close to retirement, coaxed her back into her studies. Deborah lost herself in the science and technology of radiology. Her publication of a theoretical paper on biochemical structure and radiology assured her acceptance into whatever residency program she chose. She decided on a program in San Francisco, largely to be closer to her brother. He had dropped out of school and was casting about aimlessly, his life made up of a mixture of odd jobs, marijuana, and exotic friends.

Toward the end of her training, Deborah again moved in with a man. He worked as a carpenter and eventually stopped hiding how much he drank. Their relationship was stormy, with many breakups and reconciliations. When she was offered a position as professor of radiology at a school in Los Angeles, Deborah chose to stay in San Francisco and continue her relationship. She entered a highly successful private practice, and few of her colleagues suspected the chaos in her personal life.

Finally her brother entered treatment for drug abuse. Deborah used this as an excuse to leave her boyfriend and share an apartment with her brother. After 15 months, he was doing quite well; he had gone back to school and was establishing a credible record as a pre-law major. He had also begun seriously dating a delightful high school teacher. Deborah felt more socially isolated than ever. It was around this time that a nurse gave her a book about ACAs. Deborah made an appointment with me to talk about therapy.

She entered my office dressed as a style-conscious, young, and successful professional. Her suit was gray wool; her hair, styled and in place. She appeared physically fit and attractive. Her manner was very businesslike: We were to have a discussion, doctor to doctor, about her life. She sat with her legs wound about each other, her arms folded and her eyes looking directly into mine. Everything about her appeared tightly bound and in control.

When she spoke, I felt captivated. Her words left her vulnerable, but her manner of speaking seemed to draw me into a trance. She spoke of knowing that all her apparent success had not begun to satisfy her deeper needs. Unless she could find a way to become more comfortable with intimacy, she would never find real quality in her life. She spoke of her fear of intimacy. But more than fear, she emphasized her ignorance of how to achieve intimacy in her relationships. And she spoke of her tendency to go numb whenever someone else sought increased intimacy with her.

A tremendous sadness seemed to lurk behind her voice. But never once did any spontaneous emotion begin to break through her slow and measured presentation. She was the kind of person you wanted to hug, but knew there was much more important work to do with her first.

CASE HISTORY:
THE OVERWHELMED CAB DRIVER

Alex was born in a small town in one of California's agricultural valleys. His mother was a diner waitress who periodically went off to Reno to work in the casinos and seek a quick fortune. Invariably she would have a whirlwind romance, during which her drinking got out of control, the new lover disappeared, and she found herself pregnant again. After recovering from another abortion, she would return home and attempt to reestablish an acceptable lifestyle.

During these trips to Reno, she farmed her children out to her brothers and sisters across the valley. Alex ended up most often with his aunt and maternal grandmother, both alcoholics. The grandmother had been married just long enough to the owner of a bar that she inherited it when he died of massive gastrointestinal bleeding while passed out on their apartment stairs.

Alex remembers neither living situation with any fondness. When he was with his mother, it was a fantasy world, with dreams and schemes of catching "Mr. Wonderful," punctuated by vile and angry outbursts that came without reason or warning. Overt and cruel physical abuse frequently accompanied these rampages. His mother spoke of how stern discipline was necessary if Alex was to have any chance of turning out better than his father (whoever *he* was). Stern discipline usually meant being pummelled about the abdomen and groin by his mother's fists. These rages led to Alex's running off to his grandmother's as early as age six. Out of regret and remorse, his mother tried to atone for her behavior by getting lucky in Reno.

Life with his grandmother and aunt was, if anything, even more chaotic. One or the other of them was always married to someone new. Invariably the new "stepfather" was alcoholic. Some ignored Alex. Others abused and beat him.

There was always one advantage of being with his grand-mother: Alex never doubted her love and acceptance, as he often did his mother's. Her home, such as it was, was always open to him. So was her heart, if he could catch her before 4 P.M., when she usually retired to the bar for the rest of the day. Sometimes Alex would hurry home from school just to sit next to her in the bar. She did not even have to acknowledge his presence. It was enough to be there beside this large woman.

When Alex was nine, he ran away from another of his mother's beatings. He arrived to learn from his aunt that his grandmother had died two months earlier. Alex still doesn't know how she died, and he always secretly doubted that she had. Thirty years later, this was still an unanswered question in his life.

From the time Alex can remember, he never brought any friends home. He was too embarrassed. He knew his family was different. Every weekend with his aunt and grandmother was a continuous drinking party. Patrons from the bar below felt free to wander in and out of the apartment, taking a shower or scav-enging through the refrigerator. Alex dealt with this by staying out of the house as much as possible. He joined a gang of boys that experimented with drugs and vandalism. Eventually he spent a year in a juvenile detention home for breaking into his own classroom and spraying everything with paint.

At age 16, Alex ran away and panhandled in San Francisco for two years. When he got desperate, he worked as a prostitute, although he never enjoyed this and always had to get drunk enough to tolerate it.

At 18, Alex was arrested for shoplifting. He chose to join the army instead of go to jail. The army was the first place where

Alex felt valued. He quickly advanced to the point of attending electronic maintenance school. He served two years in Vietnam, during which he saw only sporadic sniper fire. He reenlisted and planned to make the army a career. But his drinking continued to escalate until it grossly interfered with his performance. After driving an army vehicle off the road in a drunken stupor, he was given a medical discharge. He had several broken ribs and a broken leg.

After leaving the army, Alex moved back to San Francisco and became a cab driver, a "temporary" job that he is still doing after ten years. He restricted his drinking to after work and weekends. Five years ago, he met a woman with a four-year-old son. She was recently divorced and had little money, so Alex immediately began supporting them financially. He was devoted to her son from the start. They moved in together in three days.

Over the next two years, she took secretarial training and began working at a local bank. She was quickly assigned to the branch manager. Alex and his new family began attending church regularly. It was through this congregation, and in response to his girlfriend's wishes, that Alex eventually started going to AA meetings.

At first he experimented with intermittent drinking, but quit when his "son" said that he didn't like the smell of beer on his daddy's breath. Alex remembered what it was like to smell alcohol as a child. He immediately stopped drinking.

During the next two years, Alex became increasingly distressed about his relationship with his girlfriend. He longed to be close to her but couldn't trust that she loved him. He looked for clues that she was about to leave him, or that she was having affairs. He was never able to tell her about his fears. Instead, he found himself getting irritable with her. He criticized her even when he had no real reason. He was defensive whenever it seemed that she was criticizing him, and he often mistook a difference of opinion as criticism. Above all, he was ruled by fear.

He would awaken early in the morning and start planning what was necessary to avoid disaster during the day. He never felt he could relax and simply enjoy the good things in his life. Fears that it might all be taken away from him, or that his inadequacies would ruin him, constantly intruded whenever he attempted to let down his guard.

At the suggestion of his AA sponsor, Alex attended an ACA Al-Anon meeting. The meeting flooded him with feelings. Talking to people afterward, he heard about therapy for ACA issues. He contacted me the following day.

When Alex entered my office, he was dressed casually. Although he was 41 years old, he had the air of an adolescent, slumping in his chair and treating me with a mixture of deference and defiance. He began spilling out his story, freely mixing current problems with past memories. On several occasions he cried openly, then choked back his tears and went on rambling through his life history.

I had difficulty focusing his attention on a single topic. His expectations of therapy were vague. He felt immense relief, but also remained desperate for practical answers. It was clear that he had much to gain from therapy, but the first step was to note his impatience, to respect it, and to point out that it represented the greatest impediment to his treatment.

RESPONSES TO STRESS

The case histories profile two ACAs with opposite personality styles—proof that the ACA label, by itself, is inadequate as a diagnosis. As with most opposites in psychology, however, Deborah's numbness and Alex's overwhelming feelings are two sides of the same coin: persistent, unresolved reactions to stress.

What are the normal human responses to stress? What are the symptoms which result from experiencing abnormal levels of stress? Let's address these questions before going further in our exploration of ACAs.

The Stress-Response Cycle

Different people have different stress thresholds. But once that threshold has been crossed, everyone automatically begins a series of mental steps designed to chunk their experience down into manageable pieces. We all pass through the same phases in an effort to process and resolve stress. These phases are predictable, and so are the distortions in the way people experience them.

Figure 3-1 illustrates the normal human response to stress.[1]

A stressful event may trigger one of two immediate reactions: a spontaneous emotional *outcry*, or *denial*. A wrenching sob, an angry outburst, or a surge of panic is a normal response to a sudden, unanticipated stressor. If the stressor is one in a chronic series of traumas, or if it is overwhelming in its magnitude, the more likely response is immediate denial.

Denial protects us against being overwhelmed and flooded with grief, anger, or pain. The impact of the stressor seems negligible, and numbness may be the only feeling. A man reacts to news that his family has died in a plane crash by refusing to believe it. A child loses any memory of being sexually abused by her uncle. There is no need to shift perspective or call on new coping mechanisms because the significance of the event—even the reality of the event—is walled off and kept out of consciousness.

As time passes, memories and images of the event begin to pop into our awareness, often attached to minor irritations which

Figure 3-1
Phases of Response after a Stressful Event

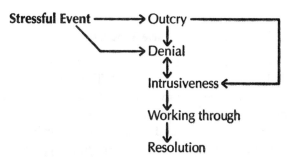

From Mardi Horowitz: *Stress Response Syndromes*

symbolically resemble the stress. This is the *intrusiveness* phase of the stress-response cycle. We work through major stresses by swinging back and forth on an internal pendulum between denial and intrusiveness. With each swing, we bite off a small chunk of the stress, chew on it, understand it, accept it, and digest it. Eventually, if nothing interferes with this process, we reach *resolution*.

Meanwhile, several recognizable themes weave in and out of our thoughts. These may have no apparent connection to the stressor itself. Although they can in some cases develop into a pathological reaction to stress, it's important to recognize that they are a normal part of the working through process, as long as they're only temporary. Common themes include fear that the stressor will recur, shame over one's helplessness, rage at the source of the stressor, guilt or shame over one's own destructive impulses, fear of others' aggressiveness, survivor guilt, and sadness.

There are also recognizable symptoms that may form during the early phases of the stress response, then gradually dissipate during the working through. Unless they persist for too long, these symptoms are normal. Common symptoms include a loss of control over thoughts and emotions, denial and numbing, repetitious or maladaptive behavior (such as compulsively returning to the source of the stress, or withdrawing from work or school), extremes of anxiety, general tension, impaired relationships, and psychophysiological disorders (such as migraine headaches or gastrointestinal problems).

Stress-Response Syndromes

A variety of factors can disrupt the natural process of working through and resolving a stressful event. They interfere with the free swinging of the pendulum between denial and the intrusion of memories. In some cases the pendulum gets stuck in the denial phase; in others, in the intrusiveness phase. Mardi Horowitz, M.D. has identified these as the two prototypical "Stress Response Syndromes."[2]

Individuals stuck in the denial phase experience a blunting of perceptions, selective attention, amnesia, depersonalization and derealization (denying the existence of an event even as it is being experienced), constriction of thought, emotional numbness, and armoring.

Individuals stuck in the intrusiveness phase experience hypervigilance, startle reactions, difficulty focusing concentration, ruminations, nightmares, flashbacks or reenactments, disorganized thinking, emotional attacks, and physical effects such as sleep disturbances, muscular tension, and cardiovascular damage.

Real people rarely present clinical material in a pure form, as therapists know. Most clients *tend* to be stuck more in one phase than the other, with their only alternative being a full and rapid swing into the other phase. They lack the ability to move freely back and forth between the denial and intrusiveness phases which is essential to working through stress. It is here, with the restricted freedom of the internal pendulum, that the therapist must begin working, and it is here that over-reliance on catharsis becomes simplistic and even harmful.

The case histories of the Numb Doctor and the Overwhelmed Cab Driver illustrate how stress responses can become so fixed that they are incorporated as enduring personality traits. When people are hindered in their social lives or their work lives by such personality traits, we can begin speaking of them, in Horowitz's terms, as exhibiting a Stress Response Syndrome.

A Stress Response Syndrome arises from an interplay between the intensity of the stress itself and an individual's tendency to respond with dysfunctional coping strategies. Successful responses to stress require *action* and *comprehension*. Action is change-oriented; either we attempt to remove the source of the stress, or we develop new skills for coping with it. Comprehension is attitude-oriented; we give meaning to events which cannot be changed.

By their very nature, some stresses cannot be affected by actions, and others remain devoid of meaning. Excessive stress, repetitive stress, and stress which involves total loss of control over one's physical safety are all examples of stresses which cannot be integrated. Concentration camp and combat experiences often fall into this category, as does child abuse, whether emotional, physical, or sexual.

Child abuse irrevocably changes a person's relationship to the world. Never again can the person claim the same degree of control over his destiny which appeared to exist before the abuse. The terror of seeing a parent out of control may be as much a source of stress as the actual assault. Once you have experienced this, you can no longer trust that your parent will keep you safe.

Although growing up in an alcoholic home is less dramatic than war or child abuse, this, too, creates stresses which cannot be integrated. For example, alcoholic families often operate according to several unspoken, self-contradictory rules like "nothing is wrong with our family, and don't you tell anyone about it." Living with such rules while trying to appear normal is chronically stressful. No amount of growth or new coping skills can reconcile the irreconcilable. This stress cannot be worked through until the rules which created it have been abandoned.

Stress generally leads to feeling a loss of control over one's life. Eliminating the stress (action) or finding meaning in it (comprehension) requires a clear-headed perspective on what you can and can't change. Alcoholic families are notoriously muddle-headed when it comes to this. As a result, COAs are saddled with dysfunctional strategies for coping with the stress in their lives. (Co-dependence, which underlies these dysfunctional strategies, is explored in detail in Chapter 4.)

Two dysfunctional coping strategies alcoholic families commonly use are denial and an over-reliance on willpower. The social network of the family rewards denial and often punishes anyone who threatens to break the denial by casting them in the scapegoat role or pushing them out of the family in some way. Although denial may make individuals unconscious of the stresses bearing down on them, it doesn't prevent those stresses from taking a toll on their lives, either emotionally or physically. Denial simply helps the COA to "cooperate" with becoming numb.

An over-reliance on willpower can lead to inflexibility and resistance to making the changes required during the working through phase. Willpower is seen as capable of controlling both the outer world and the inner world. Any failure of a person's willpower to eliminate the stressor or avoid the stress response is seen as evidence of personal inadequacy. Efforts are redoubled; more willpower is encouraged, and new methods of using willpower are sought. All of this flies in the face of reality when the stressor lies beyond the power of will to affect it. The devotion to willpower reinforces denial and inhibits the free swinging of the pendulum.

The Stress Response Syndromes framework helps to make sense of ACAs' contradictory symptoms. Both the denial-numbing syndrome, with its emotional disconnection and deadness, and the intrusive-repetitive syndrome, with its overwhelming emotions, are stress-related symptom complexes. They can also be seen as different "states of being." ACAs experience themselves as being in one state or the other. The transition can be virtually instantaneous, or it can be gradual but irrevocable once it has begun. This leads ACAs to report that they can't avoid moving from one state to the other, even when they are conscious that this is happening. Each state has its own subjective sense to it; each activates a different set of defensive maneuvers.

POST-TRAUMATIC STRESS DISORDER

In 1983, when the National Association for Children of Alcoholics (NACoA) was developing its charter statement, we wrote that "Children of Alcoholics suffer from _____." Then we sat looking at each other, wondering how to fill in the blank.

I was particularly proud of myself when I suggested the phrase, "an adjustment reaction to familial alcoholism." This seemed to solve the dilemma between (1) labeling all COAs as sick, and (2) supplying a DSM-style diagnosis capable of securing increased funding for treatment. Few people feel stigmatized by an "adjustment reaction" diagnosis.

It was not until later that I began to suspect how inadequate my suggestion was. A brief look at DSM-III-R's description of adjustment disorders reveals several problems with this diagnostic category, especially regarding *adult* children of alcoholics.

"Adjustment disorders," as defined by DSM-III-R, are *maladaptive* reactions which last no more than six months and can be expected to remit soon after the stress ceases. This description deviates significantly from the stress-related phenomena we see in ACAs, which were often quite *adaptive* originally, given the family environment in which they arose. Further, these reactions persist well into adulthood, and they don't automatically remit when the stress stops.

In other words, to label an ACA as suffering from an adjustment disorder is not only inappropriate but inaccurate. Adjustment disorders are abnormal reactions to more-or-less normal, though stressful, events. The reality in alcoholic homes is that the stress level is genuinely overwhelming. For children to build strong defenses against such an environment is not at all excessive or gratuitous. We are dealing here with *normal* reactions to abnormally stressful events.

"Outside of residence in a concentration camp," wrote George Vaillant, "there are very few sustained human experiences that make one the recipient of as much sadism [read 'stress'] as does being a close family member of an alcoholic."[3] The DSM scales (0-6) for "Severity of Psychosocial Stressors" agree. Family factors considered to be stressors for children and adolescents include "cold, hostile, intrusive, abusive, conflictual, or confusingly inconsistent relationship between parents or toward child; physical or mental illness in a family member; lack of parental guidance or excessively harsh or inconsistent parental control; . . . [or] loss of nuclear family members."[4] Divorce of parents, harsh or rejecting parents, or multiple foster home placements are rated as Severe stress (4); recurrent sexual or physical abuse, as Extreme stress (5); and the death of both parents, or chronic life-threatening illness, as Catastrophic stress (6). For adults, being held hostage and concentration camp experiences are rated as Catastrophic (6).

Most COAs experience family stress which places them at least in the Severe category, if not higher. As the saying goes, "Alcoholics do not have relationships, they take hostages." However you cut the cake, it becomes necessary to look beyond adjustment disorder to describe the primary wound caused by the stress of growing up in an alcoholic home.[5]

This brings us to the DSM-III-R (1987) diagnosis of Post-Traumatic Stress Disorder (PTSD), which represents current efforts to formulate a diagnostic category to cover the symptoms created by overwhelming stress.

The Development of PTSD
as a Diagnosis

PTSD is the latest in a long line of labels. In 1871, Jacob Mendes DaCosta noticed symptoms of palpitations, chest pain, and tachycardia in veterans of the American Civil War and the British wars in India and the Crimea. Initially known as "irritable heart," this syndrome was later renamed "soldier's heart."[6]

Over the years, this phenomenon has variously been called "neurocirculatory asthenia," "battle fatigue," "shell shock," and "combat neurosis." DSM-I (1952) introduced the diagnosis of "gross stress reactions," which was justified "only in situations in which the individual has been exposed to severe physical demands or extreme emotional stress." DSM-II (1968) replaced this with a choice of diagnoses: either "transient situational disturbance" or "adjustment reaction of adult life." The thrust in DSM-II was back toward the concept of traumatic war neurosis.

In the continuing controversy over whether the source of problems lies predominantly in preexisting flaws in an individual's personality or in the severity of the trauma, DSM-III (1980) responded to studies of Vietnam veterans with the diagnosis of "post-traumatic stress disorder." This diagnosis acknowledges that almost anyone can be adversely affected by exposure to "a psychologically traumatic event that is generally outside the range of human experience."

Today, in DSM-III-R, PTSD is listed under the heading of "anxiety disorders." Its essential feature is that characteristic symptoms arise "following a psychologically distressing event that is outside the range of usual human experience." Such a stressor "would be markedly distressing to almost anyone, and is usually experienced with intense fear, terror and helplessness."[7]

Earlier, DSM-III also claimed that symptoms of PTSD were more likely to occur if the stress was perceived as being of human origin, if a person's coping mechanisms were particularly rigid, and if environmental support systems discouraged acknowledgment of the stress or emotional reactions to it. These comments were dropped from DSM-III-R. On the other hand, DSM-III-R acknowledged for the first time that children can suffer from PTSD.

It is important to note that the list of symptoms for PTSD was developed independently of studying COAs. Like "soldier's heart," they describe the reactions people have to combat experience. The fact that many characteristics seen in COAs overlap with the diagnostic criterion for PTSD simply adds weight to the view that these characteristics are stress related. By implication, the level of stress within alcoholic families needs to be taken more seriously than it has been up to now.

The symptoms of PTSD fall into three clusters: *reexperiencing the trauma, psychic numbing,* and *increased arousal.* Symptoms must persist for at least one month before the diagnosis can be considered.

Reexperiencing the Trauma

Symptoms of Horowitz's intrusive form of Stress Response Syndrome fall into the diagnostic criterion of "reexperiencing the trauma." They include:

1. recurrent and intrusive distressing recollections of the event (in young children, repetitive play in which themes or aspects of the trauma are expressed)
2. recurrent distressing dreams of the event
3. sudden acting or feeling as if the traumatic event were recurring (includes a sense of reliving the experience, illusions, hallucinations, and dissociative [flashback] episodes, even those that occur upon awakening or when intoxicated)
4. intense psychological distress at exposure to events that symbolize or resemble an aspect of the traumatic event, including anniversaries of the trauma.[8]

Vietnam veterans reexperience the trauma of their combat experience in a variety of ways. Nearly two-thirds of combat veterans have recurrent nightmares,[9] about half of which consist of realistic dream images of the traumatic events. Other veterans complain of an inability to block conscious thoughts of combat traumas.

One of my clients told me that not a single day had passed in the ten years since his discharge that the word "Vietnam" had not come into his awareness. His efforts to will these intrusions away seemed to guarantee their appearance. Clearly, he remained unable to resolve the emotional charge connected to the combat experience, evidenced as much by the effort he put into blocking the thoughts as by the thoughts themselves.

Perhaps the most dramatic manifestations of this tendency to reexperience the trauma are flashbacks, episodes when perceptions, feelings, and behavior associated with the trauma reemerge intact in the face of events which symbolize the original stressor. It is as though the state of mind necessary to guarantee survival is suddenly revived and takes over, interfering with an individual's experience of present realities.

For example, a veteran may be walking down a city street when a car backfires or a firecracker explodes. Suddenly his palms become sweaty, his heart races, and he throws himself flat against the pavement, looking around for the source of incoming fire. Only gradually, as though waking from a dream, does he recognize that citizens are giving him a wide berth as they walk by. He rises, embarrassed, and hurries off to be alone, collect his thoughts, and calm his feelings.

Many veterans suffering PTSD have progressively modified their lives to avoid situations which could trigger such distressing intrusions. Many avoid talking to other veterans about their combat experience. In extreme cases, veterans have removed themselves from society's mainstream, even to the point of isolating themselves in wilderness settings.

ACAs report similar symptoms of reexperiencing the trauma. The saying that "alcoholic parents never die, they just lie six feet under the ground and wait for you" sums up what many ACAs believe: that it's impossible to put enough distance between themselves and their families to feel safe. Many move across the country in search of a geographical cure. One client told me that he bought a phone answering machine to monitor incoming calls, specifically to avoid being surprised by his alcoholic mother— and she had not called him for the past five years!

The following clinical vignette is an example of how ACAs experience the reemergence of old, survival-oriented feelings when confronted with events that symbolize traumas from the past.

Clinical Vignette:
The Traumatized Nurse

At 32, Linda was head nurse of her hospital's intensive care unit—the youngest head nurse in its history. Her work record was impeccable, her work habits obsessively thorough and responsible. To others, she was the picture of efficiency, maturity, and self control.

Inside, however, she felt inadequate, on the brink of flying out of control, and fearful that catastrophe was always around the corner. Conscious that the gap was widening between her inner self and her outer image, she sought therapy.

During therapy, as Linda was becoming more willing to let childhood memories emerge, she had a terrifying experience. Her daughter developed a mild fever, and Linda had to leave work several hours early to pick her up from school. After arranging to have the rest of her shift covered, and double-checking to make sure that all the orders on her patients' charts were being carried out, Linda began the 20-foot walk to her supervisor's office.

Suddenly her palms became sweaty, her heart started pounding, and she became light-headed. By the time she stood before her supervisor, she was close to a full-blown panic attack. This had never before happened to her at work. She felt herself rocking slightly from foot to foot. She was convinced that her supervisor was going to be angry at her for being "irresponsible." She felt stabbed by guilt. These feelings were extraordinary in light of the fact that Linda and her supervisor had an excellent, mutually respectful relationship.

In therapy, I asked Linda to recall the feelings she had while in front of her supervisor. As soon as she formed a vivid memory of the emotions, I asked her how old she felt. "Six years old," she answered immediately.

We began exploring her life at that age. This was when her father first lost control of his drinking, she explained. Her memories of her father's alcoholism centered on dinner time episodes when he became bombastic, sarcastic, and self-centered. At six years old, Linda quickly learned to cater to her father's needs at such times. To avoid being the target of his anger, she had to ignore her own feelings and attend to his. Authority figures were arbitrary, blaming, and uninterested in her needs. She had to take care of others at the expense of herself.

Linda had been getting close to memories like these in therapy. When she had to ask her supervisor for time to take care of her personal needs rather than her work duties, this was the symbolic equivalent of asking her drunk father to pay attention to her needs. Linda suffered an intrusion of the same old feelings. She reexperienced the trauma.

Comments

The clinical vignette brings up psychiatry's age-old debate between drive theory and trauma theory, explored in more detail in Appendix I. For now, it's sufficient to point out that the Vietnam veteran suffering flashbacks is hardly ambivalent about war. It's difficult to explain his flashbacks as a failure to resolve conflicting drives. In fact, he is likely to be remarkably *un*ambivalent about war. He *knows* he hates it.

There is a much more probable cause of his problem: At the moment he was overwhelmed by stress, new reflexes were born—reflexes consisting of perceptions, behaviors, and feelings that maximize survival. When such reflexes fail to disappear with time, and when the original threat no longer exists, they become "symptoms." Such symptoms should be seen as the direct consequences of overwhelming traumatic stress.

While Linda's behavior with her supervisor could have been the result of ambivalent and unresolved feelings about authority figures, this did not seem likely to me. There had been too many other occasions when she had dealt well with her superiors and exercised evenhanded authority over her staff. Also, her reexperience of the trauma was not generalized, as it often is in situations where drive theory applies. It happened in a highly specific set of circumstances, which is more consistent with trauma theory.

Therapeutically, the bottom line is this: No matter how challenging it may be to determine whether a specific behavior results predominately from conflicting drives or from post-traumatic effects, the treatment is different enough to make this distinction very important. Instances when ACAs reexperience the trauma often have a "flashback" quality rather than a neurotic quality, putting them on the side of trauma theory.

Psychic Numbing

Symptoms of Horowitz's Stress Response Syndrome of denial parallel the PTSD diagnostic criterion of "psychic numbing." DSM-III-R states that a person with PTSD may show:

> . . . persistent avoidance of stimuli associated with the trauma or numbing of general responsiveness (not present before the trauma), as indicated by at least three of the following:

1. efforts to avoid thoughts or feelings associated with the trauma
2. efforts to avoid activities or situations that arouse recollections of the trauma
3. inability to recall an important aspect of the trauma (psychogenic amnesia)
4. markedly diminished interest in significant activities (in young children, loss of recently acquired developmental skills such as toilet training or language skills)
5. feeling of detachment or estrangement from others
6. restricted range of affect, e.g., unable to have loving feelings
7. sense of foreshortened future, e.g., does not expect to have a career, marriage, or children, or a long life.[10]

When Vietnam veterans returned home, they often complained of feeling like they no longer "fit in" to society, their communities, even their own families. Combat experience had robbed them of their sense of belonging. Many blamed the massive social changes that occurred in the United States during those years; others blamed the vocal anti-war movement. But as therapists began hearing that many vets no longer felt that they fit in to *their own emotions*, it seemed that the origin of these feelings (or lack of feelings) had to run deeper.

A rupture had occurred between the veterans' sense of self and their emotions. This rupture had been of survival value in combat, as the following clinical vignette shows.

Clinical Vignette:
The Disassociated Soldier

Roger served as a field radio operator in Vietnam. Soon after entering a combat zone, his squad came under fire. He vividly recalls each second of the attack. He remembers taking refuge behind a tree and calling for support; he remembers the smell of the vegetation around him, the sounds of the spent bullets as they tumbled past him, and the feel of the humid air. In this moment of danger, his senses had become uniquely clear and sharp. He felt energized, excited, and strong.

When a young soldier raised his head from a nearby ditch, Roger watched as a bullet slammed through the man's forehead.

The man dropped limply, instantly lifeless. The only memory Roger has from this point on is the thought that the young soldier's life had gone out of him as quickly as a light bulb dims after it is switched off. He recalls few details of their rescue that afternoon, and none of his feelings.

Comments

At the moment traumatic stress overwhelms us, we automatically click into self-protective measures. These psychological defenses are part of our biological heritage. They swing into action like a psychic immune system, without any need for conscious prodding. They also exist without regard to a person's particular character structure, although this can affect how effective they are (just as a person's general health can affect how effective the immune system's defenses are against infection).

In Roger's case, the moment of witnessing death brought the meaning of war home to him with an impact he has still not fully integrated. As he stood behind the tree, looking at the dead soldier only feet away from him, his survival instincts took over and created a sudden gap between himself and his feelings. It was not to his advantage to begin grieving just then. It was not a good time to pull out his copy of Elisabeth Kübler-Ross's *On Death and Dying* and get in touch with his emotional reactions. It was not a good time to sit down with other soldiers for a group sensitivity session. It *was* a good time to devote *all* of his physical and psychic energies toward achieving one goal: staying alive. The rupture that leads to psychic numbing occurs at moments like these.

Most veterans assume that their estrangement from themselves and others will fade with time, but it often does not. Freud's assertion that time is irrelevant to the unconscious becomes important here. Time alone is rarely enough to heal the rupture that leads to psychic numbing. Healing requires an active process, just as many physical injuries must be actively ministered to if they are to heal.

It may at first seem trivial to compare COAs to veterans like Roger, except for those COAs who experienced physical or sexual abuse or witnessed such abuses forced on others. Recent research, however, indicates that symptoms of PTSD clearly do occur in children and adolescents. And psychic numbing is extremely common among ACAs.

Perhaps it's best to avoid making direct comparisons between the experience of combat soldiers and children growing up in alcoholic homes. Any effort to assess the relative stress each is under would be colored by our perspective as adults. Since children are naturally more vulnerable than adults, both physically and emotionally, what a child considers to be a major stress cannot be adequately assessed from the adult perspective. Also, the degree of stress one is under is directly related to the coping skills one can bring to bear against the trauma. There is no way to directly compare the experience of a six-year-old, with immature coping skills, who is leaning over a drunk mother to see if she has died or simply passed out, and Roger's experience of knowing that he just saw a man die and may well be next.

ACAs exhibit psychic numbing in a variety of forms, and with a pervasiveness, which warrants using PTSD as a framework. They frequently have few childhood memories, and they lose access to many of the most painful events they experienced. They actively avoid recalling the past, even as the past intrudes into their awareness and is reexperienced. Many have a restricted, over-controlled emotional range. And disconnection from others, from themselves, from the present moment, and from their immediate direct experience is very prevalent.

This disconnection may be severe and lasting, or subtle and transitory. As their primary defense against anxiety, many ACAs habitually withdraw their attention from the moment. You may see this as a slight glazing of the eyes, or a tightening of the facial muscles. Their expression becomes more bland and rigid. They may break eye contact or begin veering off the topic being discussed. Almost all ACAs have their own names for this experience: "going into the ozone," "phasing out," "having the wall come down" or "the curtain come across," "getting confused."

It's easy to understand how ACAs who were overtly abused would develop psychic numbing. But why would those *without* such a history have the same symptoms? As the following clinical vignette illustrates, psychic numbing doesn't always develop suddenly. It can also be fostered over a longer period of time.

Clinical Vignette:
The Boy Behind the Facade

By the time he was nine years old, Tom had already lived nine years with an alcoholic father. As an adult in therapy, he recalled an incident from that period of his life.

He and his father were standing beside the tractor, and his father was arguing that the field was dry enough to be plowed. Tom's visual image of the scene is dominated by his father's slightly bloated, ruddy face looming over him. When intoxicated, his father was oblivious to the way he invaded other people's comfort zones. Tom's impulse was to back away, but he knew this would irritate his father. So he stood his ground without any outward sign that inwardly he was retreating.

Tom knew that it made no sense to try plowing the field that day. They had gotten the tractor stuck in the muddy soil the day before, and it had rained again last night. As his father explained why he thought they could do the job anyway, Tom felt as if he were being held hostage. He knew that his father had already tried to convince his mother that they should do the plowing; she had said he was crazy. Now Tom was caught between the two. If he agreed with his father, his mother would think he was crazy, too. But if he answered his father truthfully, he would be seen as siding with his mother. It was a no-win situation.

Tom immediately went into his detached survival mode. His sole goal became to escape being held hostage. He knew that arguing rationally with his intoxicated father would only fuel the fire, and he would have to stand there for the next forty minutes. However, if he agreed with his father, he could probably get away in thirty minutes—but he would also have to struggle with the stuck tractor again. Another no-win situation! Tom chose instead to fall into Huckleberry Finn's favorite disguise: He allowed his father to see in him whatever his father needed to see. (Huckleberry's father was a drinker, too.)

He nodded a bit when his father wanted him to. He smiled a bit when it was required, but he never really responded enough to encourage his father. This required a delicate balance, something Tom had already begun to master. (Of course, his audience was intoxicated, and therefore not the best judge of how well he could hide his real feelings.) As Tom now explains, he became totally unaware of his feelings as he focused all his attention on responding the way his father required, but in very small doses. The result: He managed to escape in only fifteen minutes!

Tom adds that when he closes his eyes and calls up a picture of the scene, he literally sees the back of his own head in front of his father's face.

When Tom first recalled this scene in my office, his eyes flooded with tears. It was only much later that we were able to explore how he tended to approach me from behind the same kind of facade.

Comments

For Tom to behave as he did, he had to distance himself emotionally from his own experience. He learned how to foster the gap that was opening between himself and his feelings. He learned how to place his feelings on the other side of this gap, then widen it until his feelings were far enough away that he could focus on his father's needs and neglect his own.

To accurately interpret Tom's experience, we must remember that this was not an isolated incident. For most COAs, the experience of being held hostage to their parents' alcoholism pervades their entire childhood. It's simply too painful to live in such a world without learning to numb yourself.

Imagine this scene from another perspective—a neighbor's, for example. As you drive by, you observe what looks like an ideal relationship: Father and son are out by the tractor, discussing the spring plowing. There are no outward signs to indicate the extraordinary psychological mechanisms churning within Tom. Quiet desperation is easy to miss, precisely because it is so quiet, and because it wants to be missed (at the same time, it also wants to be seen). You can't see it; Tom's father can't see it. Tom bears it alone.

Increased Arousal

The psychophysiological aspects of trauma were first studied in the late 1920s by Walter Cannon, who described "homeostasis" and the "fight-or-flight" response. His work began to define the human *physical* response to stress. Mediated primarily by the sympathetic nervous system and the adrenal glands (via adrenaline and cortisol), this response includes increased heart rate and cardiac output, exaggerated respiration, and diversion of blood from vegetative functions to skeletal muscles.

When this state of arousal becomes permanent, as it does in PTSD, it becomes a health hazard. Symptoms of increased arousal include:

1. difficulty falling or staying asleep
2. irritability or outbursts of anger
3. difficulty concentrating
4. hypervigilance
5. exaggerated startle response
6. physiologic reactivity upon exposure to events that symbolize or resemble an aspect of the traumatic event (e.g., a woman who was raped in an elevator breaks out in a sweat when entering an elevator).[11]

Many Vietnam combat veterans found that they could not relax after returning to civilian life. Constantly on edge, constantly anticipating disaster, they were unable to redevelop trust in the safety of their world. It was as though their danger-sensing antennae were permanently raised and scanning the environment, with no way to turn them off. These veterans have remained chronically anxious, easily startled, and prone to stress-related medical problems.

Like the Dissociated Soldier's psychic numbing, increased arousal can have survival value when other human beings are trying to kill you. Not paying enough attention to danger signals, or dismissing a strange sound outside the perimeter as just a forest animal's nighttime activity, can be the last mistake a soldier ever makes. Those who remain the most vigilant, and who believe the worst of the slightest new sound, are those with the best chance of survival. Unfortunately, this hypervigilance doesn't automatically stop when the combat zone is left behind.

COAs also benefit from becoming hypervigilant. Their family environment is arbitrary and often chaotic. The sooner children can sense a parent's alcohol-induced personality changes, the sooner they can adjust their behavior to avoid being caught in the gathering storm.

One ACA told me about a time when he ran home from school with a perfect spelling test, only to suppress his excitement as soon as his hand wrapped itself around the front doorknob. He watched himself as he walked nonchalantly into the living room, where he noticed his father reading the newspaper by himself, a sure sign that he had begun drinking. He walked through to the kitchen with just a cursory greeting. His mother's mood showed that no active arguing had happened yet, so he prodded his excitement to reemerge. His mother recognized how calculated all of this was, but she responded to him as if his enthusiasm were still truly spontaneous—although its essence had been destroyed.

ACAs often have a selective sensitivity to their worlds. While they may be totally unaware of their own needs, or the affection that their friends genuinely feel for them, they may be acutely aware of any hostility, criticism, or ambivalence in the air. They constantly monitor their surroundings. They notice the slight raise of your eyebrow and interpret this as a judgment against them. They focus on the one member of their audience who yawns while the others are engrossed. Their friends and spouses sense that they are always under scrutiny, and fear that the slightest sign of rejection will be perceived as total abandonment (i.e., reexperiencing the trauma).

ACAs can be so obsessed with maintaining control that they practically have to check the sun each morning to be sure that it has risen properly. They have difficulty delegating work, convinced that it won't get done right if they don't do it themselves.

They complain of never being able to relax or play. Instead of trusting that problems will work out, they assume that they will get progressively worse.

I have been told of startle responses which occur to the sound of ice tinkling in a glass, or of the front door opening. Hyper-alertness becomes a way of life for ACAs, who perceive it as necessary for their emotional survival.

Survivor Guilt and Depression

DSM-III listed survivor guilt and depression as symptoms of PTSD. DSM-III-R mentions depression only as an "associated feature" and doesn't mention survivor guilt at all. Despite this official deemphasis, I find that survivor guilt and depression are valuable indicators of PTSD.

The development of survivor guilt is a complex psychological phenomenon. It begins with the fact that human beings cannot tolerate being forced to feel completely powerless. We try to ignore or deny the random forces that buffet our lives. Then one day a wildly flying piece of shrapnel kills the soldier standing next to us, or we walk away from a car accident in which another person died. Suddenly we are forced to confront our precarious existence in an impersonal universe. We become overwhelmed by existential anxiety.

As uncomfortable as it may be, survivor guilt is an effective avenue out of being overwhelmed. It has much in common with the defensive postures taken by victims of physical and sexual abuse.

When combat veterans are plagued by feelings that they "could have done something" to prevent a buddy from being killed, they are denying the intolerable reality of their powerlessness. The consequences of acknowledging it are too great for any of us to bear. And so we look for ways that we might have warned the victim, stopped the deadly assault, or prevented the fatal accident. We look for ways to explain our own survival—perhaps we were stronger, braver, or smarter than the other person. We search for the one thing we did, or the one quality we have, that somehow saved us. We refuse to accept that blind luck can play a part in life-and-death matters, because that would be admitting our powerlessness.

A vague sense of guilt develops—the last outpost of hope that the universe can still be controlled or predicted, if only we are equal to the task. Our guilt also stands as a monument to the dead, as if resolving it would betray the victim's memory. In the end, survivor guilt is the result of our unwillingness to recognize that the universe is ultimately out of our control, and often indifferent to our individual fates.

Many veterans found that a chronic sense of depression filtered into every part of their lives upon returning home. Others were not as pervasively affected, but were unable to enjoy the richness of their post-war lives. At times of vacation or celebration, thoughts often returned of those who never made it home. These veterans have lost the ability to abandon themselves to pleasure.

Many COAs experience survivor guilt for trying to separate themselves from their families. Clients have told me of how "callous" they feel whenever they consider acting on their own behalf instead of sacrificing their desires for the family. For example, one woman couldn't decide what to do with the $800 she had saved for a long-planned vacation. Should she go ahead and spend it on herself, or respond to her parents' plea for money to pay their rent? She had "loaned" money to her folks several times in the past to rescue them from their latest crisis. Usually they drank the money and lost their apartment anyway. In my client's mind, she could either use the money for her own pleasure and feel guilty about it, or let her parents waste the money and feel like a caring daughter.

Those ACAs who do manage to break away from their families may find themselves unable to abandon themselves to pleasure, like the depressed combat veterans. The sense of loss at having "abandoned" their families always intrudes. To them, it seems selfish to have left the sinking ship, even though staying aboard would only have added their names to the list of casualties. Unfortunately, many people perceive something "noble" about such total sacrifice, and choose it over the guilt that comes from being one of the rats that save themselves.

Even in the best, most functional families, there are many ties that must be severed before children can start living their separate lives. Imagine how much more complicated this becomes when the chaos and trauma of a parent's progressive alcoholism envelops the family. Out of their own desperation, parents may be unable to allow a needed child to leave. While some children numb themselves to their feelings in order to leave the family, others remain plagued by a sense of guilt for having put themselves first.

Children and PTSD

An important expansion of PTSD occurred when DSM-III-R formally acknowledged that children also suffer delayed symptoms from excessive trauma. Lenore Terr's research with the 25 victims of the Chowchilla school bus kidnapping helped define the symptoms of PTSD in children.[12] Terr concluded that the trauma of this incident arose primarily from the victims' total loss of control over their lives.

Within 27 hours, every child developed symptoms which persisted at least four years later. These included anxiety, mortification (profound embarrassment) at their vulnerability, suppression of memories, decline in school performance, nightmares, a foreshortened sense of the future (an obvious detriment to normal child development), and a belief in omens. These omens were actually new "memories" of events leading up to the kidnapping, invented by the victims to restore some sense of control over what had happened to them. If only they had recognized the importance of these omens, the children claimed, they might have prevented the crime.

"In a sense," Terr reports, "the child chooses personal responsibility and even guilt for the event over utter helplessness and randomness."[13] These findings apply to *all* children, not specifically to children from alcoholic homes, lending credence to my belief that many characteristics of COAs are the result of traumatic experiences.

The "profound embarrassment" which traumatized children feel cuts very deeply. Bessel A. van der Kolk points out that clinicians who treat abused children "often find the residue of self-blame and self-hatred the most resistant to therapeutic intervention."[14] While workshops for ACAs on low self-esteem have become popular, studies of PTSD argue that this approach is unlikely to make inroads into the depths from which such feelings come.

Spencer Eth and Robert Pynoos note that children who personally suffer trauma are more likely to lose access to memories of the event (protective amnesia) than children who witness trauma to others. Witnesses are more likely to experience starkly clear and terrifying intrusive memories.[15] This phenomenon may help explain why many ACAs are more able to empathize with the trauma other members of their family suffered than with their own fate.

Grief and Trauma

While it is often painfully obvious that many ACAs suffer from unresolved grief, it is not always appreciated that their failure to grieve may be due to the traumatic nature of their losses.

"Grief" refers to the experience which follows significant loss. We call the process of attenuating this grief by feeling it and adjusting to the loss "mourning." Grief and loss can occur without trauma. For example, when a child is surrounded by a supportive family and helped to understand and grieve as a parent mercifully dies after a painful illness, the loss is not necessarily traumatic.

Trauma occurs when individuals are overwhelmed by an event and experience their helplessness in the face of intolerable danger, anxiety, and arousal. When a loss is accompanied by traumatic levels of arousal, a setup exists for post-traumatic reactions (psychic numbing and/or re-experiencing the trauma) to interfere with the grief work that must be done. Efforts to grieve are interrupted by the symptoms of PTSD. Until the reflex defenses against trauma are treated, mourning is impossible.

Traumatic grief is so common among ACAs that it is almost universal. This solidifies my belief that a thorough understanding of the dynamics of PTSD, its origins and treatment, is part of the foundation required for treating children of alcoholics.

EMOTIONAL ABUSE

The high incidence of physical and sexual abuse in chemically dependent families[16] is an obvious source of trauma. But many ACAs with stress-related characteristics never received such overt mistreatment. To understand the full spectrum of stressful family environments, we must also look at emotional (psychological) abuse.

The problem with emotional abuse is that it is difficult to define. Some clients pin the "emotional abuse" label on every disappointment they experienced, or every human frailty their parents evidenced. But this is no reason to dismiss all reports of emotional abuse as self-serving or vengeful. Emotional abuse does exist. It is probably more widespread than physical and sexual abuse. It is also woven throughout physical and sexual abuse, and may be the most damaging part of each.

James Garbarino, Edna Guttman, and Janis Wilson Seeley define abuse as a concerted attack by an adult on a child's development of social competence and sense of self. It is a *pattern* of psychologically destructive behavior that results when a parent is unavailable to respond to a child's needs, responds inappropriately, or responds harshly. They have identified five forms of psychological abuse:[17]

- *Rejecting the child.* The adult refuses to acknowledge the child's worth and the legitimacy of the child's needs.
- *Ignoring the child.* The adult deprives the child of essential stimulation and responsiveness, stifling emotional growth and intellectual development.

- *Isolating the child.* The adult cuts the child off from normal social experiences, prevents the child from forming friendships, and makes the child believe that he or she is alone in the world.
- *Terrorizing the child.* The adult verbally assaults the child, creates a climate of fear, bullies and frightens the child, and makes the child believe that the world is capricious and hostile.
- *Corrupting the child.* The adult "mis-socializes" the child, stimulates the child to engage in destructive antisocial behavior, reinforces that deviance, and makes the child unfit for normal social experience.

Garbarino *et al.* have also identified four predominant characteristics among abusing adults:[18]

- they were themselves abused as children,
- they are addicted to alcohol or other drugs,
- they lead a disorganized lifestyle, and/or
- they are mentally ill.

The common thread is that "Unless parents feel materially and psychologically secure enough to move beyond concern for themselves, they will not be able to function effectively as caregivers, as instructors, or as providers of emotional support for their children."[19]

It would be impossible to outline all the ways that parental alcoholism can result in the emotional abuse of a child. Most people with any experience in an alcoholic home know this first-hand. Yet many people continue to deny the connection between parental alcoholism and abusive behavior.

It's time to consider the possibility that parental chemical dependence is *presumptive evidence* of child abuse. Just as every adult being evaluated for child abuse should be carefully screened for chemical dependence, every adult being evaluated for chemical dependence should be carefully screened for child abuse. The harder we are willing to look, the more we will find, and the closer we will come to protecting every child's right to a safe environment.

Rejecting and Ignoring
the Child

Parents can overtly or covertly reject their children and their children's needs. When intoxicated, many people lose control over their hostile impulses. They become sarcastic, mean-hearted, and selfish. Parents belittle their children for being needy and dependent, or mock them for being inferior. In extreme forms of selfishness, they may be totally unaware of their children's needs.

Rejecting fades imperceptibly into ignoring. When parents are physically absent or intoxicated to the point of stupor and unconsciousness, ignoring becomes blatant neglect and even child endangerment. A mother goes on a "crack" cocaine high, and her twins die of exposure. A professor drinks beer in front of the TV on Saturday afternoon while his six- and four-year-old boys play unsupervised in their swimming pool.

Isolating the Child

Alcoholic families isolate their children in several ways. Many COAs are too embarrassed to invite friends over to their house. Parents of their friends may refuse to let their own children visit, not wanting them exposed to "negative influences."

Over time, alcoholic families withdraw from social contacts, or narrow their contacts to others who drink. The family becomes a closed system. Eventually, everyone develops the deep belief that they "don't belong" anywhere but in the immediate family—not in the extended family, not in the community, not in society. The perception of oneself as an "outsider" becomes more and more firmly ensconced. For parents, this may be a pervasive part of their *belief system*. For children who are still in their prime years of development, it can reach down further into the very core sense of their *identity*.

Terrorizing the Child

There are many ways to terrorize children— physical and sexual abuse, threats of violence, bullying, degrading name-calling, or simply being out of control at times when they depend on you.

Alcoholic families have a high level of tolerance for inappropriate behavior, and will excuse even overtly terrifying situations to avoid confronting how deeply troubled the family really is. Children may watch one parent striking another, only to have both parents minimize or deny their perceptions later on. Terror arises not only from the threat of physical violence, but also from the sudden awareness that your parents are out of control.

To grow up believing that the universe is a safe place, we must trust that our parents are omnipotent—at least for the first several years of our lives. Once the illusion of parental omnipotence is destroyed, the universe becomes profoundly unsafe, unless we have the tools to integrate this reality. COAs are robbed of this illusion long before they are prepared to live without it. They are too young, and they don't have the tools. This in itself is a terrifying experience.

There is another form of terror COAs feel: the fear that their family is in the process of flying apart. One ACA told me how he had worried for years that his parents would divorce, only to be told repeatedly that he had nothing to worry about. When his parents' marriage did eventually end in a bitter separation, his worst fears were confirmed. He felt betrayed that his worries, which had been entirely realistic, had been dismissed as unimportant.

Many children in alcoholic homes live in constant terror. On a feeling level, they are already responding to the catastrophes which truly lie ahead if the family does not get help.

Corrupting the Child

Alcoholic families corrupt their children in one of two ways—or both. First, there are all too many instances in which children are introduced to alcohol and other drug use at a very tender age. The only avenue into being part of the family lies in joining the party. Sometimes this happens because children have seen their parents model the use of chemicals as a way to cope with life's problems. To the children, this is normal behavior. It is what big people do, and every child wants to be a big person. At other times, parents actively encourage children to become intoxicated, supplying the alcohol and other drugs and making fun of any attempts to refuse them.

Second, children are often encouraged by a nondrinking parent to relate to the alcoholic parent in very dysfunctional ways. It is corrupting to model co-dependent behavior—for example, to minimize an episode of physical abuse to keep peace with a hung-over spouse, then hold this up as a vision of maturity. This reinforces coping strategies that undercut the child's sense of self and are especially dysfunctional when generalized to settings outside the alcoholic family. Modeling such unhealthy behavior gives rise to unhealthy personality traits in children, if not overt personality disorders.

How Children Defend Themselves

Children ultimately respond to abuse and abnormal levels of stress with a single set of defensive maneuvers. Faced with a world they see as mistreating them, they unconsciously make a fateful decision to see themselves as the cause of the abuse. This decision is made on a feeling level, not a thinking level, and it is so common that it deserves to be seen as part of the human survival instinct. When looked at from the adult perspective, we can describe this decision in rational terms. But it's important to keep in mind that this is merely our adult understanding, not a true description of how a child experiences it.

Children are small. They depend on big people to sustain them physically and emotionally. To children, these big people seem to have the power of gods. When these gods act capriciously and viciously, the world becomes treacherous. Children are left to see themselves as innocent victims, which is pretty much the truth. But when they start to see themselves as "Saints" in a world of "Sinners," they are overwhelmed by their powerlessness.

There is no hope that they can control their fate. And there is anger, which is properly directed out toward the external environment. The combination of impotence and anger is a prime breeding ground for violence. Especially when the anger is directed toward the parents, this combination sets a child up to be scapegoated. My personal guess is that those children who see the reality of their situation most clearly are at increased risk of becoming early casualties. They act out their anger in ineffective, impotent gestures. They may provoke further abuse, become delinquent, run away, or lose the motivation to continue through the stages of child development.

There is one small distortion children can make to transform this scenario, and it is here that they make the fateful decision to abandon a realistic view of what is happening to them. Since children think in black-and-white terms (witness the costumes in *Star Wars* and earlier cowboy movies), the distortion which naturally presents itself is to accept the opposite view. Rather than see themselves as Saints in a world of Sinners, they can reverse the equation and begin to see themselves as Sinners in a world of Saints. While this perspective is wholly inaccurate, it has such survival value that children routinely discover it. The more horribly children are abused, the more likely they are to accept this distortion hook, line, and sinker. It becomes their reality. And this reality is incorporated into their core sense of identity. At this point the distortion is no longer a mistaken belief, to be corrected later in life. It has become a part of one's identity, and therefore more resistant to later change.

The value of recasting oneself as the Sinner in a world of Saints is that it rescues hope. Hope stems from feeling that you can exert at least some measure of control over your fate. To abused children, hope stems from believing that the abuse is somehow deserved, which means that they should be able to change their behavior enough to no longer deserve it. If only they can become good enough, smart enough, grown-up enough—whatever is being demanded of them—then surely they can return to Eden! By taking responsibility for their abuse, children can maintain the illusion that their parents are perfect. The child abuse field is replete with tragic stories of children being wheeled into surgery after savage beatings by a parent, pleading with their parent to forgive them. Such is the power of our need for love, our need for the Good Parent, and our need for hope.

Rescuing hope is no small accomplishment. It sustains the internal drive to grow. In an effort to achieve the maturity necessary to deserve not to be abused anymore, children sometimes race through the stages of their development. The distortion which creates this hope keeps children invested in themselves, or at least in who they think they could become.

The price is quite high, however. Guilt, self-hatred, and depression gradually become part of the package children buy. The guilt and self-hatred come from seeing oneself as despicable enough to deserve being mistreated. The more they are abused, the more evidence children have that there is something essentially unacceptable about them. Whatever anger they feel about this situation is turned inward. Its passive expression leads to depression. Its active expression leads to self-mutilation or suicide.

When children with victim identities (Saints) reach adulthood, it is often without the tickets needed for a successful life (e.g., education). Their victim stance continues to compound life's problems. In contrast, when Sinners reach adulthood, they possess many tickets to success, and there is often a temporary respite. They may have several years to enjoy the absence of abuse, and life feels on the upswing. But they still carry the negative image of themselves as inadequate and undeserving. Unless these distortions in their identity are eventually modified, they are building their lives on a foundation of sand. Sooner or later, the foundation will begin to shift and falter. This is frequently the point at which "successful" ACAs enter therapy.

CONCLUSION

"The wound" suffered by many ACAs refers to the extraordinary degree of stress which permeated their early years in an alcoholic family, and to the direct effects this stress had on their psychological development. Post-Traumatic Stress Disorder (PTSD) accurately describes the ways that such stress impacts their lives, both as children and later on as adults. Effective treatment of stress-related characteristics requires that they be correctly identified as symptoms of PTSD, and that therapeutic approaches be tailored appropriately. This is discussed in detail in Chapter 2 of *Volume Two: Treatment*. Readers interested in pursuing the theoretical implications of PTSD further are referred to Appendix I of this volume, "Drive Theory and Trauma Theory."

4

AXIS III:
POOR WOUNDCARE:
CO-DEPENDENCE

The lasting damage abused children suffer is only partly due to the trauma of the abuse itself. It is also a product of the shame and secrecy, the inability to openly express emotional reactions, and the lack of validation for normal feelings that go hand-in-hand with the abuse. The final effect of any trauma is a combination of how severe it is (the wound), and how well it is treated (woundcare).

When COAs receive no validation for their feelings and find no meaning in their experience, the traumatic effects of being raised in an alcoholic family go deeper and last longer. Co-dependence compounds the effects of stress on COAs by denying the wound, invalidating their emotional reactions to it, and distorting the meaning of their experience.

A NEW FRAMEWORK FOR
UNDERSTANDING CO-DEPENDENCE

I place co-dependence within the general DSM-III-R framework of personality traits/disorders. It is most directly related to narcissism, a prevalent disorder characterized by "grandiosity, extreme self-involvement and lack of interest and empathy for others, in spite of the pursuit of others to obtain admiration and approval."[1] I view co-dependence as the *complement* to narcissism—as a disorder characterized by poor self-image, extreme involvement in others, excessive empathy, and the pursuit of others for confirmation of one's existence and definition of one's identity.

Complementary psychological disorders are not simple opposites. Rather, like two sides of a coin, they rest upon the same underlying issues, but manifest them in polar opposite directions. I see co-dependence and narcissism as two ends of the same continuum. They differ primarily because relationship dynamics on this continuum flow in only one direction, *from* the co-dependent *to* the narcissist.

I propose that co-dependence is a necessary part of a healthy, balanced personality, *once co-dependence has reached its mature form.* When co-dependence remains in its original, immature form, it causes pathologic personality traits capable of developing into a full-blown personality disorder. Even so, co-dependence accounts for only a portion of the characteristics found in ACAs.

It is not possible to collapse the "ACA Syndrome" into being equivalent to co-dependence. Just as ACAs have different degrees of stress-related characteristics, they manifest different degrees of co-dependence. Also, co-dependence has been found to exist in individuals who have never been exposed to alcoholism. Since alcoholism is not a necessary condition for co-dependence, and since ACAs are not necessarily co-dependent, it's a grave oversimplification to equate being an ACA with being co-dependent.

LEVELS OF MEANING

The word "co-dependence" is surrounded by an array of definitions, many vague and metaphoric. There are two reasons for this. First, competing frameworks—family systems approaches, cognitive approaches, object relations and psychodynamic approaches, to name a few—have all created their own definitions. Second, the term has been associated with different levels of meaning.

In *Diagnosing and Treating Co-dependence*,[2] I sorted out three different ways in which "co-dependence" is used: as a didactic tool, as a psychological concept, and as a disease entity.

Co-Dependence as a Didactic Tool

In dealing directly with family members of chemical dependents, co-dependence is an important didactic tool. The word legitimizes many of their feelings and gives them permission to start focusing on their own dysfunctional behavior. Co-dependence implies that family members have their own "something" to recover from. Its value in direct client education is reason enough for mental health professionals to take the concept seriously.

Many definitions for co-dependence have developed because of their practical value in dealing with clients. Such definitions work on the metaphoric level and are specifically designed to evoke an emotional response.

For example, Charles Alexander[3] describes co-dependence as like being a lifeguard on a crowded beach, knowing you can't swim, and hesitating to tell anyone for fear of starting a panic. Or, to give another example, "A co-dependent is someone who sees *someone else's* life pass before his eyes at the moment of death." Confronted with descriptions like these, co-dependent clients are amazed. Someone else understands their internal dilemma and desperation!

Because metaphoric definitions of co-dependence help break people's isolation and reorient their focus inwardly, the term is likely to remain a valuable didactic tool, especially in the CD field.

Co-Dependence as a Psychological Concept

Psychological concepts like defense mechanisms, the ego, homeostasis, and enmeshment are critical for professionals to communicate their understanding of human behavior to each other. They enable us to identify the building blocks of personality and relationships and organize them into coherent frameworks, without reference to whether these building blocks are being combined into healthy or unhealthy patterns. Such evaluation is the business of diagnosis.

In general, psychological concepts fall into one of two broad categories: Either they refer to the intrapsychic world of the individual, or to the interpersonal world of human relationships. There are very few concepts which belong equally to both worlds. One notable exception, and perhaps the prototype for multilevel concepts, is *projective identification*, a term introduced by Melanie Klein in 1946.[4]

As an example of projective identification, a man discovers that his car has been stolen. His fear of anger (to which he gave destructive license during his active chemical dependence) causes him to immediately repress his feeling. Although his tone of voice and demeanor reveal the unconscious anger, he is only aware of feeling vulnerable and sad. The man further defends against his anger by projecting it out into the environment—specifically, onto his wife. She in turn gets uncharacteristically angry at the insurance adjuster for taking too long to respond. The man then jumps to the adjuster's defense.

This example illustrates three facets of human behavior: (1) Each person's behavior is consistent with his or her own unique personality; (2) relationships between people develop their own "personalities," with which each person's behavior is also consistent; and (3) intrapsychic and interpersonal realms intertwine and affect one another. Projective identification is concerned with the dynamics of this intertwining: how the man projected his anger outward, the wife identified with it, and the man was left with "evidence" that the anger really *did* originate outside himself—hence his defense of the insurance adjuster. In projective identification, one person's projections are absorbed and confirmed by another person's behavior. This single concept applies simultaneously to intrapsychic and interpersonal behavior.

Co-dependence as a psychological concept also points to interactions between intrapsychic and interpersonal dynamics. It focuses on relationships which are sustained by one member's tendency to mold herself (including her very sense of identity) around the projections of the other. Whereas therapists tend to see projective identification as being initiated by the *projector*, the concept of co-dependence highlights the active role played by the *receiving* partner in eliciting, and absorbing, projections. The concept of co-dependence refers simultaneously to the personality of this receiving partner and to the relationships entered into, normally with a narcissistic partner. An understanding of this complex dynamic forms the basis for therapeutic interventions.

Efforts to define co-dependence as a psychological concept have been hampered by the natural desire to *simplify.* The truth lies in the opposite direction. Co-dependence can be understood only if we recognize that it is a highly complex concept, speaking to the interface between intrapsychic and interpersonal realms. Viewed in this light, co-dependence stretches our powers of abstraction to their limits.

Co-Dependence as a Disease Entity

For the purpose of clinically assessing individual clients, the word "co-dependence" is used diagnostically. CD therapists speak of family members as being "affected by co-dependence" or "actively co-dependent." Such diagnostic assessments imply that a consistent pattern of traits and behaviors is recognizable across individuals, and that these traits and behaviors can create significant dysfunction. In other words, co-dependence is used to describe a disease entity in the same way phobia, narcissistic personality disorder, and PTSD are diagnostic entities.

I first proposed a set of diagnostic criteria for co-dependence[5] in 1986 to focus and clarify debate regarding its definition as a clinical entity. Without such criteria, no standards exist for assessing the presence and depth of pathology, developing appropriate treatment plans, or evaluating the effectiveness of therapy. The proper course for proving whether co-dependence exists as a specific entity is the testing of these or similar criteria for validity and reliability. Until we begin gathering such data, co-dependence will remain confined to clinical impression and anecdote.

This chapter proceeds under the assumption that co-dependence can be defined as a personality disorder with a complementary relationship to narcissism. This relationship can never be reduced to a few simple rules. Rather, it is a tapestry, filled with all the complexity of human life. Narcissism, a strong element in addiction, is the warp, and co-dependence is the woof.

Both have their origins in defective mirroring, which occurs when parents (or other primary caretakers) withdraw emotionally as their children begin to develop their own unique personalities. The resulting mixture of co-dependent and narcissistic characteristics is determined by the specific nature of the mirroring defect (e.g., is the empathic connection between parent and child excessive or deficient?), and the frustration or overstimulation of two primary needs: to have one's developing capabilities appreciated, and to have an ideal parent care for our every need. All of these points are explained more thoroughly later in this chapter.

In brief, I view co-dependent personality traits as capable of creating sufficient dysfunction to warrant the diagnosis of Personality Disorder, Not Otherwise Specified (NOS) as outlined in DSM-III-R. Viewing co-dependence as a personality disorder has implications for its causes and its treatment. Understanding these implications is essential to treating many ACAs.

EXPANDING THE MYTH
OF NARCISSUS

Mythology has often been used to illustrate basic patterns of human personality. In our search to understand co-dependence, we can turn to the Greek Myth of Narcissus, which is normally used to illustrate the prototypic self-centered personality. Perhaps properly called the Myth of Narcissus *and Echo*, it contains a great deal of ancient wisdom.

Echo was the fairest of the wood nymphs, and quite a talker. Her gift of gab got her into trouble with Hera, wife of Zeus. Known for her jealous outbursts, Hera suspected that Echo was distracting her with amusing chatter while Zeus was cavorting with her friends. The goddess condemned Echo to remain speechless, except for repeating what was first said by others.

This curse was hardest to bear when Echo, like many maidens before her, fell in love with Narcissus, a young man of great beauty. Echo had no way to tell Narcissus how she felt. All she could do was follow him about, hoping for a scrap of attention.

Her big chance came one day when Narcissus called out to his companions, "Is anyone here?" Echo was thrilled, but too shy to meet him face-to-face. Instead she remained hidden behind a tree and called back, "Here . . . here!" Narcissus looked around but saw no one. "Come!" he shouted. That was what Echo had been waiting for. Stepping forward, she beckoned to Narcissus and said sweetly, "Come."

But Narcissus turned away in disgust from her outstretched arms. "I will die before I give you power over me," he declared. To which Echo responded forlornly, "I give you power over me." His rejection left her feeling ashamed. She could not be comforted, yet she continued to love Narcissus.

It is a misconception that Narcissus' fatal flaw lay in becoming enamored of his own reflection. This was actually a punishment visited on him by Nemesis, the goddess of righteous anger, because he scorned those who adored him and was oblivious to their affection. Furious over his treatment of Echo, Nemesis caused him to lean over a clear pool for a drink—and fall hopelessly in love with what he saw there. Consumed by the futile desire to have his affection returned, Narcissus gradually wasted away.

When death eventually overtook Narcissus, Echo was helpless to reach out to him until he breathed his last. As he said his final "Farewell, farewell," to his own image, she repeated the same words to him.

After Narcissus' death, Echo's flesh became increasingly insubstantial, while her bones became cold and turned into stone. Today, all that can be found of Echo is her voice, in canyons and caves, still repeating only what others have said.

This myth clearly outlines a complementary relationship between two partners, one of whom is primarily involved in mirroring the other. It is consistent with both of their personalities that the whole myth was named after Narcissus alone. If Narcissus is the prototype for pathologic narcissism, then Echo is the prototype for pathologic co-dependence.

Freud acknowledged this complementary relationship when he wrote, "[One] person's narcissism has a great attraction for those who have renounced part of their own narcissism and are seeking after object-love."[6] This statement is full of meaning which must be explored slowly and deliberately. (However, "object-love" is an unfortunate phrase which simply means "being loved by another person." For reasons of history and tradition, it remains part of the language of our field.)

First, Freud described a "chemistry" which exists in the relationship between anyone who is self-centered (for example, because of chronic intoxication) and someone who is other-centered. Narcissists have a need to feel special, and co-dependents have a unique talent for helping them feel that way. The two have a passionate affinity for each other, like opposite poles of a magnet, or like a warm glove and a cold hand. This "chemistry" can be experienced in a variety of ways, from falling in love, to an immediate sense of familiarity ("It's as if we've known each other for years!"), to the excitement and drama of compulsive attraction—even "relationship addiction," a recently invented phrase that sums up what it's like to be harmfully enmeshed in a narcissistic/co-dependent twosome.

Second, Freud mixed pathologic and normal narcissism into the same discussion. Today we distinguish between the two. During early childhood, extreme self-centeredness is normal. With maturity, a *balance* develops between self-centeredness and other-centeredness. But the impulse to center the world on yourself is not entirely lost. It simply exists in healthy proportions—except in co-dependents. One characteristic of co-dependence is that all narcissistic impulses, even healthy and mature ones, are renounced. As a result, co-dependents turn themselves into empty caricatures of maturity, and become very attractive partners for people with an excessive need to be the focus of attention.

Freud also suggested a theoretical void which co-dependence appears to fill: "The disturbances to which the original [normal] narcissism of the child is exposed, the reactions with which he seeks to protect himself from them, the paths into which he is thereby forced—these are themes which I shall leave on one side, as an important field for work which still awaits exploration."[7] To date, most of the work done in this field has focused on adults whose narcissistic traits have become solidified and excessive.

Alice Miller[8] and others have gone on to explore the intergenerational effects of narcissistically wounded parents. However, very little work has been done in the area of those who "seek object-love" by *renouncing* part of their own narcissism. These "Echo personalities" are the other half of the story during our "Age of Narcissism." The attention now being paid to COAs gives us an excellent chance to increase our understanding of Echo, the original co-dependent.

Precisely why Narcissus was impervious to affection is unclear. It may have had something to do with how the Oracle at Delphi responded when Narcissus' mother asked how long her son would live. "As long as he shall not know himself," was the answer. Did Narcissus avoid bonding to others because he was in search of eternal life? After all, it is only through letting ourselves be loved that we come to know much of who we are. Apparently Narcissus felt that a true relationship with another would threaten his existence. Compare this to the co-dependent, whose existence is threatened by the *absence* of relationship.

Human existence and connection to others are inextricably intertwined, and it is in this dynamic that narcissism and co-dependence find their meeting ground. What differentiates the two is *whose* existence is threatened when connection with others is broken. Narcissists can not see *others* as existing separately from themselves; co-dependents can not see *themselves* as existing separately from others. They are opposite ends of the same continuum.

However, their subjective experience is quite different. Narcissists have great difficulty forming human connections except when others mirror them. Co-dependents gain their sense of self through connecting with others they mirror. Together, they form the perfect couple for demonstrating projective identification.

Bonding with autonomous individuals is inconceivable to the narcissist, since such people provide inadequate mirroring. And existence without mirroring someone else is inconceivable to the co-dependent.

The myth illustrates the powerful attachment between narcissist and co-dependent created by these complementary dynamics. Other maidens had fallen in love with Narcissus, but he could have cared less. However, when confronted by Echo's exact mirroring, Narcissus was touched emotionally for the first time. We know this because of his outburst that he would die before giving Echo power over him. Statements like these are generally good evidence that one member of a couple has penetrated the other's defenses.

Remarkably, the specific effects of growing up with an alcoholic parent have been largely ignored throughout the history of psychoanalytic thought, despite the intense interest in narcissism. As difficult as the alcoholic's narcissism is for other adults to deal with, its impact on children is exponentially greater. Although there is no simple equation linking active alcoholism with clinically significant narcissism, the AA "Big Book" is clear about the connection (recall the quote, "Selfishness—self-centeredness! That, we think, is the root of our troubles . . . [The] alcoholic is an extreme example of self-will run riot, though he usually doesn't think so.").[9]

It's clear that parental alcoholism not only subjects children to chaos and abuse, but also exposes them to damaging levels of self-centeredness. As a result, many children are molded into becoming little Echoes.

CO-DEPENDENT PERSONALITY TRAITS AND DISORDER

In *I'll Quit Tomorrow*,[10] Vernon Johnson described the "ism" of alcoholism as being the same illness as co-dependence (or "co-alcoholism," as it was originally known). Overstating his case a bit, he wrote, "The only difference between the alcoholic and the spouse, in instances where the latter does not drink, is that one is physically affected by alcohol; otherwise both have all the symptoms."

Despite the fact that this "ism" is still only vaguely defined, most CD therapists believe they can identify when it exists clinically. And the concept of co-dependence has become increasingly accepted as family therapists have impacted the CD field with their systems theories. But the lack of a clear definition continues to bar it from the broader mental health field.

Currently, co-dependence is starting to attract attention from clinicians outside the CD field who have become aware that it exists in family systems with no history of addiction. Just as narcissism exists without chemical dependence, so does co-dependence. Furthermore, work with COAs has shown that individuals can develop a co-dependent personality early in life and carry it into a series of dysfunctional adult relationships. Apparently we are dealing with a phenomenon with broader implications and applicability than was first believed.

Two major roadblocks remain to making co-dependence a formal diagnosis: its apparent ubiquity and the lack of a clear, clinically useful definition to guide research necessary to support its inclusion in DSM.

Described by some critics as "a condition of the 20th Century," co-dependence is often dismissed as social commentary. If nearly everyone seems to be co-dependent, the argument goes, then how can co-dependence be considered a disease? The answer lies in DSM-III-R's distinction between personality *traits* and personality *disorders*.

According to DSM-III-R, personality traits are "enduring patterns of perceiving, relating to, and thinking about the environment and oneself . . . exhibited in a wide range of important social and personal contexts."[11] Together these traits comprise the "characteristic" way each of us goes about our lives. If we are passive in nature, we will drive a car passively, relate to other people passively, and play cards passively. If we are aggressive in nature, we will drive aggressively, relate aggressively, and play cards aggressively. Personality traits give our identity a sense of continuity. But personality traits become disorders when our personality is narrowed down to only a few traits which have become "inflexible and maladaptive and cause either significant impairment in social or occupational functioning or significant subjective distress."[12]

In other words, while co-dependent *traits* may be widespread, the diagnosis of Co-dependent Personality Disorder can only be made in the face of identifiable *dysfunction* resulting from excessive rigidity or intensity associated with these traits. Narcissistic traits are also nearly universal, but Narcissistic Personality Disorder only exists in the face of significant objective dysfunction. We should be able to apply the same line of reasoning to co-dependence.

The question of ubiquity having been addressed, what about the lack of a definition? In *Diagnosing and Treating Co-dependence*,[13] I advanced a set of specific diagnostic criteria. As with the criteria for other personality disorders, it is their distinct overall *pattern* which constitutes the diagnosis. No single criterion is necessary or sufficient to make the diagnosis.

The process of testing these criteria for validity and reliability, then revising and retesting them, should eventually achieve a level of diagnostic sophistication at least comparable to that which exists for currently accepted personality disorders.

Diagnostic Criteria for Co-Dependence

   A. Continued investment of self-esteem in the ability to control both oneself and others in the face of serious adverse consequences.
   B. Assumption of responsibility for meeting others' needs, to the exclusion of acknowledging one's own needs.
   C. Anxiety and boundary distortions around intimacy and separation.
   D. Enmeshment in relationships with personality disordered, chemically dependent, and impulse disordered individuals.
   E. Exhibits at least three of the following:

1. Excessive reliance on denial
2. Constriction of emotions (with or without dramatic outbursts)
3. Depression
4. Hypervigilance
5. Compulsions
6. Anxiety
7. Alcohol or other drug abuse
8. Recurrent victim of physical or sexual abuse
9. Stress-related medical illnesses
10. Has remained in a primary relationship with an active alcoholic or other drug addict for at least two years without seeking outside support.

Time and again, research has shown that the specific personality disorders identified by the American Psychiatric Association's *Diagnostic and Statistical Manual* are not mutually exclusive. Each blends into several others, much as the peaks in a mountain range are simply distinguishable landmarks, not individual mountains totally separate from one another. As a result, DSM has a tradition of recognizing that personality disorders exist outside the formally accepted categories. When features of more than one personality disorder are present but do not meet the full criteria for any specific category, the newly revised DSM-III-R permits the diagnosis of "Personality Disorder Not Otherwise Specified (NOS)."

To take advantage of this "catch-all" category, the criteria for Co-dependent Personality Disorder borrow heavily from the traditional disorders. In the records for my own clinical practice, I diagnose co-dependence as "Personality Disorder [or Traits, depending on the severity], NOS (Co-dependent type)."

Differentiating Co-Dependence

For co-dependence to be accepted as a legitimate personality disorder, it must be differentiated from established diagnoses. This differentiation can begin by using the three personality disorder clusters outlined in DSM-III-R.[14] I place co-dependence more into Clusters B (dramatic, emotional, or erratic) and C (anxious or fearful) than A (odd or eccentric), which contains Paranoid, Schizoid, and Schizotypal disorders. (The relationship between co-dependence and self-defeating personality is explored in Appendix II.)

Differentiating Co-Dependence from Cluster C Personality Disorders

Cluster C includes Dependent, Avoidant, Obsessive Compulsive, and Passive Aggressive Personality Disorders, each of which has one or more traits in common with co-dependence.

• *Dependent Personality Disorder.* Dependent and co-dependent personalities overlap considerably, especially in their fear of rejection, preoccupation with fears of abandonment, and willingness to do unpleasant or demeaning things to get other people to like them.

There is a primary distinction between co-dependent and dependent personalities, without which the two might collapse into the same disorder: the secretly willful and manipulative nature of the co-dependent's relationship to the world. Dependent personalities are passive, submissive, self-effacing, and docile. While co-dependents may appear this way on the surface, they are nonetheless trying to control their world, or feeling deep guilt for being unable to.

This internal contradiction—feeling impotent while having a grandiose sense of what willpower ought to be able to accomplish—is parallel to the internal contradiction within narcissistic personalities between grandiosity and depression. The co-dependent's distorted relationship to willpower is also identical to the alcoholic's prideful need to maintain self-esteem by denying his or her loss of control.

This distorted relationship to willpower makes co-dependents more vulnerable to rejection than dependent personalities. Because willpower lies at the core of co-dependence, and because

denial of their own narcissistic needs is so prominent, co-dependence deserves to be differentiated from simple dependent
personality. A further justification for this differentiation lies in
the reactions each has to therapeutic interventions regarding
willpower. This subject is explored in Chapter 3 of *Volume Two:
Treatment*.

• *Avoidant Personality Disorder*. Although co-dependent personalities possess many of the same social discomforts as avoidant
personalities (e.g., being easily hurt by criticism, feeling embarrassed in front of other people), they generally demonstrate a
degree of enmeshment in relationships not seen in avoidant
personalities. When co-dependents avoid social contacts, this is
usually counterphobic behavior, not a core dynamic.

• *Obsessive-Compulsive and Passive-Aggressive Personality Disorders*.
Co-dependents can demonstrate many obsessive-compulsive
qualities (especially perfectionism, indecisiveness, and using
compulsions/addictions to avoid underlying feelings), but they
usually do not lack generosity, even without the promise of
personal gain. Similarly, co-dependents can be quite passive-
aggressive, but they are unlikely to protest, without justification,
that others make unreasonable demands on them, or to avoid
obligations, as is typical of passive-aggressive personalities.
When passive-aggressive behavior *is* seen in co-dependents, it is
more likely to result from accumulating years of resentment and
is not a core dynamic.

Finally, these last three personality disorders—avoidant,
obsessive-compulsive, and passive-aggressive—do not speak in
any way to the distorted relationship to willpower and sacrifice
of identity for intimacy, both central themes in co-dependence.

Differentiating Co-Dependence from Cluster B Personality Disorders

Cluster B contains Antisocial, Histrionic, Borderline, and Narcissistic Personality Disorders.

• *Antisocial Personality Disorder.* Antisocial personalities are almost the antithesis of co-dependents. Even features like a disregard for the truth, which co-dependents demonstrate in relation to their own inner feelings, stem from an entirely different internal dynamic.

The other three Cluster B disorders do overlap with co-dependence.

• *Histrionic Personality Disorder.* Histrionic personalities are similar to co-dependents in at least three ways: They turn to others for protection, they constantly require acceptance and approval, and they are exquisitely sensitive to the moods and thoughts of those they wish to please. But the histrionic's intolerance for delayed gratification is quite different from the co-dependent's long-suffering martyrdom. And while histrionics demonstrate a general shallowness, co-dependents do not necessarily.

• *Borderline Personality Disorder.* It can be very difficult to distinguish between Borderline and Co-dependent Personality Disorders, especially when the latter is particularly severe. To further complicate matters, the two syndromes can and do coexist.

The features they most commonly share are chronic feelings of emptiness, efforts to avoid real or imagined abandonment, and a blurring of interpersonal boundaries. For the co-dependent, this blurring of boundaries usually occurs during periods when the interpersonal distance from others is changing or needs negotiation. Like borderlines, co-dependents do best when those around them maintain stable boundaries, and they don't have to depend on their own ability to hold on to their identity.

The fact that borderlines are more severely disturbed creates a qualitative difference between them and co-dependents. This severity leads to an intensity of emotional instability, a depth of identity disturbance, and a tendency to cycle rapidly between extremes of loving (idealizing) and hating (devaluing) others that go beyond what is usually seen in co-dependents.

Perhaps the most significant similarity between co-dependence and borderline disorders is that both confuse fusion (mingling identities with another person) with intimacy (a mutually empathic understanding of each other's subjective experience). They do it for different reasons, though. Borderlines, by definition, are incapable of maintaining stable interpersonal boundaries; co-dependents have this capacity, but voluntarily tear down interpersonal boundaries in a misguided quest for intimacy.

Finally, since personality disorder diagnoses depend on *patterns* of symptoms, borderline disorders can also be distinguished from co-dependence by a history of instability that outstrips most co-dependents.

• *Narcissistic Personality Disorder.* Narcissistic Personality Disorder is inextricably bound to Co-dependent Personality Disorder. The same core dynamics operate in each (although often in opposite directions), and the same life issues are emotionally charged.

These issues include specialness, grandiosity or insignificance, continuous hypersensitivity to the evaluation of others (although the narcissist breaks contact with critics and the co-dependent tries harder to please them, both are similarly obsessed), entitlement or lack thereof, fantasies of power, and the existence or lack of empathy in their relationships. Narcissists are concerned about their partners' empathy for them; co-dependents are concerned about their empathy for their partners (although this is based on fear of abandonment rather than on altruism).

Because both co-dependents and narcissists focus on the same person (the narcissistic member of the relationship), their interaction is symmetric and synergistic. They incite and feed on each other. Narcissists stimulate co-dependents to be *more* co-dependent, and vice versa.

There is an element of existential all-or-nothingness in both narcissism and co-dependence. If someone around the narcissist stops mirroring him, the relationship ends. The narcissist can no longer relate to someone who becomes autonomous. In his eyes, that person ceases to exist. For the co-dependent, if the relationship ends, it is her own existence that is threatened. Co-dependents do not develop the narcissist's pseudo-autonomy. If they are not mirrors, they are nothing.

The essential relationship I am suggesting between co-dependence and narcissism opens many questions. Are the two complementary—two ends of the same continuum—as I am suggesting? Or is co-dependence merely one form of narcissism, perhaps the result of a defensive response to narcissistic traits?[15] Or is co-dependence just another name for narcissism itself? Perhaps there is some other relationship between co-dependence and narcissism that I haven't yet been able to see.

There are, at present, no firm answers to these questions. Whatever answers are eventually discovered, I believe that the concept of co-dependence fills a long-standing gap in our psychology of personality.

HOW CO-DEPENDENCE AND NARCISSISM DEVELOP

Assuming for the moment that co-dependence is a legitimate constellation of personality traits capable of becoming a true disorder, it is useful to reflect on how it develops.

Clinical experience quickly teaches that co-dependence has no single origin. While some clients were raised in highly abusive and dysfunctional families, and consequently recreate similar interpersonal dynamics in a series of relationships throughout their adult life, other clients present an entirely different picture. Their family of origin does not seem to contain more than the usual amount of dysfunction found in the average American home. Their marriage appears relatively normal at first, but then their spouse develops active alcoholism. Gradually there is a slide into more and more profoundly co-dependent behavior.

Jael Greenleaf[16] was the first to described the distinction between these two clinical pictures. She coined the word "para-alcoholism" to describe the effects of growing up co-dependent, and "co-alcoholism" for those who slip into co-dependent behavior as adults. The "co-alcoholic" has a vision of sane behavior to "recover." The "para-alcoholic" lacks such a vision and must build it from the ground up as an adult. Similarly, Terrance Gorski refers to "child onset" and "adult onset" co-dependence.[17]

I prefer the terms "primary" and "secondary" to make the same distinctions. Primary co-dependence becomes integrated into a child's core identity; secondary co-dependence results from regressive use of less mature defenses during adulthood, often in response to a gradually deteriorating relationship with a chemically dependent spouse. A working knowledge of primary co-dependence is more relevant to an understanding of ACAs and will be our focus at this point. Outlining its causes and its relationship with narcissism will also shed light on secondary co-dependence.

James Masterson's work on narcissism[18] is a useful starting-point for exploring the roots of co-dependence. His outline of the main clinical characteristics of narcissistic personality disorder opens the door for its relationship with co-dependence. Masterson describes the narcissistic patient as being grandiose, extremely self-involved, lacking interest in and empathy for others, and endlessly motivated "to find others who will mirror and admire his/her grandiosity."[19] Where do those "others" come from? Theories of co-dependence are efforts to answer this question.

When Masterson traces the origins of narcissism through child development, he gives us a template for conceptualizing the origins of co-dependence as well. The necessary and sufficient causative agent in narcissism, according to Masterson,[20] Heinz Kohut,[21] and Alice Miller,[22] is defective mirroring. Defective mirroring occurs when parents (or primary caretakers) withdraw emotionally as a child begins to develop her own unique personality. To the parents, the child's autonomy is not permissible. What the child is does not meet the parents' needs. In order for their own emotional balance to be maintained, the child has to be shaped in their own image.[23] As Miller poignantly writes, "[Probably] the greatest of narcissistic wounds . . . is not to have been loved just as one truly was."[24]

Miller's descriptions of how narcissistically wounded parents wound their own children—by not seeing them for who they really are—seem to fit equally well for those children who develop narcissism, and those who develop co-dependence.

ACAs who satisfy the criteria for co-dependence often have vivid and painful memories of an intoxicated parent who could not focus on his or her child's needs, but demanded instead (overtly or covertly) that the child attend to the parent's needs. The prize for complying was connection with the parent; the price for not complying was the loss of this connection. How many children are willing to break the bond with the most important person in their lives? When this tension is present during the earliest stages of development, it permanently affects the individual's character structure.

If defective mirroring causes both narcissism and co-dependence, this again raises questions about their relationship. Is there any essential distinction between the two clinical diagnoses, or is co-dependence merely one form of narcissism? Or are different needs within the child "defectively mirrored," bending personality development toward narcissism or co-dependence? And are there substantially different kinds of defective mirroring, with each kind having different consequences for the child?

I propose that defective mirroring leads to *both* narcissism and co-dependence. Which one develops in a given child depends on an interplay between the *specific needs* within a child which are defectively mirrored, and the *specific defect* in mirroring experienced by the child.

The Specific Needs

Whether a child becomes predominantly narcissistic or co-dependent is determined primarily by which of the child's specific needs are most defectively mirrored. This line of reasoning stems from the work of Heinz Kohut,[25] who identified two complementary needs that arise when a child first senses that she is a separate human being. He labeled them "healthy, age appropriate narcissistic needs." They are:

1. the need to have one's developing capabilities validated, and

2. the need to form an idealized image of one's parent with
   which to merge.

Or, in other words,

1. the need to be unconditionally loved and focused upon as
   the center of the world (i.e., "I am perfect"), and
2. the need to depend totally on perfect parents for safety and
   happiness (i.e., "You are perfect, and I am part of you").

To put this in even simpler terms, all children pass through a
period when they need to be immersed in a relationship with a
totally *appreciative* and *appreciated* adult.[26]

Kohut acknowledges that these two needs "are, of course,
antithetical. Yet they coexist from the beginning and their individual and largely independent lines of development are open to
separate scrutiny."[27] Each need matures through a process of
"optimal frustration," which means that children lose their fantasies about their relationship with their parents a little at a time,
and only as they are prepared to integrate the loss. Failure to lose
these fantasies aborts the child's maturation; too traumatic frustration of them throws a child prematurely into a state of feeling
abandoned and overwhelmed.

Ideally, the need to be wholly appreciated gradually matures
into adult forms of positive self-esteem and self-confidence, and
the need to be wholly appreciative matures into adult forms of
admiration, empathy for others, and enthusiasm. When these
needs fail to mature, the first remains in its archaic form as the
Grandiose Self, and the second remains in its archaic form as the
image of an Idealized Parent.

I propose that these two complementary needs be reframed as
age-appropriate "interpersonal needs" consisting of:

1. the narcissistic need for omnipotence (the need to be
   unconditionally appreciated), and
2. the echoistic (i.e., co-dependent) need for dependence and
   merging (the need to be unconditionally appreciative).

These two needs emerge in tandem as the child moves out of what Mahler, *et al.*[28] called the initial symbiotic phase of life. During this phase, which lasts only a few months, a child has no sense that there is any difference between "me" (the child) and "you" (the parent). It is only when the child begins experiencing that difference that it becomes important which way emotional energy flows between the two.

The symbiotic phase of development gives way to the two intertwined processes of separation and individuation, during which children first become aware that they are separate beings, with their own unique characteristics. It is at this point (the separation-individuation phase) that interpersonal relationships first begin, and that the two complementary interpersonal needs emerge.

Children are unable to experience *mutual* interactions at first. Their cognitive capacity has not yet moved beyond black-and-white, all-or-nothing thinking. They alternate between needing to be fully appreciated and needing to be fully appreciative. In other words, the narcissistic and echoistic interpersonal needs cannot be met simultaneously while still in their archaic forms. As a result, these needs are initially antithetical, even though they emerge in tandem during the moments when children first become aware of the separation between themselves and their parents. Once children become aware that separation from their parents exists (i.e., once humanity has been cast out of Eden), they must face the whole question of how to be in relationship with anyone.

Ultimately, children must come to some acceptance of their growing sense of separation, and incorporate this awareness into relationships with others. Many of the temper tantrums and tears of the first two years of life are a revolt against accepting what amounts to "the human condition"—the paradox we all experience between being individuals and social animals at the same time. Mahler labeled the successful resolution of this struggle *rapprochement* (French for "reestablishing cordial relationships"). In order for children to become comfortable with the paradox of being-in-relationship-while-being-separate, they must mature each of their interpersonal needs enough that they are no longer starkly antithetical, and can be experienced simultaneously (just as love and hate can be felt at the same moment, toward the same person).

In light of the two interpersonal needs outlined above, the basic "narcissistic" wound becomes a dual phenomenon, encompassing both narcissistic and echoistic needs. Everyone suffers some wounding to each of these basic interpersonal needs. Everyone carries into adult life bits and pieces of each of these needs still in their archaic form.[29]

The wounding of each interpersonal need leads in one of two directions. Frustration of a need may lead to its being disowned, while stimulation may lead to its remaining in the original archaic form. The classic, purely narcissistic personality has disowned echoistic (co-dependent) needs while harboring unmatured narcissistic needs. The classic, purely co-dependent personality has disowned narcissistic needs while harboring unmatured echoistic needs.

Before we explore the specific types of mirroring defects, let's entertain two questions: What happens to each interpersonal need if Narcissus is a child's only parent? And what if Echo is the only parent? Figure 4-1, below, suggests some answers.

The Narcissus parent invalidates (ignores or rejects) his child's narcissistic needs. The child's "See me!" meets the parent's "Only as a reflection of myself." When the parent's response fails to meet the child's narcissistic needs, the child concludes that "what I am is inadequate or bad." As a protection against such shame, the narcissistic needs may be disowned.

On the other hand, the Narcissus parent stimulates the child's echoistic needs. The child's "You're great!" meets the parent's "Yes, I *am* great." The child is left feeling that she can be valuable, and connected, to the parent, but only as a reflection of the parent's greatness. Echoistic needs are never optimally frustrated, and thus do not mature out of their archaic form, while narcissistic needs are disowned. (Remember Freud's comment that one person's narcissism has a special attraction for those who have disowned their own narcissism in an effort to make themselves

Figure 4-1
Defective Mirroring of Complementary Interpersonal Needs

If the Parent's Personality is . . .	and the Child's Interpersonal Needs are . . .		then the Child's personality becomes . . .
	Narcissistic	Echoistic	
Narcissistic (Narcissus as only parent)	Ignored/Rejected "What I am is inadequate or bad"	Stimulated "I am valuable, but only as a reflection of you"	Co-dependent
Co-dependent (Echo as only parent)	Stimulated "I am always enough"	Ignored/Rejected "My needs are unimportant or bad"	Narcissistic

lovable.) The child develops an echoistic (co-dependent) personality structure.

The Echo parent stimulates her child's narcissistic needs. The child's "I'm great!" is unconditionally confirmed by the parent's "Yes, you're great," and no optimal frustration, and therefore no maturation, of these needs occurs. The child concludes, "I am always enough." Meanwhile, echoistic needs are ignored or rejected. The child's "You're great!" encounters the parent's "Only as a reflection of you." The child feels abandoned and potentially ashamed of her dependence needs. Narcissistic needs do not mature out of their archaic form, and echoistic needs are disowned. The child develops a narcissistic personality structure.

Specific Mirroring Defects

A weakness in traditional theories of narcissism lies in their use of the undifferentiated concept of "defective mirroring." Reviewing the developmental period during which narcissism and co-dependence begin, and unpacking the concept of defective mirroring into its different components, reveals that it comes in a wide variety of forms, with markedly different consequences for children.

As noted earlier, it is generally accepted that narcissism (and by extension, co-dependence) has its origins in the first three years of life—during the developmental stages Margaret Mahler labeled *symbiosis, separation-individuation,* and *rapprochement.* A closer look at the dual processes of separation and individuation will help us look at the range of mirroring defects which actually exist. In healthy development, separation and individuation proceed in such harmony that there is little to distinguish one from the other. It is in the pathological situation that the difference between separation and individuation becomes more important. Figure 4-2 illustrates how the development of autonomy consists both of separating and differentiating into a unique individual.

Figure 4-3 lists the different attitudes a parent may have toward his child's growth from dependence to independence (i.e., separation), and from being identical to being individuated (i.e., individuation). The parent can be *unaware* (i.e., neglect the child), *intolerant* (reject the child), *needing* (excessively stimulate the child), or *unpredictable* mixtures of all three. These are all different kinds of defective mirroring. The *accepting* parent is one who accurately mirrors the child's actual feelings.

Parents may adopt *any* of these attitudes toward *any* part of a child's development. For example, narcissistic parents may be so self-obsessed that they are literally unaware or highly intolerant

Figure 4-2
The Dual Processes of Separation and Individuation

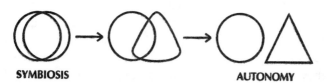

SYMBIOSIS   AUTONOMY

Figure 4-3
Potential Parental Attitudes toward Each Part of
the Developmental Process

Parent's Attitude	Child's Development	Parent's Attitude
	SYMBIOSIS ⟶ AUTONOMY	
Unaware		Unaware
Intolerant		Intolerant
Needing	DEPENDENT (Separation) INDEPENDENT	Needing
Unpredictable		Unpredictable
Accepting		Accepting
Unaware		Unaware
Intolerant		Intolerant
Needing	IDENTICAL (Individuation) INDIVIDUATED	Needing
Unpredictable		Unpredictable
Accepting		Accepting

of a child's dependence, and need the child to develop independence. At the same time, they may send the mixed message that they need the child to be a perfect mirror and not individuate if the bond between them is to remain intact ("Don't depend on me, but be like me").

In contrast, co-dependent parents may define themselves so much through others that they remain fused with their child. They remain unaware, or become intolerant, of the development of independence. At the same time, they may send the mixed message, out of their own sense of shame, that they need the child *not* to be a reflection ("Depend on me, but don't be like me"), thereby stimulating individuation.

Narcissistic parents would end up encouraging independence but discouraging individuation; the co-dependent parents might encourage individuation (so they would have something to mirror) but discourage independence. Both kinds of parents intensify the emotional charge surrounding issues of separation and individuation. In both cases, the children are not being loved for who they are, as unique individuals—to paraphrase Alice Miller, "just as one truly is." This is the primary wound which generates both narcissistic and co-dependent personalities.

Other parents, perhaps because of intermittent intoxication, psychosis, manic-depressive illness, or borderline instability, may alternate unpredictably in their attitudes toward the different elements of their child's development, from lack of awareness, to intolerance and need. To the extent that a parent's personality structure is a mixture of narcissistic and co-dependent elements, there will also be a certain amount of unpredictability and arbitrariness in the messages which a child receives ("Don't be like me, but don't be different").

Many other combinations of disturbances could exist that are not further explored here. For example, schizoid parents may be unaware of all facets of the developmental process in their child. Depressed parents may alternate between needing their child to be dependent and independent, and they may also need their child to individuate as much as possible ("the more you are like me, the more I have failed as a parent"). What's important to keep in mind about all this is that defective mirroring exists in enough different forms that we should expect the consequences to vary widely. A considerable amount of further study is called for in this area.

Although the matrix of parental attitudes illustrated in Figure 4-3 seems to be an accurate description of observable clinical phenomena, its complexity creates a theoretical quagmire. In other words, I have seen everything on this chart in real clients, but the theoretical implications of what I have seen are difficult to calculate in fine detail. Instead of trying to sort through the whole complexity at once, it may be useful to narrow our inquiries. Let's turn to others for guidance.

Complementary Forms of
Defective Mirroring

William Fairbairn[30] introduced the idea that pathogenic interactions with a parent can be either "rejecting" or "exciting." In other words, an age-appropriate need can be either traumatically rejected, or encouraged beyond the point that it is still age-appropriate. In both cases, the parent is responding predominantly to his own needs, not the child's.

For example, a narcissistic parent may shame a child's willful efforts to get his way (i.e., rejecting the impulse to individuate) while stimulating acts of compliance (i.e., exciting the impulse to be identical). In alcoholic families, this might take the classic form of labeling a child who confronts the drinking "bad," and rewarding a child who supports and shares the denial.

Daniel Stern's[31] concept of "affect attunement," a refinement of the concept of mirroring, adds an important dimension to our understanding. Affect attunement requires that a parent determine a child's feeling state by observing the child's behavior, then respond in a way that goes beyond mere imitation. What this does for the child is confirm that her feeling state has been accurately perceived.

For example, when a child totters on the edge of a bed and finally pulls himself back to safety, he has a set of body sensations that rise suddenly in intensity, waver momentarily, then gradually diminish. If a parent spontaneously reproduces this same sequence vocally—by saying "Whoooooa!" in a voice that rises suddenly in volume, wavers, then diminishes over the same time period as the child's experience—this tells the child something very important. It gives him indisputable evidence that, despite the separation between himself and others, the parent has been able to *understand* his subjective experience and *communicate* this understanding. This is healthy mirroring.[32]

It is through affect attunements, or the lack of them, that parents communicate their focused attention and their true feelings about a child's existence and development. Parents who need a child to be dependent form a reinforcing human connection with those feelings—a connection which is jeopardized when physical growth drives the child toward independence. For example, a parent may attune to a child's fears (rather than her daring) as she climbs a tall slide for the first time. On the other hand, parents who cannot tolerate a child's dependence will connect with and reinforce only those feelings which strive toward independence—like the parent who neglects the child's fears as she climbs the slide, but attunes only to her courage.

No facade on the parent's part, such as a forced smile to conceal irritability, can override the affect attunements that are actually taking place, or should be taking place but aren't.[33] For a child to accept a facade as reality, she must be old enough to develop a false self. Only then can the child react to the *content* of what a parent says instead of the *way* the parent says it. Once a false self develops, the child can enter into duplicity with the parent. From this point on, the relationship is between facades, not people.

The wounds creating co-dependence and narcissism occur before a false self develops, and they nurture its development. One reason why co-dependent and narcissistic personality structures become stable is because they make a child less vulnerable to further wounding.

In an environment of what Stern calls "deficient affect attunements" (this corresponds to Fairbairn's "rejecting" interactions), the child must maintain the bond with the parent by contributing more than the normal amount of emotional energy to the relationship. For example, instead of the parent maintaining connection with a child who wanders to the other side of a playground by getting up off the bench and quietly following, the child must maintain connection by noticing that the parent is engrossed in his newspaper and move back closer to regain his attention. The child who can't do this becomes disconnected and chronically depressed. In the most severe cases, autistic traits may develop. The core sense of inadequacy and low self-esteem is so deep that the child is consumed by feelings of emptiness. Even the child who *can* supply the extra emotional energy required develops a core sense of inadequacy. He may form the habit of excessive empathy, but continually experience the failure of his greatest efforts to earn a response in kind. Affect attunements by the parent are scarce, and usually made to their own projections (as in the case of the parent who attunes to his child's sense of daring while climbing a slide, and totally misses the fears which are also present). The only way for the child to achieve any sense of connectedness is to identify with the parent's projections. Narcissus' children never feel entitled to be in a mutual relationship.

In an environment of "excessive affect attunements" (Fairbairn's "exciting" interactions), the child must fight off the parent's constant efforts to fuse with her if she is to achieve any independence. For example, a child may have to actively reject a clinging parent's presence in order to spend some time alone in fantasy play. A core sense of grandiosity develops as the child becomes the center of her parent's life. The parent's tendency to be a perfect mirror gives the child unlimited opportunity to manipulate the parent, and little chance to experience mutuality in the relationship. No empathic connection from child to parent is necessary for the bond to remain intact. Echo's children always feel entitled to be the center of their relationships.

Synthesis

Now that the traditional concept of how "defective mirroring" creates "narcissistic wounds" has been unraveled, we can start to see some important distinctions between the specific needs being defectively mirrored, and the specific mirroring defects.

Narcissistic parents tend to produce co-dependent children by (1) rejecting their children's normal narcissistic needs and stimulating (but not maturing) their normal echoistic needs, and (2) creating a general atmosphere of deficient affect attunements, requiring their children to provide most of the bonding energy necessary to hold the relationship together. This causes children to (1) disown their own normal narcissism and abort maturation of their echoistic impulses, and (2) develop a core sense of inadequacy and other-centeredness in their relationships. When echoistic needs remain in their archaic, childhood forms during adulthood, they become pathologic echoism—or co-dependence.

Co-dependent parents tend to produce narcissistic children by (1) stimulating (but not maturing) their children's normal narcissistic needs and rejecting their normal echoistic needs, and (2) creating a general atmosphere of excessive affect attunements, requiring their children to shy away from the bonding energy to maintain even a semblance of independence and individual identity. This causes children to (1) abort maturation of their normal narcissism and disown their echoistic impulses, and (2) develop a core sense of grandiosity and self-centeredness in their relationships. When narcissistic needs remain in their archaic, childhood forms during adulthood, they become pathologic narcissism.

These wounds can happen very early in a child's life, and it's wise to assume that *no* child is too young to be impervious to their effects. Daniel Stern places the development of a core sense of self between the second and six months of life. It is then that a child first manifests evidence of a coherent sense of himself—his own body, feelings, and ability to affect the world. For the child to flourish, the parents must attune to these new feelings and abilities. Between months seven and fifteen—a time when, according to Stern, children become aware that their inner experiences can be communicated to others—it is critical for a child's own internal reality to be attuned to by adults. One common way parents do this is by playing peek-a-boo. The child's pleasure at seeing and being seen is enjoyed and reflected back to her.

When a child experiences defective mirroring during these very early stages of development, his core sense of self is affected. Primary co-dependence (and narcissism) exists at this basic level, within the very structure and experience of one's self, and not simply at the level of a conflict among drives or a set of dysfunctional beliefs. It is for this reason that we are justified in including co-dependence among the personality disorders.

Neither the narcissist nor the co-dependent successfully separates and individuates. Arrests and disturbances at such early stages of a child's development cause adult life to be permeated by fragments of primitive, all-or-nothing emotional energy. Kohut defines narcissism primarily by the nature or quality of this primitive energy,[34] and I find that precisely the same quality of energy disrupts relationships in co-dependence. But narcissists and co-dependents are differentiated by their core feelings of grandiosity versus inadequacy, and by the defenses they develop against these archaic feelings.

The narcissist develops a pseudo-autonomy to defend against further wounding. This defense is based on feelings of grandiosity, and protects against the disowned urge to be dependent. Because the basis for this "autonomy" is an unrealistic omnipotence, access to the true self, which must be based in reality, is lost. Despite their defensive stance of self-reliance, narcissists remain unable to achieve either true separation or true individuation. They can not relate to authentic autonomy in others, because their only sense of human connectedness comes when they are being mirrored by others.

The co-dependent takes the opposite tack by developing a pseudo-dependence to guard against further wounding. This defense is based on feelings of inadequacy, and protects against the disowned urge to be the center. By over-assuming responsibility for others, co-dependents attempt to assure that their dependence on relationships will be tolerated. Because their dependence is based on a continual fusion with someone else's identity, co-dependents also lose access to their true selves. They remain unable to achieve true separation or true individuation because their only sense of self comes when they are being the perfect mirror. Autonomous individuals cannot relate to them.

Buried beneath the grandiosity of the narcissist and the inadequacy of the co-dependent are the stark emotions of rage and terror—the child's reactions to abandonment. Rage and terror protect against deeper feelings of depression, despair, and apathy. The narcissist's grandiosity more easily admits to feeling rage, because feelings of terror would acknowledge inadequacy. The co-dependent's core sense of inadequacy more easily admits to feeling terror, because feelings of rage imply a sense of being entitled to be heard.

Reframing Kohut's two basic needs, and differentiating between types of mirroring defects (i.e., deficient versus excessive affect attunement), leads to a formulation of the complementary relationship between narcissism and echoism (co-dependence) with several important implications:

1. It expands the complementarity of co-dependence and narcissism across generations. A narcissistic adult will not only seek out his complement in a co-dependent mate, but will also mold children in the same direction. Conversely, a co-dependent adult will mold children toward narcissistic personalities.

2. It answers the question regarding whether narcissism or co-dependence is primary and the other a derivative. If the two needs postulated by Kohut are seen as contemporaneous, equal, and possessing their own independent lines of development, then narcissism and echoism are both primary phenomena. They bear a relationship to each other which is present within the basic needs themselves, which Kohut describes as "antithetical." In healthy development, these two needs mature beyond their archaic forms at the same time that a child's sense of self grows in sophistication. Mahler's concept of rapprochement can now be seen as the threshold a child crosses when she first becomes able to tolerate the paradox of feeling both these needs simultaneously. Neither the narcissist nor the co-dependent personality has successfully traversed rapprochement. Each has aborted the conflict between interpersonal needs by disowning one of them.

3. Freud's description of the attraction that narcissism has for those who have renounced part of their own narcissism is now explained, as is the attraction that echoism must have for those who have renounced part of their own echoism (i.e., for narcissists who are phobic of dependence). By the process of mutual projective identifications, both narcissists and co-dependents serve as the hand for the other person's glove. Narcissists own their need to be seen as capable, but disown and project the need to be dependent. Echoists own the need to be dependent, but disown and project the need to be seen as capable. Each identifies with the other's projections, and each is attracted to the other's acceptance of the shadow side within themselves. The "chemistry" of human emotional attraction is present in full force.

4. Clinically, narcissism and co-dependence rarely exist in pure forms. In most cases, they exist as an admixture. While one stance predominates in each individual's personality, the other stance is disowned and projected onto others. As a result, it is not uncommon to see a narcissistic client temporarily re-own his projections and become thoroughly co-dependent in the face of a crippling narcissistic injury (i.e., events which force the narcissist to become aware of his inadequacy or vulnerability). For example, as someone's love (which the narcissist wears as an achievement badge) is withdrawn, there may be a sudden willingness to be whatever the other person wants in order to regain her love. On the other hand, it is also common to see elements of grandiose thinking underlying co-dependents' belief that they can make anyone love them if they are compliant enough. During treatment, as co-dependents begin to re-own their normal narcissistic needs, this often takes the uncharacteristic form (for them) of archaic feelings of entitlement.

Differentiating Secondary and Primary Co-Dependence

Clinicians often are faced with thoroughly co-dependent clients whose family of origin history gives no clue of enough dysfunction to explain the severity of their personality disorder. Is this an example of denial, or does it argue against the framework presented above?

I believe that such cases are usually examples of secondary (adult onset) co-dependence. We are now in a position to understand better what secondary co-dependence is and how it develops.

Secondary co-dependence occurs when a person with co-dependent personality traits enters into relationship with someone with narcissistic tendencies. Through a gradual process of mutual projective identifications, each has her particular traits intensified until they cross the line into becoming full-blown personality disorders.

George Vaillant's work helps explain how secondary co-dependence develops.[35] In his discussion of the immature defenses normally found in adolescence (projection, fantasy/denial, acting out) and common to most alcohol/drug addicts, Vaillant writes, "Immature defenses effect a merging of personal boundaries. They induce a breakdown of clear knowledge of what is mine and what is thine."[36] Defenses such as projection, blaming, and denial have great power to manipulate, because humans universally take immature defenses personally. In doing so, their capacity to remain objective and reasonable begins to erode, and they are drawn into meeting character disordered individuals on their own terms.

Therapists who have been manipulated by the immature defenses of a persuasive sociopath may recognize their own over-personalizing in the intensity of anger and blaming they felt toward the client. If this tendency to have our own immature defenses activated by encountering the same in others is part of the human condition, then individuals with co-dependent traits will be especially susceptible.

For example, if the intensity of co-dependent traits could be rated from 0 (absent) to 100 (in complete control of one's personality), we might postulate (arbitrarily) that the line between traits and a co-dependent disorder lies at 75. Below this level, no significant dysfunction occurs, although the quality of life may be directly limited.

We may also postulate (again arbitrarily) that the intensity of co-dependence within the average population lies within the 40-60 range. Clearly, individuals rated near 60 and above are more susceptible than individuals rated at 40 or below to having their co-dependent traits further activated to the point of crossing over into true disorders.

Primary co-dependents score above 75 while still youngsters, and have little or no chance of entering into healthy relationships as adults. But neither the individual rated at 40 nor the one rated at 60 are "bound" to enter into a dysfunctional relationship in the same way as primary co-dependents, although the higher score is at greater risk than the lower.

This framework also introduces a certain element of luck as an important determinant in our lives. For example, two couples, both rating 60, marry. Twenty years later, one of the spouses begins to develop active chemical dependence. This couple may enter into a downward spiral of gradually increasing self-centeredness and immature defenses on the alcoholic's/drug addict's part, all of which his spouse takes too personally. He mirrors her projections of blame, reinforcing her co-dependent traits. Ever so gradually, the one couple swirls off the deep end, while the other couple remains relatively healthy.

In the co-dependent who began at 60 and gradually experienced rigidification and intensification of her co-dependent traits until the line was crossed (75) into disorder, the core personality structure still has the capacity to operate at its original level. The client is suffering an adjustment disorder to an identifiable stress which is occurring on top of a susceptible character structure. In line with calling this an adjustment disorder, the assumption is that greater health would automatically be reestablished if the stressor were removed. And this is often what happens.

The vast majority of people with secondary co-dependent personality disorders can improve significantly simply by getting out of the dysfunctional relationships they are enmeshed in. The speed with which very dysfunctional clients (often indistinguishable from active borderlines) can pull back from the precipice of extreme character pathology seems to argue against co-dependence as a personality disorder. I believe that such dramatic reversals are neither flights into health, nor are they examples of deep characterological change. Instead, they are cases of secondary co-dependence which respond rapidly to being extracted from the dysfunctional system which feeds into the co-dependents' pathology. When looked at carefully, such cases usually reveal an underlying character structure with co-dependent traits.

A Final Caveat

Analysis and theory building simplify reality. Real clients rarely present pure forms of whatever our theories have led us to expect. Children grow up with parents who possess mixtures of poorly matured and disowned narcissistic and echoistic impulses. Many children are influenced by two parents, each with his or her own unique mixtures of these elements. Some parents are more co-dependent with their spouse, more narcissistic with their children. Many children are exposed to one, or more, step-parents as well. And finally, if there is a narcissistic defense against borderline pathology, there must also be a co-dependent defense against the same. Further exploration of complexities like these lies beyond the scope of this book. Meanwhile, let us never forget that theory only approximates life.

MORE TOOLS FOR DIAGNOSING CO-DEPENDENCE

There are three more tools that can help in the clinical assessment of co-dependence in ACAs: alternative diagnostic criteria, based on the complementary relationship between narcissism and co-dependence; a lay "translation" of the alternative diagnostic criteria; and a "motive versus behavior" approach.

Alternative Diagnostic Criteria for Co-Dependence (Based on Complementarity with Narcissism)

The criteria for diagnosing co-dependence presented earlier in this chapter were first suggested in 1986.[37] At that time, I was beginning to explore the relationship between co-dependence and narcissism, but I had not yet concluded that it arises from two complementary needs lying at the core of early child development. Had I understood this, my criteria for diagnosing co-dependence might have been more tightly tied into those already accepted for the diagnosis of narcissism.

Out of curiosity, in order to put my framework to the test, I constructed a mirror image of each of the DSM-III-R criteria for narcissism. Given the arguments presented in this chapter, it should come as no surprise that the following criteria serve remarkably well as signs and symptoms for co-dependence.

Alternative Diagnostic Criteria

Co-dependence is a pervasive pattern of inadequacy (in fantasy or behavior), excessive empathy, and hypersensitivity to the evaluation of others, beginning by early adulthood and present in a variety of contexts, as indicated by at least *five* of the following:

1. Reacts to criticism with feelings of fear, shame, or embarrassment (even if not expressed)
2. Is interpersonally exploited: permits others to take advantage of him or her to achieve their own ends
3. Has an inadequate sense of self-importance; e.g., minimizes achievements and talents, expects to be ignored except insofar as achievements are continuously present (the extreme extent to which this characteristic exists often reveals a submerged, inverse grandiosity)
4. Believes that his or her problems are unique and can be understood only by other special people
5. Is preoccupied with fantasies of unlimited failure, impotence, catastrophe, evil, or ideal love
6. Lacks a sense of entitlement: has an unreasonable expectation of especially unfavorable treatment; e.g., assumes that he or she must wait in line so others can be taken care of first
7. Has a constant desire for attention and admiration; e.g., keeps fishing for compliments, but has a highly developed capacity for delayed gratification
8. Lacks empathy for himself or herself, in conjunction with excessive empathy for others; is unable to recognize and experience how he or she feels
9. Is preoccupied with feelings of guilt.

Lay Translation of Alternative
Diagnostic Criteria

One significant difference between narcissism and co-dependence is the grassroots willingness of co-dependents to look at their own problems. Of course, this might result as much from the specific type of pathology seen in each (i.e., narcissists feel entitled to be seen as healthy, co-dependents assume that they *are* the problem), but the end result is that large numbers of co-dependents are seeking recovery.

Since most clients would not self-identify with the formal diagnostic criteria, I also have a lay "translation" describing five symptoms of co-dependence.[38] It is included here to aid therapists in their work with clients. Familiarity with this translation may help the therapist formulate questions more effectively during clinical evaluation interviews.

Lay Translation

1. *Changing who you are to please others.*

   Co-dependents exist through their relationships with other people. Being able to please someone else is their only avenue to feeling real.

2. *Feeling responsible for meeting other people's needs at the expense of your own.*

   Co-dependents are so other-directed that they get more upset if someone else's needs go unmet than if their own do.

3. *Low self-esteem.*

   Co-dependents suffer low self-esteem for two reasons. First, they have turned their identities over to other people to such a degree that they often have very little sense of self to esteem. Second, co-dependents often enter into relationships with partners who are less than fully mature.

4. *Driven by compulsions.*

   Compulsions serve two purposes for co-dependents. First, they add drama to their lives. Second, compulsions occupy a lot of time and effectively block co-dependents from becoming aware of deep, painful emotions.

5. *Denial.*
Co-dependents tend to deal with problems largely through denial and willpower. In particular, they deny that they are living their lives through others, or use willpower to prevent being other-directed from damaging their lives.

Motive versus Behavior

Finally, regarding motive versus behavior: In defining narcissism, Heinz Kohut places emphasis on the "nature or quality of the instinctual charge" which is motivating an individual, rather than the target of that charge.[39] This is another way of saying that there are no specific behaviors which by definition are, or are not, narcissistic. What qualifies a particular action as being narcissistic is the primitive, archaic quality of feeling which underlies it. As noted earlier, this same quality of archaic energy motivates co-dependence as well.

This distinction between motive and behavior is useful when trying to evaluate a specific client's behavior. There are no rules for determining which behavior is a manifestation of healthy generosity and the desire to help, and which is a manifestation of co-dependence. Every given piece of behavior could be either— depending on the "nature or quality of the instinctual charge" underlying it.

I use three axes to evaluate the degree to which any specific action is a sign of co-dependence: relationship to willpower, relationship to personal needs, and level of autonomy from others.

A. Relationship to Willpower.

To what degree is an individual acting in order to gain a sense of pride in what he is capable of making happen? To what degree is he involved in trying to control the world beyond realistic limits? When it seems likely that an individual is gaining self-esteem by forcing solutions harder and harder, despite negative consequences, he is probably being actively co-dependent. When an action is excessively willful, it is often a sign of co-dependence.

B. Relationship to Personal Needs.

To what degree has an individual acted to meet someone else's needs, rather than her own? Or, if the individual has acted in line with her own needs, how much guilt is she feeling as a result? Many acts of kindness are performed out of a sense of obligation. If this sense of obligation is unnecessary or resented, the actions may be examples of co-dependence.

C. Level of Autonomy from Others.

What does the act in question imply about the individual's separateness from—or fusion to—others? Has he acted out of choice, or out of a compulsion to earn others' approval? When an individual feels compelled to be kind in order to keep others happy and to avoid the risk of being abandoned, it is likely that he is being co-dependent.

The three operative words in assessing the degree of co-dependence underlying specific behaviors are *pride, shame,* and *doubt.* Pride refers to one's willfulness; shame, to feelings about one's needs; and doubt, to uncertainty about who one is when apart from others.

Co-dependents often vacillate between pride and shame, which is confusing and frustrating both to themselves and to those around them. Therapists who understand the complementary relationship between co-dependence and narcissism will be better prepared to shift with clients between these two sides of the same coin.

CONCLUSION

The framework presented in this chapter, postulating an essential, complementary relationship between co-dependence and narcissism, is obviously speculative. The value of such speculation is that it enhances the usefulness of the concept of co-dependence, providing it with increased explanatory power.

I believe that the framework I have developed increases my understanding of the basic nature of co-dependence, places it into its proper developmental context, and outlines the cross-generational dynamics of its causes.

A host of ACA characteristics result from co-dependent personality traits. In some ACAs, these traits rigidify into overt co-dependent personality disorder. In others, narcissism may predominate, either at the trait or the disorder level. And all ACAs will possess some mixture of archaic co-dependent and narcissistic needs and vacillate between them.

Unless the primary co-dependence found in ACAs is conceptualized on the level of being an intrusion of very old, developmentally arrested interpersonal needs, therapy is likely to remain superficial, or to flounder in a morass of unresolvable projective identifications between therapist and client.

5

AXIS IV:
UNDERLEARNING

In Chapter 1, underlearning is defined as "insufficient experiences requisite to learning adaptive behaviors"—or insufficient exposure to normal behavior. At Genesis, underlearning is our fourth evaluation axis. Because it is so intimately connected to each individual's specific and unique experiences, constructing a general theory of how it occurs and the deficits it produces is more difficult than for the first three evaluation axes (biology/genetics, the wound, and poor woundcare).

It is also difficult to diagnose underlearning, except by observations made during the course of therapy. Because many ACAs have constructed successful lives around their learning gaps, sometimes without being aware that these gaps even exist, underlearning may be impossible to document during initial evaluation sessions. As a result, this chapter must touch on treatment more than others in this volume.

With these caveats in mind, it's still important to explore (as far as we can) how underlearning creates its own distinct set of characteristics, and what therapists can do about them.

UNDERLEARNING:
NOT KNOWING
"WHAT NORMAL IS"

The feeling that one doesn't know "what normal is" is endemic among ACAs—in their relationships with others, and in their understanding of their own emotions. This feeling is similar to the disorientation alcoholics often experience when they first become abstinent. They no longer occupy their time, manipulate their feelings, and organize their lives around drinking, but they still have little or no idea of how "normal people" live.

The concept of recovery implies that alcoholics forget what "normal" is during the active stages of their illness, and must gradually recover those memories through disciplined Twelve Step work. But ACAs often have no such memories to "recover." For them, the concept of normal behavior may be an empty category.

Clinical Vignette:
The Outsider

Ellen often lamented that she "didn't know how to deal with" her relationship to me. In our work together, she had become aware of how she remained isolated from me emotionally, always only tenuously vulnerable. She continuously kept one foot out of the relationship, ready to run in case we drew too close, or if it looked like I was abandoning her. It was painful to watch her growing awareness that this was a bankrupt stance and she didn't know how to behave any differently.

At times she almost begged for me to show her how to be in a healthy relationship. Whenever I urged her to explore what she could do to lessen the distance between us, she claimed ignorance and demanded that I take the lead or tell her what to do.

Part of Ellen's behavior stemmed from her resistance to risk something new, such as talking more openly about her feelings about me. The pain of not changing was still less than the anxiety of trying something different. Another part of her behavior may have been motivated by her desire to be rescued by me, or even to frustrate me in a hostile way. But these traditional interpretations do not shed light on the moments when Ellen stared the unknown squarely in the eye, was ready to relinquish her painful, self-imposed isolation—and had no idea what to do next. She simply had no concept of a healthy relationship.

Ellen grew up in a profoundly disturbed family. Until Ellen was four years old, her mother had tied her wrists and ankles to keep her "safely in her crib" while the parents went out drinking. Although her mother is abstinent today, without the aid of recovery or therapy, she still chuckles at the image of Ellen being "tucked in" for the night. No one in the family seems aware of the distress that this action caused Ellen then and continues to cause her today.

By the time she was six years old, most of Ellen's evenings were filled with chaos. Typically, her parents fought over dinner, her mother passed out on the living-room floor, and her father left the house. Later, after dark, Ellen often walked around her neighborhood, searching for houses where the blinds had been left open. She would stand quietly and watch the scene inside, studying what the people were doing and wondering what they were saying. It was a world as distant from hers as the images on a television screen. But she watched with fascination because, even at six, Ellen wondered what "normal" families looked like.

Comments

While some ACAs, such as Ellen, are plagued by the awareness that they don't know what normal is, others merely feel "different—interlopers in the mainstream of life." It's important to emphasize that feelings of being "different" and of "not belonging" are primary for many ACAs. By "primary," I mean that they have been integrated into the ACA's core sense of identity. The feelings are free-floating and exist without specific content. Very often, when ACAs state that they don't know "what normal is," they are simply trying to make sense of their global feelings of separateness.

Ellen, for example, had a diminished capacity to connect with other people. By continually calling attention to the differences between herself and "normal" people, she could make sense of her feelings of isolation. However, even in situations where she could not identify a difference between herself and others (for example, in an ACA group), she still was unable to feel a strong sense of belonging. Her sense of separation was a primary feeling, with an autonomous life and dynamic independent of objective realities.

For many ACAs, the sense of not being normal comes from the family's view of itself as cut off from the world. This view is incorporated into the ACA's identity like an impurity trapped in a growing crystal. The crystal is increasingly distorted, even as the impurity is hidden ever deeper within.

LEVELS OF UNDERLEARNING

There are at least three levels on which underlearning affects ACAs: the cognitive/behavioral (thinking/acting) level, the affective (feeling) level, and the identity (characterological, sense of self) level. The therapeutic approach to each differs, and treating one often leads to the awareness that deeper levels still exist.

The Cognitive/Behavioral Level

Underlearning exists on the cognitive/behavioral level when ACAs simply do not know how humans normally interact. Not having experienced healthy interactions, they are left to guess at what works for most people. Even when their guesses are correct, ACAs may lack confidence in what they have figured out. Treatment of underlearning at this level consists of providing information where appropriate, and actively validating a client's healthy decisions.

Growing up with alcoholic parents can pervasively alter the flow of one's daily life. Basic routines are modified, family rituals are disrupted, and problem-solving behaviors are skewed. For children, a parent's alcoholism[1] results in a major constriction of experience.

Two topics are nearly always capable of evoking reactions among ACAs: dinner time and Christmas. The intensity of reaction to these two important family events confirms the depth to which alcoholism affects both mundane and special facets of the young COA's experience. Children reach adulthood with only fantasies, often fostered by television images, about how families and adults behave.

There are numerous concrete examples of cognitive/behavioral underlearning among ACAs. For example, many ACAs report never having seen an argument which did not lead to violence; the possibility that conflict can be resolved and lead to intimacy is inconceivable to them. Other ACAs report never having had a friend sleep overnight at their house. Still others have never seen an extended family gathering, a family Thanksgiving dinner, or a sit-down dinner of any kind. Some ACAs have never seen an adult with a responsible work ethic. Few have seen a loving relationship between two independent adults.

Children in alcoholic homes may not learn the most ordinary things. When Rick, a successful lawyer, went to be fitted for a new suit, a young sales clerk abruptly asked him where he had learned to tie his shoes. Rick was immediately embarrassed, and said defensively that he tied them "the same way everyone else does." The clerk pointed out how the bows were crooked, then showed him how most people tie their shoes. In relating this incident to me, Rick recalled the day his alcoholic mother had "taught" him to tie shoelaces. In a fit of impatience, she had cuffed him on the side of the head and told him to figure it out for himself. Rick remembers going out to the back yard and working for a couple of hours until he had discovered how to twist his shoelaces around enough to keep his shoes on tightly.

In my own experience, I recall only one family vacation as a child—an event that was only partially successful by any standards. As an adult, preparing for the first vacation after my child's birth, I began feeling uncharacteristically anxious. At one point, I considered looking for a book on vacations—one that would tell me what to pack and how to plan. It finally struck me that I was almost as inexperienced in family vacations as my child was, and that my anxiety stemmed from imagining that all "good fathers" were old hands at such things and could take care of the details effortlessly.

After listening to me discuss my anxieties, my wife gave a few simple suggestions on how to prepare for a successful vacation. I understood them and was able to carry them out without difficulty. Her suggestions made immediate sense—one of the characteristics of underlearning. When alternative behaviors are suggested, the ACA with cognitive/behavioral underlearning is often able to comprehend and act on the new information quite quickly.

Evaluating Cognitive/Behavioral Underlearning

The most effective way to evaluate this level of underlearning is to observe how an ACA client responds to new information. For example, when Rick told me that he was worried about an overdue evaluation from his supervisor, we started by exploring his feelings around this matter. It soon became apparent that he genuinely wanted to know how he was doing, but didn't know how employees normally initiate a meeting with their supervisor. He was surprised that such a thing was possible. We problem-solved the different approaches he could take, and by the next week's session, Rick had acted on one of them. All he had needed was validation that this behavior was possible and acceptable.

There are dangers to giving clients such direct help. The client's natural tendency to see the therapist as a Teacher or Guru may be reinforced, which can be an obstacle to entering deeper levels of therapy later on. Other clients may feel patronized. The process of exploring emotionally important material may be sidetracked or aborted as the therapist runs to the rescue with information about what is normal. And the client's fantasy that all problems have "right answers" which "normal" people know may be reinforced by the therapist who seems to know them all.

Powerful techniques have been developed for working on this first level of underlearning, but they can be abused in individual cases where their appropriateness is limited. For example, techniques to replace destructive self-judgments with daily affirmations can actually feed into an ACA's pathology. An over-reliance on willpower has led more than one ACA to believe that the internal chanting of affirmations ought to have the power to *control* his feelings. When this fails to happen, it becomes just another sign of one's basic inadequacy.

When techniques such as affirmations fail, it should be taken as evidence that the underlearning runs deeper than the cognitive/behavioral level. A willingness to take on one belief system after another, or one lifestyle after another, is part of the ACA's problem. When the damage has reached down into the identity level, the question has to be asked, "*Who* is doing the believing?" Many times, it's not the belief system which must be changed, but the identity of the believer.

In most cases of true character pathology, cognitive/behavioral changes have limited ability to reach down and dramatically affect the characterological level. Until real character change takes place, the individual keeps trying to make cognitive/behavioral changes in the only way she knows how (a clear example of being "hoisted upon one's own petard"). Efforts to change one's underlying character structure require more than new information. Therapists cannot educate people out of character deficits; nor can clients think themselves into new identities. As outlined in Chapter 3 of *Volume Two: Treatment*, characterological change occurs through *experiencing* relationships differently.

On the other hand, there are dangers to withholding helpful information. Therapy may be prolonged. The therapeutic alliance may be strained by the therapist's unwillingness to address concrete problems, or inability to see that the client simply doesn't know how to act. For alcoholics early in recovery, therapists[2] have come to recognize that a full course of therapy often must start on a more behavioral level than is needed later in the treatment. Unless the alcoholic learns how to live in the sober world, relapse may abort deeper therapy. Skilled therapists meet the cognitive/behavioral needs of early recovery in a way that builds trust and creates a bond that facilitates the eventual move into deeper work.

Therapists treating ACAs who appear to display cognitive/behavioral underlearning should provide some concrete information the client requests early in the therapy. This will lead to one of two possible outcomes: Some clients will put the information to use immediately, confirming that the cause of their confusion and inaction is simple underlearning. Others will continue to be inhibited by underlying ambivalence. In these latter cases, it is useful to clarify (to oneself, and to clients, when clinically useful) that lack of information is not the true cause of their confusion, and to move more directly toward working with resistances which remain out of the client's awareness.

The Affective Level

Underlearning on the affective level takes three forms. (1) Some ACAs have no model for the full range of human feelings, having never seen feelings such as tenderness or anger expressed in their families. (2) Some have never learned to experience or label their own feelings, having never had their emotions validated. (3) Some have inadequate models for the effective expression of feelings, having seen little but drunken emotional displays or the pervasive constriction of emotional expression.

For clients who display affective underlearning, each step toward expressing feelings openly—especially feelings about their therapist—is more than a venture into unexplored territory. It is a discovery that such territory even exists, and entering it requires a leap of faith. A few facilitating comments can be remarkably helpful for ACAs struggling to express "forbidden" feelings about a family member, or direct feelings about the therapist. At times it is even appropriate to "guess" a client's feelings before they have actually been spoken.

Alice Miller strongly urges that therapists take seriously the childhood events clients report, to the point of becoming their advocate in cases where trauma is suspected. "In the majority of cases," she writes, "it is not difficult to point out to the patient . . . the way he has dealt with his feelings and needs, and that this was a question of survival for him."[3] In contrast to the more traditional psychoanalytic approach of viewing such reports as condensed screen memories (see Appendix I) fueled by the client's own internal drives, Miller suggests that the therapist act as an auxiliary ego in the struggle to acknowledge the absolute reality of past traumas. "[A] child can only experience his feelings when there is somebody there who accepts him fully, understands and supports him," she explains. Lacking that, the child "cannot experience these feelings `just for himself' but fails to experience them at all."[4]

When a client first reports memories of physical or sexual abuse, it is critical for the therapist to acknowledge the importance of this information. Failure to react, Miller argues, calls the client's perceptions into question once again, a subtle retraumatization that may affect the course of therapy.

On the other hand, there are considerable dangers to becoming the client's ally. Leading clients too actively into acknowledging their feelings may work against their learning to take responsibility themselves. Worse yet is the risk that boundaries may blur between the clients' and the therapists' psychodynamics—a special problem for therapists whose own personal histories have been touched by parental chemical dependence or abuse.

Overtly allying with clients is so hazardous that it should be avoided, except that traumatized individuals often benefit from such therapy. There are two reasons why. First, a therapist's reaction to hearing a history of abuse provides important modeling for the client who suffers from affective underlearning. Traumatized individuals often grew up in families which failed to notice or react to the most inappropriate behavior. When a therapist displays no reaction to information about childhood abuse, this may confirm that such experience is "unimportant," and in some cases can even retraumatize the client. But when a therapist immediately responds with an acknowledgment of the significance of the abuse history, an expression of caring, and willingness to let the client decide when to explore this material further, this may be the first appropriate reaction the client has ever witnessed.

Second, traumatized individuals often require a level of validation for their emotions which therapists can provide only by becoming empathic allies. Without such validation, these clients may never become aware of buried emotions or overcome their fear of expressing them.

ACAs with affective underlearning have no reason to trust that their potentially overwhelming emotions will be seen, permitted, or respected. Neither do they have reason to trust that their feelings will not invite retaliation or overwhelm others. We all learn from experience, and ACAs have little or no experience of others reacting to their feelings in healthy ways. It is here that therapists can work most directly to create what Franz Alexander termed "corrective emotional experiences."[5] This is accomplished by achieving the proper balance between advocating for clients' feelings and remaining detached (i.e., empathic attunement within the context of firm interpersonal boundaries).

The most effective therapeutic stance is one that simultaneously *models* and *validates*. It models normal reactions to abuse by the therapist's willingness, within limits, to react spontaneously to what the client is saying. For example, I will not remain stony faced when a client first tells me about a history of sexual abuse. Rather, I will allow the mixture of concern and sorrow that I feel to register subtly on my face. Effective therapy also validates clients by facilitating awareness and expression of their feelings, and normalizing them when necessary. For example, if a client reports a history of physical abuse while forcefully resisting his emotions, I am likely to comment that most people who have had similar experiences have strong feelings about it. If the client shows interest in this comment, I may add that it is also common for people to feel they have to keep their strong feelings in check, but that the therapeutic setting is a safe place to begin experiencing them openly. This combination of modeling and validation gradually permits clients to experience their feelings fully, without being overwhelmed or fearing they will overwhelm the therapist.

As affective underlearning is corrected, catharsis begins. At this point in therapy, ACAs frequently gain easy access to their past, allowing the free flow of deep passions. This is often extremely gratifying to therapists. Gestalt and psychodramatic techniques can further massive, and impressive, discharges of emotion. For some clients, this is life-changing.

Unfortunately, such catharsis also has its dangers. (1) It can be regarded incorrectly as the whole of therapy; (2) it can be used inappropriately with clients suffering from PTSD; and (3) it can be used in situations which don't permit adequate follow-up care.

The impulse to view catharsis as the essence of therapy, as opposed to an essential aspect of therapy, has been present throughout the history of modern psychiatry. Freud himself originally believed that Charcot's use of hypnosis to cure hysteria by catharsis was the quintessential model for all of psychotherapy. His experience gradually tempered this opinion. For psychotherapy to be effective, there must be a balance between catharsis and cognition—between feeling and understanding.[6] Catharsis alone seldom leads to permanent change unless a framework of cognition is present as well, giving form to unlocked emotions and integrating them into new psychic structures. It is an oversimplification, encountered too frequently among therapists treating ACAs, to assume that getting clients to express their feelings is tantamount to treating their "ACA issues".

Techniques for evoking buried feelings are often used as dramatic demonstrations in ACA workshops and conferences, but these settings rarely screen adequately for the appropriateness of such work for individual participants. These techniques do not discriminate between activating vivid memories and triggering an actual re-experience of the original trauma. For ACAs with stress-related characteristics, in particular, becoming awash in re-experiencing traumatic feelings is of no benefit, and may even intensify problems. At worst, clients can be retraumatized and experience the "therapy" as more dangerous than continuing to live with their problems.

It is not enough for therapists to assume that individual clients must take personal responsibility for doing work at such an intense level. The sheer power therapists wield in these settings demands that they take responsibility as well. Naive clients cannot be expected to understand the nature of the experience such techniques may evoke. And, once the experience is in progress, they may lose the capacity to assess their ability to handle it.

Many clients have sought my help after completing an intense inpatient treatment program for ACAs and being left with their wounds open and raw. In its enthusiasm to provide innovative treatment, the CD field often fails to meet the complex needs of ACA clients, especially in terms of psychological evaluations and adequate follow-up treatment. Thorough diagnostic evaluation is necessary to formulate individualized treatment plans, but inpatient programs do not always take this measured approach. Instead, they accept most clients who seek admission, and use the same burst of therapeutic artillery on them all. The power released by activating primitive emotions connected to childhood experiences can be very fragmenting and disorienting, making follow-up treatment essential. Instead, the CD field offers aftercare—a continuation of the same work undertaken during inpatient treatment—which often does not adequately meet the needs which have been opened during the residential phase of treatment.

Once permission to experience ancient, buried feelings has been granted and catharsis begins, ACAs often need to use their therapists as containers for the released feelings. If the therapists are primarily interested in exploring and resolving their clients' dependence on them, they will interfere with the work their clients must do. Therapists serve as adequate containers by (1) remaining in an empathic mode rather than fusing with their clients, and (2) being willing to "hold" their clients in the sense described by D. W. Winnicott.

Therapists in the empathic mode do not take on the same feelings their clients are experiencing. If they did, their clients might dampen their feelings out of fear of overwhelming the therapists. Rather, therapists experience their own feelings of empathy and avoid fusing with their clients.

Winnicott's concept of "holding" clients refers to the process of supporting their growth without dominating it. The prototypic "holding" occurs within a mother's womb. In the therapy setting, "holding" clients during cathartic moments means permitting them to be absolutely dependent and vulnerable while keeping them separate and whole in your mind.[7] It means taking full responsibility for maintaining the proper boundaries, which is a way of lending ego strength to your clients' struggles. It means accepting the legitimacy of their dependence on you for mirroring and validation; accepting whatever developmental level they are experiencing; and communicating your acceptance simply by your presence, and often primarily by your gaze.

For many ACAs, it is deeply liberating to have their childhood feelings heard and respected. Before, their lives were on hold, but now there may be movement on a wide variety of fronts—as though an ice jam has broken up and the river is free to flow again. Defenses begin lessening, relationships begin resolving, and a new softness may develop. Any and all of these changes are evidence that affective underlearning has been present, and corrective emotional experience is acting as an antidote.

However, a substantial number of ACAs will experience only temporary relief from the catharsis of expressing long withheld emotions. The ice jam begins to reform. Three directions seem to lead from this difficult choice point. Some clients return to cathartic situations, compulsively trying to make them "work." Some experience a painful sense of betrayal and hopelessness, respond with increased bitterness and apathy, and terminate therapy. And some choose to deepen their therapy.

Evaluating Affective Underlearning

Just as the most effective way to evaluate cognitive/behavioral underlearning is to observe how ACAs respond to new information, evaluation of affective underlearning is best done by observing how clients respond to being given permission to have their feelings, and validation for expressing them.

How does the client respond to modeling? For example, when clients relate episodes of abuse from their past, it is often useful for therapists to demonstrate some reaction to what they have heard, perhaps even a brief grimace. Or, when clients are blandly listing one loss after another which they are currently suffering, therapists might model an emotional reaction by placing a hand on their own chest (i.e., "clutching their heart") as they ask how the client has made it through such loss.

When affective underlearning is present, clients usually respond to such modeling with increased access to their feelings. Emotions bubble up and catharsis begins. Some clients are surprised at first that their story affects someone else; others are genuinely confused that there has been a reaction. What's important is that the therapist has taken the lead in permitting feelings to be present. As with cognitive/behavioral underlearning, clients with affective underlearning quickly follow the therapist's lead, demonstrating that the block to their feelings was not psychic numbing, a symptom of PTSD.

How does the client respond to validation and facilitation of her feelings? Is there a willingness to enter into feelings once it is clear that feelings are accepted?

Facilitation can take many forms. For example, the therapist can work with the client to develop a language of feelings. Clients with affective underlearning never had the chance to learn a lexicon for all the feeling states humans experience. Often all they have are a few global words ("I'm feeling bad, or upset") which do not differentiate between emotions such as sadness, anger, and hurt. On an emotional level, such clients are like adults who never traveled more than ten miles from their birthplace. They have no concept of other lands. When therapists help them to develop a language of emotions, many clients become aware of subtleties in their feelings which they never knew existed. Those who suffer from affective underlearning quickly put this new language, and new awareness, into use as a practical tool.

Facilitation can also take the form of guessing what a client is feeling. This technique can be dangerous, especially with co-dependent clients, who are susceptible to feeling whatever others suggest. However, with clients I suspect of having affective underlearning, I may take the chance of guessing the feeling they are struggling to identify. For example, when clients have difficulty articulating the neediness they feel toward a lost parent,

I may say that it sounds like they are feeling a longing for their mother, or father. This technique can only be used if clients have the ability to consider the suggestion, and to reject it if it doesn't fit, without getting into a battle with me around whether I am right or not. When this ability is present, it leads me to trust more deeply that affective underlearning is present.

Facilitation can also take the form of both active and passive support for clients. Active support is represented by Alice Miller's belief that it is sometimes useful for therapists to become a client's ally. For example, a client who was sexually abused as a child may have access to her feelings, but is unwilling to express them unless she is repeatedly convinced that the therapist is "on her side." Until this experience is integrated, it must be continually reinforced. Therapists may find themselves fighting on behalf of clients' hidden emotions.

Passive support entails giving clients a safe enough environment, clear enough boundaries, and a strong enough ego on the therapist's part that clients can trust that their feelings will be contained, and will not fly destructively out of control. Clients who only witnessed emotions when someone in their family was drunk may have no experience that others can tolerate strong emotions without being overwhelmed. Therapy may be their first experience of this.

As always, the sign of underlearning is clear: Once clients have been introduced to a concept, a tool, an alternative, or a new experience, they demonstrate the capacity and willingness to make use of it. The conclusion that underlearning is present is even more warranted when clients' childhood histories give reason to believe that they had never been exposed to the experience they quickly made use of, once they were exposed to it in therapy. The concept of underlearning is especially valuable when it prevents therapists from assuming that "resistance" is always unconsciously motivated.

The Identity Level

Some therapists seem to think that addressing the first two levels of underlearning—cognitive/behavioral and affective—

constitutes the whole of therapy. There are several reasons why they make this mistake (which, incidentally, is not restricted to therapists who work with ACAs).

First, many clients don't require therapy beyond these two levels. Second, the training needed to work on cognitive/behavioral and affective underlearning is easier to get than the training needed to work on characterological (third level) underlearning. As a result, some therapists have little exposure to this level, especially if their education relies more on classroom instruction than on direct clinical supervision. Third, some therapists have not explored the foundations of their own character structure in personal therapy and are ill-prepared to accompany clients along this path. And finally, many clients in need of third-level work have difficulty moving beyond wishful thinking that half measures are enough. They overvalue the more concrete and dramatic nature of therapy that addresses the first two levels, and willingly accept that therapy stops there.

But correcting underlearning on the cognitive/behavioral and affective levels does not lead to sufficient change in all cases. Most of my ACA clients know that there is a wider range of possible behaviors than those they saw modeled by their families of origin. Most have also experienced at least the beginnings of a new relationship with their own feelings. They can now experience previously forbidden emotions, plumbing and expressing their true depths. But their self-esteem remains fragile, based primarily on others' opinions. Their basic sense of self is no different; their character structure has not shifted. The most difficult and most rewarding work still lies ahead.

It may seem strange to include the need for characterological change under the rubric of underlearning. Clearly we do not achieve such change by gathering factual information, force of logic, or intensity of feeling. The fulcrum upon which characterological change turns is clients' willingness to experience all facets of the client-therapist relationship. The healthy interpersonal interactions experienced during such exploration permit and fuel characterological change.

The identity level of underlearning points to the lack of experience ACAs have with those forms of relationship which are transforming—those which help develop new and healthier character traits and create a freer, more authentic sense of self. Such transformations go beyond being corrective emotional experiences, and instead constitute corrective *relational* experiences. They begin when therapist and client enter into work on the transferential level—when the client transfers childhood feelings about the parent to the therapist.

Working in the Transference

Working in the transference is basically a four-step process:

1. The therapist identifies expectations and misperceptions which the client brings into the therapeutic relationship.
2. The therapist focuses on those expectations and misperceptions which stem from the client's childhood experiences.
3. The therapist generates a hypothesis about the child developmental issues which remain unresolved and continue to adversely affect the client's relationships.
4. Guided by this hypothesis, the therapist molds interventions to assist the client's efforts to accomplish unfinished developmental tasks.

The assumption underlying transference work is that the human personality is largely a product of interactions with other people. For the basic character of a client's personality to change, powerful interpersonal forces must be brought to bear. The most powerful of all human interactions occur during childhood, when the effects of relationships are built directly into the foundation of one's personality. By symbolically recreating the parent-child bond and addressing unresolved childhood issues, the therapist provides a unique opportunity for remedial work at the level of the client's basic character structure. The core sense of self is given a second chance to complete its growth.

Two important aspects of this process are worth noting here. First, just as children are not consciously aware of the developmental issues that motivate their behavior, the bulk of the work done in the transference takes place in the client's unconscious. Therapists must be content to let their actions stir unconscious forces within the client, and they must know how to read the signs that progress is being made. The urge to enlist conscious cooperation from the client is like expecting children to understand multiplication before they have learned to count.

The practice of speaking directly to the unconscious through the client-therapist relationship leads into a second important aspect of working in the transference: the hierarchical structure of that relationship. The developmental issues a client brings along originated in the past, between a small child and a powerful parent. Any expectations and misperceptions the client now has because of those childhood experiences inevitably cause hierarchy issues to be emotionally charged. Meanwhile, the therapist's task is to facilitate growth which the client is unable to comprehend until after that growth has taken place. To accomplish this, client and therapist must find a way to work together within the transference.

The need for this becomes clear when we understand the disturbances at the level of self which ACAs experience. Barbara Wood nicely summarized what underlearning at the identity level can do:

> It is the fundamental assumption here that many of the problems adult children experience, including the failure to separate from the family of origin and become a true individual, the inability to establish stable commitments in love and work, the compulsive engagement with hopeless persons and causes, and the severe depletion of self-esteem, can all be understood as the result of damage to the structure of the self. This damage is rooted in the troubled parent-child relationships that are characteristic of alcoholic families, and which lead to severe disturbances of the internal object relationships which form the foundation of the self.[8]

It is through our relationships with significant others that we gather the stuff to build our sense of self. In developing the principles of self-psychology, Heinz Kohut repeatedly emphasized this basic point, stating that "the unfolding, structuralization, and crystallization of the healthy self depends, in great part, on parents' ability to provide an emotionally responsive and empathic psychological environment for their children."[9] Parents must be able to grasp their child's "inner life more or less accurately so that their responses are attuned to his needs."[10]

Alice Miller echoes Kohut's theories when she asserts that we come to know who we truly are only through being loved as we truly are. Since the very essence of interactions with active alcoholics involves their inability to empathize, COAs are at very high risk of developing disturbances in their sense of self.

When underlearning exists on the identity level, it means that a client has not had enough quality relationship experiences to build a strong sense of self. Cognitive/behavioral and affective solutions alone cannot substantially change that, but the client-therapist relationship can. Working in the transference, both the client and the therapist let the fears, distortions, and projections originally directed toward the client's parents emerge toward the therapist. The client assumes a vulnerable position, and the therapist becomes an authority figure who defines the boundaries of the relationship.

It is here that the therapeutic relationship becomes acutely similar to the parent-child relationship, both symbolically and in substance. The client allows the therapist to *be* the therapist in the fullest sense by permitting a relationship like that which exists between a child and an older, hopefully wiser, parent. This represents a true leap of faith for the client. Prior experience has taught him that such relationships lead to incredible disappointment and pain. To voluntarily re-enter one is an act of profound courage, foolhardiness, or desperation.

Evaluating Underlearning at the Identity Level

There are three ways the therapist can evaluate underlearning at the identity level. The first is simply to assume that every human has aspects of self which are incompletely developed. The therapist must then decide whether a particular client is available to enter into work capable of healing residual damage on this level. Since it is impossible to force clients into such work, the therapist can only invite, often by facilitating open discussion of the client-therapist relationship. When a client is willing to consider this relationship while allowing the therapist to maintain the position of participant/observer, the work has begun.

Second, once corrective work has been done on the cognitive/ behavioral and affective levels of underlearning, if significant change still seems to be blocked, it is likely that the client's self has to be repaired. The difference between the first two levels and the third can be expressed as a metaphor: When a construction crew is failing to build the house they are supposed to, is it because they lack some of the tools they need (cognitive/behavioral and affective levels), or does the crew itself need to be restructured to increase its effectiveness (identity level)? The therapeutic question moves beyond, "Do you have all the knowledge and access to all the feelings you need?" to "*Who* is it that has this knowledge and these feelings?"

Third, the strength of a client's self can be evaluated in terms of its *cohesion, vitality,* and *functional harmony.*[11] Cohesion is evaluated by finding out how resistant the client is to fragmentation—does he demonstrate increased splitting (e.g., black-and-white thinking) when under stress? *Continuity,* a related concept, is cohesion in a temporal sense—does the client's sense of self remain stable over time? Vitality relates to the vigor of a client's self—the degree of psychic energy at the self's disposal. Functional harmony refers to the degree of consistency or internal contradiction among the parts of one's self.

In line with the framework for narcissism and co-dependence outlined in Chapter 4, these three aspects of the self can be seen as resulting from (1) the maturation of narcissistic needs (which leads to stability of self-esteem), (2) the maturation of echoistic, or co-dependent, needs (which leads to the ability for enthusiasm), and (3) the successful integration of the two (which is the intrapsychic facet of successfully resolving Mahler's rapprochement crisis).

CONCLUSION

The concept of underlearning points to the consequences of insufficient experience on each of three levels: cognitive/behavioral, affective, and identity. Because underlearning occurs on such disparate levels, and because the unique details of underlearning differ widely from individual to individual, no umbrella theory is capable of describing all three. It suffices to say that underlearning leads ACAs to feel that they don't know what constitutes normal behavior, normal emotions, and a normal sense of self.

Underlearning on the cognitive/behavioral level leaves ACAs ignorant of possible behaviors and appropriate choices in a wide variety of situations. When underlearning exists only on this level, ACAs quickly convert new information into new behavior.

Underlearning on the affective level leads ACAs to believe that restricting feelings is a proper measure of maturity. When underlearning exists primarily on the affective level, catharsis releases an adequately structured self from bondage, and external change can rapidly follow as the false self drops away.

Underlearning at the identity level results in damage to the structure of the self, which leaves ACAs incapable of changing even when underlearning at the first two levels has been corrected. Here is where characterological change becomes necessary. Working in the transference, the client experiences increasingly healthy interpersonal dynamics and integrates them into a more cohesive, vital, and functionally harmonious self.

6

AXIS V:
DUAL DIAGNOSIS

The warning "ACA is a label, not a diagnosis" has particular relevance to the question of dual diagnosis. Studies of psychopathology in ACAs differ in their findings, but the one conclusion they all support is that the full range of human mental disorders can occur in people with alcoholic parents.

In addition to having the characteristics outlined in preceding chapters, ACAs may be schizophrenic, manic-depressive, and/or mentally retarded; they may have major depressions, borderline personality disorder, and so on. The frequency of these illnesses among ACAs has not yet been established, but this is of little significance in evaluating specific individuals. What's important is that therapists not take the narrow perspective of trying to fit all of a client's signs and symptoms under the "ACA issues" umbrella.

When therapists fail to look for psychopathology which is not specifically related to being an ACA, the result may be inappropriate treatment. For example, validating the traumatic nature of a client's childhood is not the best way to deal with psychotic episodes. Grief work is not the answer to episodes of major depression when the client's body has become so involved in the depression that psychological work is temporarily blocked. *The fact that a client is an ACA is no guarantee that every symptom he or she has is related to this fact.* This is the reason dual diagnosis is our fifth axis for evaluating ACAs at Genesis. Making it a necessary part of our evaluation process compels us, in every evaluation interview, to consider the widest range of diagnostic possibilities to explain the data before us.

Our dual diagnosis axis emphasizes borderline personality disorders, which present perhaps the most difficult differential diagnostic challenge. COAs are subjected to many of the early childhood influences which produce borderline symptomatology. Severely active co-dependence can be nearly indistinguishable from borderline conditions. And, since group therapy is frequently the treatment of choice for ACAs, it becomes extremely important to recognize borderlines in order to avoid disrupting a therapy group which can not accommodate borderline issues.

Unfortunately, there are no certain ways to detect borderline pathology in the course of a brief evaluation, especially in its milder and well-compensated forms. The following framework aids in this challenging task.

THE RELATIONSHIP BETWEEN BORDERLINE AND NARCISSISTIC/ECHOISTIC PERSONALITY DISORDERS

It is important to differentiate between ACAs who are borderline and those who are narcissistic/echoistic, because the therapeutic approaches to each differ significantly. To make this differentiation easier, let's return briefly to theoretical considerations.

But first: Despite continuing disagreements among clinicians and researchers over the precise nature of borderline pathology, we as therapists must be as clear as possible in our thinking about it. We also must come to terms with a seeming paradox in our theoretical framework: the fact that borderline issues can be more debilitating than narcissism or echoism, even though borderline disorders are believed to get their start later in child development. This seems to violate the common-sense notion that the earlier problems form during child development, the more severe dysfunction they cause.

What Is Borderline Pathology?

Just as with co-dependence, there is disagreement about whether "borderline" is a concept or a diagnosis. There is even deep dissatisfaction with the term itself, with noted therapists rejecting it because it "neither connotes nor communicates a behavioral pattern that portrays distinctive stylistic features . . . *the label, borderline, is perhaps the most poorly chosen of all the terms selected for the DSM-III.*"[1] Many therapists struggle to develop a coherent framework for understanding borderline phenomena long after they have come to terms with other, better defined character disorders. They keep struggling because, despite the lack of clarity about borderline symptoms, every therapist encounters clients who demonstrate them.

The word "borderline" has been used to refer to a psychological concept, a measure of symptom severity, and a formal diagnosis. Kernberg[2] argues that borderline issues represent an entire *level of personality organization*, and contrasts it with neurotic and psychotic personality organizations. Neurotic personality structure uses high-level defenses such as repression. Borderlines use more primitive defenses, such as splitting (dividing the world into black and white, good and bad), but maintain reality testing (the capacity to distinguish fantasy from reality). Psychotics use primitive defenses *and* lose the capacity to reality test.

Theodore Millon believes that "borderline" represents a degree of personality disorder *severity*.[3] He contends that borderline develops insidiously as an advanced or more dysfunctional variant of other personality disorders, particularly dependent, histrionic, compulsive, and passive-aggressive disorders.

Finally, John Gunderson and his colleagues assert that "borderline" is a discrete personality disorder *diagnosis*, characterized by intense affect, frequent depersonalization, impulsivity (leading to self-destructive acts and alcohol or other drug abuse), identity disturbances, brief psychotic episodes, and interpersonal relationships that vacillate between superficiality, dependence, and manipulativeness.[4] DSM-III-R follows this latter course, emphasizing a "pattern of unstable and intense interpersonal relationships characterized by alternating between extremes of overidealization and devaluation."[5]

While Gunderson's diagnostic description is clinically useful, it does not distinguish borderline from personality disorders which cycle between co-dependent and narcissistic symptoms. Two additional considerations are useful in making this difficult distinction. First, I am aided in my understanding of borderline personalities by applying Kohut's approach to defining narcissism: It is not so much specific behaviors as it is the "nature or quality" of subjective experience in the client which makes the diagnosis. Second, while clients can vacillate between narcissism and co-dependence, each of these stances is relatively stable. This is in marked contrast to the essence of the borderline's experience, which results from extreme instability within one's very sense of self. Such instability leads to the deep existential anxiety and sense of internal void characteristic of the true borderline.

It is also difficult to distinguish ACAs who are very actively co-dependent from ACAs who are borderline. Their symptoms and subjective experiences overlap; both feel deeply uncertain about who they are. But there is a distinction. The co-dependent's uncertainty comes from a split between the false and the true self ("I look good, but feel bad"), while the borderline's comes from an instability within the basic organization of the self ("I am either all good, or all bad"). It is in this sense that the diagnosis of borderline personality disorder indicates a deeper pathology.

The Genesis of
Borderline Pathology

Exploring child development issues which give rise to borderline pathology helps differentiate this disorder from co-dependence and narcissism. Even theorists who disagree on the underlying personality structure of borderlines agree that the problem stems from an inability to resolve the rapprochement phase of development. For example, Kernberg notes that Margaret Mahler's (1971) proposal "that borderline pathology is related specifically to the rapprochement subphase of the separation-individuation process seems to me to coincide with my proposal that the problem with borderline patients is not the lack of differentiation of self from nonself but the lack of integration of 'good' and 'bad' self and object representations."[6]

In discussing narcissism and echoism in Chapter 4, I emphasize the factors which lead to an inability to leave the symbiotic phase (i.e., "separation of self from nonself"). In discussing borderlines, we must move further along in the separation-individuation process to rapprochement, for it is here that the borderline has become stuck—in a perpetually unresolved rapprochement crisis.

According to Mahler, "the rapprochement struggle has its origins in the *species-specific* human dilemma that arises out of the fact that, on the one hand, the toddler is obliged, by the rapid maturation of his ego, to recognize his separateness, while, on the other hand, he is as yet unable to stand alone and will continue to need his parents for many years to come."[7] Children go through an immense struggle, both internally and with their parents, during the last half of their second year. Tremendous ambivalence develops. The child wants to do it on his own, but also wants his parents to help. He wants to be completely independent, but also wants his parents to keep him safe. Impossible demands are made; temper tantrums reappear. Underlying all this is the child's conscious realization that he is truly separate from his parents. The illusion of being "at one" with his parents has been destroyed. Symbiosis has ended. It is time to rebuild the relationship between self and parent on a new, more realistic basis, one which takes into account new feelings such as being finite and limited.

Up until now, the child has imagined that he can have it all: "I'll become independent, but keep the cozy feeling of being in total union with my parents." During the rapprochement crisis, it becomes clear that this is no longer possible. The child realizes that there is a price for separateness and independence. The question of how to maintain closeness with the parents, minus the illusion of "oneness" with them, is what constitutes the crisis.

This can be a profoundly terrifying period. The child no longer knows the safety of being in union with others, and does not yet have the maturity to achieve closeness with real, whole people. Narcissists and echoists never quite reach this point. They still harbor the illusion of union. Neither has fully differentiated from others. Narcissists expect you to take your identity from them; echoists expect to take their identity from you. Both avoid the rapprochement crisis in favor of earlier dreams of union. To accomplish this, they must disown one of their incompatible interpersonal needs (i.e., the narcissist disowns the need to be dependent, while the co-dependent disowns the need to be the center). Once this occurs, there is less internal tension to propel a child into rapprochement. A stable (although not healthy) personality configuration ensues—either co-dependence or narcissism, depending on which basic interpersonal need has been rejected.

Borderlines go further out on a limb: They experience separation, but fail to develop any avenue back into relationship. Unable to achieve rapprochement, they also fail to achieve the relative stability of co-dependence or narcissism. Caught in an unremitting war between primitive narcissistic and echoistic needs, borderlines put increasing amounts of psychic energy into defending against being overwhelmed by their internal tensions. The very instability of the borderline's personality renders these defenses ineffective. Over time, the defenses become exaggerated, and the internal tensions are projected out into the world. Borderline symptoms begin appearing.

Why would a child be unable to resolve the rapprochement crisis? And, failing this resolution, why would a child remain in the destructive limbo of a prolonged rapprochement phase, rather than retreat to the more comfortable stability of a narcissistic/co-dependent personality structure? The answers to these questions are not known, but I give considerable credence to the framework proposed by Bessel van der Kolk, who notes that the role of actual parental abuse in creating borderline children has never been systematically studied. He writes:

Clinical descriptions of borderline personality disorder . . . are remarkably congruent with descriptions of chronic post-traumatic stress disorder (PTSD), and especially with the form of the disorder described in patients who have been subjected to repeated trauma over a considerable period of time. In both syndromes, major disturbances are found in the area of affect regulation, impulse control, reality testing, interpersonal relationships, and self-integration."[8]

The implication, which still must be supported by research, is that the emotional intensity and high levels of general arousal stemming from repeated abuse simultaneously interfere with the maturation process (thereby preventing resolution of the rapprochement crisis), and with achieving the stability of a narcissistic/echoistic personality structure (thereby aborting the crisis by backing away from it).

The Effects of Borderline Pathology

The borderline's fundamental instability disrupts subsequent development more than the blind-alley compromises of codependence and narcissism. By identifying with one interpersonal need and disowning the other, narcissists/echoists achieve a stable internal structure. Borderlines, on the other hand, tend to oscillate (sometimes rapidly) back and forth between the two incompatible interpersonal needs. Either they expect their capabilities to be appreciated, or they seek an ideal parent to fuse with. Neither need becomes dominant, but neither does the borderline mature to a sense of self which can incorporate both needs. A core sense of instability ensues.

This instability becomes an important part of the borderline's subjective experience, gradually oscillating into greater extremes of idealization and punitive rage. The stuff out of which the borderline's character is made does not differ from the narcissist's or echoist's. But the organization of this stuff does differ, as does the stability of this organization. The personality of the narcissist/echoist stabilizes around the illusion of union with others. The borderline remains unstably rocking between the desperate hope for union and the impulse for revenge.

The borderline structure is an improvement on narcissism/ echoism in the sense that maturity requires the presence of both interpersonal needs. Finding a measure of stability by denying one or the other aborts the need to reconcile them at some point. The problem for borderlines is that neither interpersonal need matures sufficiently to permit integration with the other. The two remain at loggerheads. As a result, borderlines can never form an image of themselves or others that corresponds to the richness of human emotional reality.

In particular, borderlines can never reconcile the reality that each of us is a mixture of good and bad characteristics, generous and self-centered motives, power and limitation. As a result, both self and others are always seen through a lens which makes everything either black or white. Therefore, whenever the therapist displays a trait or behavior which violates the borderline's image of the therapist, the borderline feels betrayed and lied to: "The therapist has really been someone else all this time!" The borderline is unable to conceive of the therapist as having a mixture of contradictory facets, all of which are integrated by the therapist's underlying sense of self. Because the borderline's own sense of self is so fragile, this feeling of being betrayed fully reopens the wounds of abandonment/abuse inflicted by the parents during rapprochement. The client suddenly relives the original crisis. This tendency to re-experience earlier traumas fits van der Kolk's suggestion that parental abuse plays a role in creating borderline symptoms.

Doubly confusing to borderlines are the times when their own contradictions leave them feeling tossed about upon an inner sea. Without a broad enough sense of self to integrate internal contradictions, a borderline's identity alternates between extremes. The worst of these have to do with feelings of hostility and dependence toward others—difficult feelings for any of us to hold simultaneously toward the same person. Borderlines are consigned to dividing the world into those upon whom they can utterly depend, and those toward whom they feel deep rage. Whenever borderlines attempt to enter into intimate relationships, these two feelings end up being directed toward the same person. Alternating between idealization and rage causes relationships to be intense, and often short-lived.

Comments

It is beyond the scope of this chapter to solve the riddle of why an individual might progress beyond the narcissist/echoist level, but get stuck in the rapprochement phase and become borderline. It may even be beyond the scope of our current thinking to provide clear and concise perspective on this issue. Two comments in this direction will have to suffice.

First, the origins of borderline processes can be found on both sides of the nature-nurture spectrum, and it may be that genetics play a more significant role in the genesis of borderline than in other personality disorders. Second, as James Masterson asserts, "the great majority of the mothers of the borderline adolescents we studied were indeed borderline. . . ."[9] In other words, borderline parents may create an environment which fosters borderline processes in children. Such an environment would present children with no model for being able to integrate "good" and "bad" human traits, no attunement with children's efforts to accomplish such integration, an atmosphere of intense instability, and parent-child interactions which would solidify children's natural tendency to organize the world, including their internal image of themselves, into black-and-white categories. It could be that such a chaotic environment, which can also be created by parental abuse, plays the most significant role in creating borderline personality disorders.

ACAs AND BORDERLINE PERSONALITY DISORDER

It should be fairly obvious, from descriptions of alcoholic family dynamics and the influences on developing children leading to narcissistic/echoistic problems, that COAs are also at high risk of developing borderline personalities. This is especially true in those families where an alcoholic parent's pre-existing borderline traits are catapulted into a full-blown disorder by the development of alcoholism, or where profound and early abuse occurs. The real question is one of why borderline pathology does not occur more frequently among COAs.

The answer to this may lie in the fact that chronic alcoholism tends to impose self-absorption, self-centeredness, and narcissism upon people's basic personalities more than it imposes borderline issues. Nevertheless, an alcoholic home is a good breeding ground for some children to develop borderline personalities, a possibility the therapist must entertain whenever she evaluates an ACA for treatment.

Recognizing borderline pathology is important because the treatment for borderlines is complex and may be quite taxing. Borderline pathology in clients leads to specific responsibilities for the therapist. Here, perhaps more than anywhere else, a therapist's love for the client is inadequate as a curative factor unless it is joined by a disciplined and well-informed psychodynamic approach. The therapist must set boundaries clearly and consistently. The therapist must recognize that transference issues are going to be activated almost immediately, and will tend to be acted out. And therapy must be entered into with the up-front knowledge that borderlines have "an idiosyncratic sensitivity to the unconscious of others, particularly their rewarding and withdrawing responses."[10] Although the obvious content of therapy may revolve around "ACA issues," the underlying dynamics will be pervasively consistent with borderline issues.

Generally speaking, borderline issues cannot be effectively addressed by treatment plans derived from ACA-oriented frameworks. Until the therapist has had enough experience with borderlines to integrate a clear and effective approach into his or her psychotherapeutic framework, ongoing supervision is recommended.

EVALUATING BORDERLINE SYMPTOMS

The question still remains, "How do I recognize a borderline client?" The following framework and interview techniques are helpful in evaluating the presence of borderline pathology.

The psychiatric interview not only pays attention to information clients provide, but also concentrates on interactions between therapist and client. The therapist observes firsthand how a client's behavior and personality may be related to his complaints. The goal is to go beyond observations at the symptom level to observations of the very structure of the client's personality (or, in Heinz Kohut's terms, how cohesive, vital, and harmonious is the client's sense of self?).

To activate and diagnose such structural characteristics, Otto Kernberg[11] developed a hierarchy of increasingly powerful interventions. Understanding these interventions and incorporating them in sequence into the evaluation interview increases the therapists' chances of correctly diagnosing borderline conditions.

Kernberg's Interventions

Clarification

Kernberg's first intervention "refers to the exploration, with the patient, of all the elements in the information he has provided that are vague, unclear, puzzling, contradictory, or incomplete."[12] Clarification neither calls the material into question nor implies negative or positive judgment. Rather, it "aims at evoking conscious and preconscious material without challenging the patient."[13]

The therapist should be genuinely interested in what the client has to say, curiously following certain threads out as far as possible to understand their implications. At the same time, the therapist should attempt to discover the client's own understanding or confusion regarding what still remains unclear. Clarification explores the limits of the client's self-awareness.

Confrontation

For the second intervention, the therapist simply, and again without judgment, presents the client with areas of information that seem contradictory or incongruous.

Confrontation exists at two levels of intensity. The less intense involves placing on the table two incompatible things the client has said about herself and seeking some clarification. For example, a client may say at one point in the interview that her marriage is wonderful, then mention at another point that she is thinking of getting divorced.

The more intense level of confrontation addresses contradictions which somehow involve the interaction occurring between client and therapist. For example, a therapist may note that a client is smiling while talking about feelings of sadness. Or the therapist may call attention to the disparity between a client's request for help and his refusal to entertain a suggestion the therapist makes. Ideally, the therapist also raises the possibility that such behavior has a bearing on the client's current problems.

"Confrontation, thus defined, requires tact and patience," Kernberg explains. "[It] is not an aggressive way of intruding into the patient's mind or a move to polarize the relation[ship] with him."[14] If confrontation is done properly and the client begins to feel intruded on, becomes hostile, or otherwise polarizes the relationship between herself and the therapist, this is suggestive of borderline symptoms.

Unfortunately, the word "confrontation" carries connotations for some therapists (particularly within the CD field) which are not intended here. It is particularly important for the therapist to avoid any sense of confronting clients with the force of his or her own character. The confrontation should have nothing to do with motivating the client to change; its sole purpose should be a respectful effort to better understand him. The therapist should leave it up to the client to misinterpret the confrontation as a tug-of-war, if the client is so inclined. Such misinterpretations (i.e., over-personalizing the confrontation) represent precisely the sort of diagnostic information this level of intervention seeks.

They increase the likelihood that the client being evaluated is borderline.

Interpretation and Transference
Interpretation

After clarification has led to a mutual understanding of what the client is saying, and confrontation has identified incongruities and contradictions in this material, interpretation offers possible explanations for these contradictions by hypothesizing unconscious forces.

For example, a client speaks of divorce soon after praising her spouse. The therapist might offer the interpretation that the client feels afraid of, or guilty about, her anger at her spouse, and tends to compensate with excessive praise. In Kernberg's words, "interpretation focuses on the underlying anxieties and conflicts activated. Confrontation brings together and reorganizes what has been observed; interpretation adds a hypothesized dimension of causality and depth to the material."[15]

What's important about interpretation during an initial interview is not that the therapist be *right*, but that the client's reactions be *observed*. Is the client able to enter into the spirit of introspection, or does he feel intruded upon by what he misperceives as the therapist's efforts to define who he is? Such misperceptions may represent symptoms of borderline personality structure.

Interpretations have even greater power when they involve transference. Transference refers to the presence of feelings and behavior that stem from the unconscious reenactment of relations with significant people in the client's past—often one's parents. It is usually triggered by something in the present which resembles that past experience, either concretely or symbolically. The quality, and intensity, of feelings that occur in the transference is comparable to the quality, and intensity, that the feelings had in the past.

Commenting on transferences developing in the relationship between client and therapist brings them into here-and-now awareness. For example, if a client smiles while reporting feelings of sadness, the therapist might suggest that the client is embarrassed to reveal such intimate details to someone she fears might judge her, perhaps as other authorities in her life have done. As Kernberg puts it, the value of transference reactions is that they "provide the context for interpretations linking the here-and-now disturbance with the patient's there-and-then experience."[16]

Comments

Kernberg's own summary of his interventions is helpful here:

> *Clarification* is a nonchallenging, cognitive means of exploring the limits of the patient's awareness of certain material.

> *Confrontation* attempts to make the patient aware of potentially conflicting and incongruous aspects of that material.

> *Interpretation* tries to resolve the conflicting nature of the material by assuming underlying unconscious motives and defenses that make the previously contradictory appear logical.

> *Transference interpretation* applies all these preceding modalities of technique to the current interaction between the patient and the diagnostician.[17]

The interview techniques outlined above subject clients to a certain amount of stress, which must simultaneously be balanced against the need to initiate an empathic, therapeutic relationship. This balance is hard to maintain. Unless an empathic connection is forged, clients may not enter into therapy, no matter how valuable the evaluation interview has been to the therapist. But, unless the interview has explored the depth of disorganization in a client's personality structure, or the rigidity of defense against such disorganization, therapists will not be able to individualize treatment effectively. It is useful to remind oneself that the purpose of such an interview is not to see how the client behaves while under stress, but rather to see how stressed the client becomes by successively penetrating interventions.

I use the word "penetrating" because it suggests the subjective reaction borderline personalities are likely to have to the interventions. The more severely borderline a client is, the more intruded on she will feel by the therapist's interventions. In extreme cases, the process of clarification will generate significant anxiety. Such anxiety in a borderline goes beyond neurotic performance anxiety ("Aren't I doing this well enough to please the therapist?") and tends toward a paranoid sense of being persecuted ("Why won't the therapist understand me?"). A feeling may develop that "the therapist is trying to put words in my mouth." The belief that the therapist "isn't satisfied with what I'm saying" leads the severe borderline to suspect that her story is being "taken over" by someone else. This in turn produces an existential anxiety ("Do I even exist in this relationship?"). All-or-nothing, black-or-white, good-and-bad thinking—splitting—begins to occur as the client becomes convinced that either he or the therapist must be "right."

When confrontation is added to clarification, some clients may further regress. If the client's defensiveness begins to predominate over introspection, this may be evidence that the client is perceiving the therapist as aggressive. It is precisely the borderline client's inability to integrate contradictory material which causes her to flee into a defensive posture at this point. When interpretations then attempt to provide this integration, the borderline feels a loss of self, and the therapist is now seen as defining who the client is. To accept the interpretation is to surrender one's identity to the aggressor. More and more profound regression may occur until distortion of reality "borders" on being psychotic.

ACAs who are not borderline may still be sensitive to clarifications, confrontations, and interpretations, perhaps even misperceiving them in the same way as the borderline. In such cases, therapists must focus on what happens next. Do these misinterpretations start escalating into borderline defenses? If so, does an avenue remain open for exploring this with the client? Or do the therapist's efforts to address the misperceptions add fuel to the fire? In either case, the likelihood increases that the client is borderline.

CONCLUSION

ACAs are subject to the full range of psychopathology seen in the general population, including borderline personality disorder. It is critical to their care that evaluations continuously entertain the possibility of dual diagnoses. This chapter lays the groundwork for including the possibility of borderline pathology in the evaluation of ACA clients. Kernberg's graded interventions (clarification, confrontation, and interpretation) are valuable tools we can use to make this diagnosis. By incorporating them into initial evaluation interviews, therapists can better elicit information needed to individualize treatment plans and to prevent therapeutic misadventures with those clients for whom changing therapeutic direction is especially difficult. At best, use of these techniques is an art, and far from an exact science.

7

AXIS VI:
EVALUATING RECOVERY

Our sixth and final axis for evaluating ACAs involves assessing their recovery. By "recovery," we mean both the process of surrendering compulsive behaviors (such as alcohol abuse and co-dependent rescuing) and the specific program of action outlined by Alcoholics Anonymous (AA) to promote healing.

The concept and practice of recovery encompassed by this axis arose within the chemical dependence (CD) field. Therefore, this chapter begins by exploring the differences in how the CD and psychotherapy (PT) fields relate to recovery. Next, it outlines frameworks for evaluating where individual clients are in their own recovery, and how well they have been able to use Twelve Step principles as tools to facilitate this process.

PERSPECTIVES ON RECOVERY

In its most general sense, "recovery" means the return to a normal state of affairs, and it was in this sense that the early pioneers of AA believed that alcoholics could be "restored to sanity." The main purpose in writing the AA "Big Book" was "to show other alcoholics *precisely how we have recovered* [italics added]."[1] Later, as medical descriptions of the disease of alcoholism outlined its progressive development, recovery was envisioned as the mirror image of a spiral into more and more severe symptoms.[2]

As the CD field took shape, the concept of recovery *from the specific disease of alcoholism* became the touchstone of treatment. Recovery and treatment became nearly synonymous, in keeping with the CD perspective that the bulk of treatment for alcoholism must be self-prescribed and self-administered if it is to be effective. The measure of a person's recovery from alcoholism was and remains the degree to which he has dismantled his denial and embarked upon a way of life incompatible with intoxication.

In medical terms, recovery is tantamount to a person's voluntary compliance with treatment, through the development of behaviors and attitudes which maintain sobriety. These healthy behaviors and attitudes evolve in predictable stages after people become abstinent.[3] It is for this reason that recovery can be seen as a developmental process, capable of being evaluated.

Within medicine, physical conditioning and physiotherapy are analogous to the CD concept of recovery. When doctors counsel exercise, rest, and a nutritious diet, they are outlining a program designed to "recover" and maintain a person's full physical health and vigor. Such a program can be of value to a wide range of people, from the recent heart-attack victim to the Olympic athlete. Obviously, the daily practices would differ for these two extremes, but the underlying principles are similar. The recovery process is the psychological equivalent of pursuing an active program of physical conditioning.

Within the mental health field, the concept of recovery can be seen in principles underlying the human potential movement, which holds that individuals can take responsibility for their own healing by strengthening their mental, emotional, and spiritual "muscles." Human potential therapists function in part as guides, advising people in their striving toward greater health.

I would also include the specialized field of Christian therapy here. Therapists in this tradition assess the state of a client's faith and spiritual practices, much as CD therapists evaluate a client's recovery. The assumption that a strong faith and its disciplined practice will augment therapy and promote healing is similar to the CD field's view of recovery as a way of life.

Most psychotherapists justifiably balk at the prospect of prescribing lifestyles for clients, or too directly suggesting specific solutions for problems. This often constrains therapists from encouraging their clients to get involved in Twelve Step-oriented self-help groups. The distinctly different perspectives the PT and CD fields take toward recovery are due to both practical and theoretical considerations. On the practical level, psychotherapists see a wider range of mental disorders. No single developmental model of healing describes their clinical experience, as recovery does in the CD field. On the theoretical level, there are deep philosophical differences between the two fields, which I believe should be identified, analyzed, and looked upon as a source of strength for each. Chapter 1 of *Volume Two: Treatment* explores these philosophical differences in some detail.

No matter what treatment framework is being used, there is value in being able to evaluate the status of a client's recovery. When clients remain in denial and lack basic information about how alcoholism and other drug abuse affects families, therapists will quickly understand which therapeutic interventions would be most helpful. When clients have already benefited by "entering into recovery," therapists will understand the tools which are already at the clients' disposal. And it is always best for therapists to avoid discouraging clients from entering treatment by having no understanding of how recovery has helped save their lives.

THE RECOVERY PROCESS

As noted in Chapter 2, the process of recovery from alcoholism has been well described by Stephanie Brown[4] in a developmental model encompassing four stages, each with its own tasks. This model has direct relevance to ACAs, a topic we'll explore after outlining Brown's framework in greater depth.

The Drinking Phase

The first stage of recovery is dominated by the belief that control is possible. The alcoholic believes that he can control his drinking after he has started, or that he can control how alcohol affects his brain and personality.

Gregory Bateson[5] described the alcoholic's stance on control as essentially "prideful," carrying the seeds of its own inevitable destruction. In Bateson's words, this pride "is an obsessive acceptance of a challenge, a repudiation of the proposition `I cannot.'"[6] In this sense, it is the embodiment of the narcissist's grandiosity.

The internal struggle with being limited is externalized and turned into a battle with alcohol. The individual becomes a tragic hero in the classic sense—railing mightily against superior forces, indomitable in spirit if not in fact. His sense of self-worth becomes attached to the intensity of the struggle, but the struggle involves a drug over which he has no possibility of exerting the kind of control he desires. There is no concept of acknowledging defeat without simultaneously losing access to the one avenue to self-esteem he can imagine—drinking with control. Naturally, denial can keep much of this dynamic out of his awareness.

According to Stephanie Brown, therapeutic tasks at this stage focus on cognitive and behavioral levels. Denial must be dismantled, and dysfunctional beliefs about control must be broken through. Behavioral suggestions are designed to facilitate these cognitive shifts. Until the conflict is properly internalized, progress is limited and characterological change is unimaginable.

Obviously, the continued harmful effects of alcohol and other drugs on the brain lower the individual's cognitive capacity at this critical juncture. In many cases, a period of abstinence is necessary before cognitive changes can occur.

The Transition Phase

Massive changes occur on many fronts during this phase. Behaviorally, the individual shifts to abstinence as the norm (although this does not have to be continuous). Cognitively, she drops denial and makes a more realistic assessment of her lack of control over drinking. Perhaps most importantly, she makes a critical shift in identity—from *not* being an alcoholic to *being* an alcoholic. This shift means that the conflict has been internalized and the boundaries of the self have changed. This change can be as important as an infant's move out of the symbiotic stage into separation and individuation. It may feel like a new self has been born.

We have a phrase for such fundamental shifts in identity— shifts which bring the self into new relationship with the rest of the world. We call them "spiritual experiences." They can be blazingly dramatic, or hide their profundity in a cloak of subtlety.

The transition phase may take hold tenuously, cycling back and forth between the drinking phase and this new identity. Because the stakes in alcoholism are so high (life-or-death in some cases, "living-or-dying" in others), the tasks appropriate to this stage focus on the transitions being made. Behaviorally, there is an emphasis on actions which promote continued abstinence, such as regular attendance at AA meetings, avoidance of drinking situations, and development of sober friends. Cognitively, large amounts of information are integrated as denial is dismantled. A new identity as an alcoholic must be firmly established to inoculate against the easy return of denial. The individual's attachment turns away from alcohol toward AA meetings, literature, and new friends among the recovering community. Therapists should actively promote these attachments.

Early Recovery

Once drinking behavior is no longer an immediate threat, the individual is ready to move beyond the narrow focus on abstinence fostered during the transition phase. These initial forays into self-exploration must incorporate a new foundation for one's identity, or denial may return as a sense that the problem has been licked.

The overriding task of early recovery is to ensure that all aspects of one's life and personality are based on the reality that one is an alcoholic. This doesn't mean that one's identity is restricted to being an alcoholic. Rather, it means that one must not begin identifying with aspects of oneself which are incompatible with being a recovering alcoholic.

Two facets of early recovery illustrate the most important tasks of this stage. First, feelings begin to emerge more fully. If the individual maintains the same relationship to his feelings as he had during the drinking phase, he will likely try to dictate to them, control them, and evaluate his self-worth on the basis of how he feels, as opposed to how he responds to his feelings. Being an alcoholic means that an individual is prone to complicating his life by attempting to control the uncontrollable. Recovering alcoholics recognize that they pay a very high price (i.e., increased risk of returning to drinking) for being in denial about their lack of control over both the external and internal world. One task of early recovery is to develop a healthier relationship to one's emotional life.

Second, self-worth must now be built on a new foundation, one based on being an alcoholic. This task is paramount. It represents the narcissist's challenge to develop self-esteem which is not based on grandiose fantasy, or on gratification of the primitive need to be fully appreciated.

For many individuals, early recovery is a time of finding ways to feel good about oneself "despite being an alcoholic." The ultimate goal is integration of a benevolent attitude toward oneself which transcends this identity. This is most often attained through spiritual or therapeutic discipline, such as prayer, meditation, or long-term psychotherapy which works in the transference to recapitulate basic developmental tasks.

Ongoing Recovery

In Brown's words, "Much of the process of ongoing recovery is the development and fine tuning of the self in relation to the larger whole."[7] The individual who has completed the tasks of the first three stages now has the foundation to do uncovering, psychodynamic work with much less risk of returning to alcohol.

The lessons learned so far have given the client new and powerful tools for understanding herself. Recognizing denial, and taking active steps to dismantle it, have made her more introspective. Acting before fully understanding why—as a way to gather more information about oneself—has made her less likely to use intellectualization as a defense. She is comfortable with paradox, having regained some control over aspects of her life by accepting that she cannot control other aspects. She is prepared to take leaps of faith into the unknown, rather than demanding that the unknown be revealed first.

The first three stages have established a firm and realistic identity. This now permits the task of developing and fine-tuning this new sense of self in relation to a larger whole. The individual can begin to experience relationships with others in the fullest sense, including the transferential relationship which develops with the therapist.

Comments

I have outlined Stephanie Brown's recovery model for two reasons. First, it underscores the fact that children of alcoholics must contend not only with their parents' active drinking, but also with profound psychological disturbances which may last well beyond the point where abstinence begins. Abstinence in and of itself does not guarantee the opportunity to be in relationship with a healthy parent. There are many more barriers the parent must cross before this becomes possible. Meanwhile, the children continue to pass through their own development.

Second, many facets of Brown's model for alcoholics are identical for ACAs. Herb Gravitz and Julie Bowden[8] outlined six stages of recovery for ACAs: Survival, Emergent Awareness, Core Issues, Transformations, Integration, and Genesis. The Survival stage is marked by continued denial and a sourceless sense of pain. Emergent Awareness refers to the breaking of this denial and acknowledgment of the psychological and genetic vulnerabilities acquired from one's alcoholic family. The Core Issues stage is a time of taking responsibility for how one's distrust and excessive use of willpower continue to permeate one's current life. During the Transformation Stage, ACA characteristics are turned into effective tools (for example, hypervigilance is used to notice how frequently black-and-white thinking takes over). During the Integration Stage, people begin behaving in ways that increase their sense of integrity, rather than in ways that are designed to control other people's impressions of them (i.e., the True Self emerges more fully). Finally, the Genesis stage is a time of spiritual growth. (It is from this last stage that Genesis Psychotherapy and Training Center took its name.)

In *Treating Adult Children of Alcoholics*,[9] Brown describes recovery for ACAs in terms of the same four stages she used for recovering alcoholics. Her stages are built upon the recognizable steps taken by alcoholics who are discarding an identity based on a distorted relationship to willpower, and developing an identity with a more realistic relationship to control issues. The fact that COAs learn most of what they know about willpower at the knee of an alcoholic parent makes this process equally relevant to ACAs.

Briefly, ACAs in the "drinking phase" remain in denial of their parents' alcoholism and unable to break out of co-dependent behaviors. The transition phase marks the dawning recognition of parental alcoholism. Early recovery signals construction of a new identity based on acknowledgment of being an adult child of an alcoholic. Finally, the core of ongoing recovery, and of uncovering psychotherapy, is an ongoing challenge of the defenses ACAs developed in their families of origin and continue to use in the world at large.

EVALUATING RECOVERY IN ACAs

Combining the work of Brown and Gravitz and Bowden with our own experience at Genesis, we evaluate an ACA's recovery from two perspectives: 1) the evolution of a client's relationship to willpower, which is vitally related to potential for characterological change, and 2) the activation of natural healing forces.

Evolution in the Relationship to Willpower

The word "evolution" implies orderly transition along a predictable continuum. At Genesis, we evaluate the status of an ACA's recovery using the following four points along this continuum.

The Survival Stage

We call the first stage in the evolution of the ACA's relationship to willpower the *survival stage*. Psychologically, there is little difference between the ACA at this stage and the alcoholic in the drinking phase. Denial is present on many different levels. There may be denial that a parent is alcoholic, sometimes despite the most blatant evidence to the contrary. There may be denial that one feels one way or another about a parent's alcoholism—which amounts to a denial of one's need to be seen, and one's longing for an ideal parent to merge with. This turns into denial of normal human feelings, and ultimately denial of self. Finally, there may be denial that a parent's alcoholism and one's feelings about it have any relevance to one's current life. This is clearly the result of a mistaken belief that we can exercise willpower over what affects us and what doesn't.

It is not just the extent of denial, but also its quality, which characterizes the survival stage. To many ACAs, denial seems necessary for sheer survival. Dismantling denial seems to threaten self-dissolution, and existential anxiety wells up. Many ACAs can talk about the curious state of mind which comes over them as they dig their heels in, knowing they are sliding ever more deeply into defensiveness, but having no way to halt the slide. Denial is maintained to appear normal, to hold things together, to survive.

Throughout this stage, there is a sourceless sense of discomfort. Since denial prevents one from being aware of the real reasons for the pain in one's life, there is an endless searching for "the answer"—something that will make sense of the feeling.

The goals for the ACA at this stage are the same as for the alcoholic in the drinking phase. Until denial can be recognized, voluntarily dismantled, and relinquished, therapy remains very difficult. In essence, therapy can only be supportive until clients are willing to explore the lack of reality that permeates their unconsciously held beliefs about willpower.

For the alcoholic, internalization of being an alcoholic is unlikely unless he can be honest about his harmful involvement with alcohol, and recognize that alcohol is the source of his problems, not their solution. The first stage ends, and real recovery begins, only when he is willing to take on the label of being an alcoholic. It is this label which initiates internalization.

The ACA has to accomplish the inverse process. As denial is broken, the fact that a parent is alcoholic is seen as the cause of much of the stress in one's life. But while alcoholics must internalize this cause, ACAs must *externalize* it, rather than continue to inappropriately take the blame for family problems over which they had no control. As denial dissipates and the ACA accepts the label of being the child of an alcoholic, it becomes increasingly difficult to feel responsible for a parent's alcoholism and guilty for how one was treated as a child.

The Reidentification Stage

We call the second stage in the evolution of the ACA's relationship to willpower the *reidentification stage*, emphasizing its central feature. At this point, it becomes necessary to grapple with the subtle, but critical, difference among ACAs who acknowledge that they *have* an alcoholic parent, and those who acknowledge that they *are* children of alcoholics.

Too many ACAs achieve the former and stay there, stuck in resentment and anger. They externalize too much and become unable, or unwilling, to take responsibility for their own healing. They are "victims to recovery," now feeling the pain of old wounds, but without any hope for healing that pain. They are analogous to alcoholics who recognize that they are harmfully involved with the chemical, but resist acknowledging their own alcoholism.

Ultimately, if further healing is to become possible, the identity of *being* an ACA must become palpable. Only then can one attend to issues within oneself, including the distorted relationship to willpower. Only then does one realize that many of one's own beliefs about willpower may be inaccurate, and must be brought out and investigated in the light of day. The mere act of becoming willing to explore the limits of willpower is a deviation from the ACA's earlier belief that those limits can be expanded "at will."

This second level of acknowledgment, in which individuals take on the label of being an ACA and focus internally on unresolved control issues, is the eye of the needle in recovery. Passing through it heralds the simultaneous contraction and expansion of the self—or, to put it more precisely, disconnection from the false self and connection to the true self. This true self is more realistic, less grandiose, and more human; flawed, but more vital.

For many ACAs, the first concrete reality which must be faced—without attempting to change it or take the blame for it—is their parents' alcoholism. This fact must be integrated as the backdrop for their entire childhood history. While this may feel more painful than continued denial, it provides a view of the past which is much closer to what really happened.

The Core Issues Stage

The third stage in the evolution of the ACA's relationship to willpower is called the *core issues stage*. It begins when the client accepts that distorted control issues permeate her life. During the survivor and reidentification stages, recovery consisted of ending denial of a parent's alcoholism and accepting that willpower cannot change this reality. The core issues stage begins when this new perspective on the past is applied to the present as well.

The core issues stage may also be seen as the time when both

ACAs and alcoholics start to deal with their co-dependence. Healing proceeds from this point through an exploration of all the ways in which a distorted relationship to willpower influences one's life. Ideally, clients eventually explore the subtle ways they are attempting to control therapy—and the therapist—in order to manufacture the experience they believe they need. Every effort to achieve a healthier relationship to willpower is seen to contain the very flaw it is intended to resolve.

This is the stage when clients are willing to be backed into the corner of their own making, until total bankruptcy occurs. This is comparable to moments in Reichian therapy when a client realizes that he can't stop trying to *make* his breathing become more spontaneous. Even efforts to stop forcing spontaneity are excessively willful. One's characterological flaw is simultaneously evident and still in control.

The core issues stage can be a time of great deflation and humbling. New strategies avail nothing, as long as the basic sense of self remains unchanged. Efforts to change the basic sense of self are gradually seen as stemming from one's "ideas" about health, and each new strategy is simply one more way to disguise one's basic character. Without the support of the therapist, or of other healthy persons, the ACA may become hopeless or apathetic. And this signals the beginning of deeper change. It is realistic to lose hope that the same old strategies for change can finally be made to work by redoubling one's efforts once again. The only avenue available to create real change is to unequivocally abandon what has not worked.

The Integration Stage

The curtain rises on the *integration stage* as an individual begins to abandon (or "abstain from") basic characterological traits even before replacements are present. This willingness to act before there is a clear idea of "how to be" is reminiscent of the leap of faith which initiated recovery. The therapeutic goal at this point is to help a client open up to a deeper sense of herself than she has previously experienced. The therapist's empathic connection to the client's true self facilitates the disconnection of energy from the false self. This real self may not be all that the client expected, and rarely is it what she hoped for. But it emerges with two clear advantages: It carries the force of reality, rather than the bluster of facade, and it ushers the client into a more vital relationship with the therapist and others.

Clinically, the stages leading up to integration are characterized by systematic attacks on a client's self-esteem by her own fundamental beliefs. ACAs frequently allude to this by describing a "committee" inside their heads, made up of a constant stream of negative beliefs. This committee swings into action in the face of accomplishments, compliments, and positive feelings about oneself. During integration, a new voice develops, one that legitimizes self-acceptance. As beliefs emerge to support one's personal rights and self-worth, there is a shift from guiding one's behavior by other people's opinions to guiding it by a new feeling: the sense of peace which comes from being in the presence of one's true self. Integrity becomes a matter of following this internal feeling, rather than reacting to external cues.

Comments

To the therapist familiar with the signs along the recovery path, it makes a great deal of difference where a client happens to fall. Recovery stages suggest the therapeutic tasks the client is facing. They also caution the therapist about levels of therapeutic work which might be contraindicated.

In the early stages, therapeutic efforts should focus on guiding the client through the recovery process, always helping to clarify which steps must be taken next. In the later stages, therapy will be enhanced by the therapist's ability to call on tools developed during earlier stages of recovery. At no time do therapy and recovery have to disagree.

Although dividing recovery into stages can be quite useful, it is not without pitfalls. It tends to oversimplify the recovery process, and clients may use it to judge rather than guide themselves. Clients often work on tasks from several stages at once, and not always in the order suggested by the stages; some must develop a sense of integrity before they can relinquish denial.

For these and other reasons, it is not enough to evaluate ACAs only by the evolution of their relationship to willpower. A second evaluation perspective is necessary.

The Activation of Natural Healing Forces

The second perspective we use at Genesis to evaluate an ACA's recovery serves as a practical guide for assessing the momentum of a client's recovery.

Consider the way we treat physical wounds—for example, a cut on a child's finger. We wash the wound, apply antiseptic and a dressing, and give the child antibiotics when needed. The active role we play obscures the fact that the wound heals without any conscious thought on our part about how blood proteins create a clot, how white blood cells scavenge infection, or how the body repairs connective tissue. These natural healing forces go about their business without needing us to be aware of their existence or understand their mechanisms. All we have to do is create the environment in which they can be most effective.

The healing of psychic wounds is no different. There are forces within the mind that we could not create, cannot control directly, and have no need to comprehend fully, yet they heal our psychic wounds. It is our job to create the environment in which these forces can be most effective. In psychotherapy, this consists primarily of the client-therapist relationship. Through this relationship, therapist and client together activate the natural healing forces by systematically engaging in three activities: 1) honesty, 2) experiencing feelings, and 3) entering into community. The disciplined pursuit of honesty, feelings, and community gives the mind freedom to heal itself.

It is often possible to assess the degree to which clients are actively engaged in each of these activities. A commitment to honesty dismantles the denial which contaminates a person's relationship to the world. I believe that real healing does not begin until one's mind is focused on reality.

I also believe that the mind heals itself best when one experiences one's feelings as well as acknowledging them intellectually. When clients commit to openly experiencing their feelings, they no longer take a master-servant approach to their emotional life. Feelings are invited into awareness (and into the body) as honored guests.

I further believe that perceiving oneself as part of a larger whole is invariably healing. To enter into community, we must let others see our real selves, rather than relating to them through a facade.

Attempting therapy with an individual who refuses to activate himself in any of these three ways is difficult—like trying to train an Olympic sprinter who refuses to stop smoking. In evaluating an ACA's recovery, I look specifically at his willingness to work toward honesty, to experience feelings, and to enter into community. Whenever one of these is missing, I assume that therapy will ultimately be more successful if this can be changed. For example, a client who actively pursues intellectual self-understanding, but refuses to tolerate any feelings, is cutting off some of the natural healing forces within himself. A client who refuses to experience feelings except when she is alone is missing the benefits of entering into community.

WORKING A PROGRAM
OF RECOVERY

At Genesis, when we talk about "working a program of recovery," we mean developing a disciplined way of life which practices honesty, feelings, and community. Psychotherapy is an excellent avenue toward this end. So are Twelve Step programs.

It is essential for ACA therapists to comprehend "The Program," as it is embodied in today's self-help organizations. In the vast majority of cases, ACA clients will either already be involved with a Twelve Step program before they encounter a therapist, or their therapy would benefit greatly if they were referred to one. Recovery from the self-help perspective involves two things: working the Twelve Steps, and attending Twelve Step meetings governed by the Twelve Traditions.[10]

The Twelve Steps

All current Twelve Step self-help programs trace their origins to the fellowship of Alcoholics Anonymous. In the mid-1930s, AA codified the principles of recovery into a series of Twelve Steps and developed a set of Twelve Traditions to guide its meetings. Figure 7-1 shows the Twelve Steps; the Twelve Traditions are found on pages 194 and 195.

Figure 7-1
The Twelve Steps of Alcoholics Anonymous

1. We admitted we were powerless over alcohol—that our lives had become unmanageable.
2. Came to believe that a Power greater than ourselves could restore us to sanity.
3. Made a decision to turn our will and our lives over to the care of God *as we understood Him.*
4. Made a searching and fearless moral inventory of ourselves.
5. Admitted to God, to ourselves, and to another human being the exact nature of our wrongs.
6. Were entirely ready to have God remove all these defects of character.
7. Humbly asked Him to remove our shortcomings.
8. Made a list of all persons we had harmed, and became willing to make amends to them all.
9. Made direct amends to such people wherever possible, except when to do so would injure them or others.
10. Continued to take personal inventory and when we were wrong promptly admitted it.
11. Sought through prayer and meditation to improve our conscious contact with God *as we understood Him,* praying only for knowledge of His will for us and the power to carry that out.
12. Having had a spiritual awakening as the result of these steps, we tried to carry this message to others, and to practice these principles in all our affairs.

Ernest Kurtz[11] has documented how the Twelve Steps relied heavily on precepts of the Oxford Group, a turn-of-the-century spiritual movement. The Oxford Group's members were attempting to return to the purity of primitive Christianity. Their "Five Procedures"—to give in to God, to listen to God's direction, to check guidance, to make restitution, and to share—reflect a uniquely American brand of theology. A form of evangelical pietism, it amounted to a belief that salvation comes from outside oneself as a gift (pietism), and that this "good news" should be joyfully proclaimed (evangelism).

Through the study and practice of the Oxford Group's procedures, alcoholics such as Bill Wilson and Dr. Bob, the original members of AA, began to achieve sobriety. As AA coalesced and grew, the founders tried to clarify the simple steps they believed had freed them from the tyranny of their obsession with alcohol. The core of this recovery was the freedom and relief that came from accepting that their control over the world was limited. The Twelve Steps they developed are a condensation of wisdom from across the ages, tailored to lives that have been disrupted by alcohol. It should not be surprising that this wisdom also has value for ACAs.

Relevance to ACAs

Familiarity with the Twelve Steps and how they are worked enables therapists to assess clients on several useful levels. For example: How concrete and literal is a client? How capable is the client of abstraction? Are denial, rationalization, and intellectualization curtailing the client's ability to work the Steps? Is the client capable of introspection? How rigid is the client? Is the client open to reassessing her relationship to willpower? And on and on. The information available is almost endless, if the therapist understands how to use the Twelve Steps like Rorschach inkblots. Exploring clients' resistance to self-help programs, the distortions they project upon them, and the issues these programs activate can help therapists to focus their own work more effectively.

The Twelve Steps are relevant to ACAs in the following specific ways.

• *The First Step* ("We admitted we were powerless over alcohol— that our lives had become unmanageable").

Until they accept the First Step, many ACAs continue to feel guilty that they are not clever enough or strong enough to get their alcoholic parents to stop drinking. It may never occur to them that it is literally impossible to *make* other people stop drinking. It *is* possible to *ask* that they stop drinking, to *suggest* that they stop drinking, to *refuse* to be around them when they are drinking, to *confront* them with the damage they have done to their own lives and the lives of people who love them, to *invite* them to spend some sober time with you, etc. But none of these approaches has the power to *force* them to stop drinking.

The first half of the First Step challenges the basic co-dependent belief that any of us can somehow be responsible for the alcoholic's behavior, either by "causing" his drinking or getting him to stop. The second half offers the same challenge to an ACA's misguided efforts to control other aspects of her life which cannot be directly influenced by willpower alone. It suggests that she is compounding her problems and wasting energy trying to control what is beyond her limits and then feeling shamed by her failures. It says that the reason she can't keep parts of her life under control isn't because she is inadequate; rather, it's because those parts of her life lie outside the ability of any human being to control.

The First Step relieves ACAs from co-dependent delusions by confronting their denial about what is and isn't under their control. Implicit in it is the suggestion that a person's emotional life is not under his conscious control, so it makes no sense to be ashamed of one's feelings, no matter what those feelings might be. This is analogous to the release from shame alcoholics feel when they first accept that alcoholism is a disease, not a character flaw.

• *The Second and Third Steps* ("Came to believe that a Power greater than ourselves could restore us to sanity," "Made a decision to turn our will and our lives over to the care of God *as we understood Him*").

These steps suggest that an individual's conscious mind is not the pinnacle of creation, nor is it obliged to stand alone against the stresses of the world. The leap of faith these two steps require creates a new sense of belonging and a greater acceptance of one's feelings.

The single most effective way to recapture the capacity to belong is through a leap of faith toward God. The important point is that you leap toward where you feel God might be. Being right or wrong is secondary to being willing to act on your belief. Communion with God, however you conceive such a Higher Power, reopens the capacity to belong and to feel "at home"—two feelings ACAs long to experience. The capacity to belong affects our relationships with both the outside and inside worlds. It permits us to enter into friendships with a feeling that we are welcome. It also permits us to enter into a new relationship with our own emotions. As we start to feel at home within ourselves, we can begin welcoming our feelings as legitimate parts of who we are.

• *The Fourth and Fifth Steps* ("Made a searching and fearless moral inventory of ourselves," "Admitted to God, to ourselves, and to another human being the exact nature of our wrongs").

The Fourth Step is an exercise in self-honesty. It requires a thorough inventory of all of one's character traits, good and bad. Past behaviors must be recorded with as little embellishment as possible. The Fifth Step suggests that this inventory is complete and objective only when you share it with someone else. The ultimate goal is to stand before your God and to speak the truth about yourself, as best you know it, without dramatizing your shortcomings or understating your virtues.

Steps Four and Five require absolute honesty, particularly when it comes to evaluating your virtues, as most of us are convinced that we will recover faster if we give special emphasis to the harm we have done to others. Such emphasis is a form of manipulation by which we attempt to impress our Higher Power.

• *The Sixth Step* ("Were entirely ready to have God remove all these defects of character").

For ACAs, this step suggests that they become "entirely ready" to have God remove all the character defects exposed in the Fourth and Fifth Steps. This requires another great leap of faith. If the initial response is paralysis from fear of the unknown (as it often is), the Program advises starting over again with the First Step, as a reminder that you are powerless to erase fear of the unknown. Such fear is normal, but you don't have to handle it alone. You can rely on your Higher Power to help you move through it.

Refusal to rely on a Higher Power may be one of the character defects listed in the Fourth Step's inventory. Admitting it to yourself, another person, and God will move you one step closer to being "entirely ready" to be free of it. The Twelve Steps are a continuously self-reinforcing process of becoming more honest, accepting your feelings, and entering into community—all of which promote the healing which is gaining momentum even before it has begun creating concrete behavioral changes.

• *The Seventh, Eighth, and Ninth Steps* ("Humbly asked Him to remove our shortcomings," "Made a list of all persons we had harmed, and became willing to make amends to them all," "Made direct amends to such people wherever possible, except when to do so would injure them or others").

These three steps continue the process of being completely honest with oneself, turn it into a way of life, and deepen the willingness to bring new levels of honesty into current relationships. ACAs actively working these steps will benefit from having their attention focused on what *is* under their control in the present, rather than focusing primarily on the past.

• *The Tenth Step* ("Continued to take personal inventory and when we were wrong promptly admitted it").

Once the past has been dealt with honestly, the Tenth Step is a commitment to keep the slate clean. You will never again accumulate a "backlog" of guilt—as long as you continue to be honest in the here-and-now, and promptly acknowledge any harm you do to yourself or others.

Working the Tenth Step provides a solid internal foundation upon which to base self-esteem. The willingness to deal honestly with yourself becomes the guiding standard. A sense of integrity becomes more important than the impressions you make on others. This way of life runs directly counter to active co-dependence.

• *The Eleventh and Twelfth Steps* ("Sought through prayer and meditation to improve our conscious contact with God *as we understood Him,* praying only for knowledge of His will for us and the power to carry that out," "Having had a spiritual awakening as the result of these steps, we tried to carry this message to others, and to practice these principles in all our affairs").

The final two steps bring fullness to one's spiritual life, and thus bring fullness to one's healing. They solidify a sense of identity which includes the *capacity* to belong. This is in marked contrast to the tendency ACAs have, when still actively co-dependent, to borrow their sense of identity from others, while paradoxically feeling isolated.

The Twelve Traditions

The Twelve Steps are of value in helping ACAs to make deep characterological change. But a program of recovery includes more than just working the steps. It also includes a willingness to enter into the recovering community, which usually means regular attendance at self-help meetings.

The fellowship in these meetings, structured by the Twelve Traditions of Al-Anon, shown in Figure 7-2, provides a vessel in which an ACA's identity can be contained during the precarious process of abandoning dysfunctional characterological traits. While the Twelve Steps outline a path toward identity transformation, it is the relationship members foster with their Higher Power and the fellowship of the recovering community at meetings which helps them feel safe enough to abandon the roots of a dysfunctional identity and leap into the unknown.

Figure 7-2
The Twelve Traditions of Al-Anon
(Adapted from Alcoholics Anonymous)

1. Our common welfare should come first; personal progress for the greatest number depends on unity.
2. For our group purpose there is but one authority—a loving God as He may express Himself in our group conscience. Our leaders are but trusted servants; they do not govern.
3. The relatives of alcoholics, when gathered together for mutual aid, may call themselves an Al-Anon Family Group, provided that, as a group, they have no other affiliation. The only requirement for membership is that there be a problem of alcoholism in a relative or friend.
4. Each group should be autonomous, except in matters affecting another group or Al-Anon as a whole.
5. Each Al-Anon Family Group has but one purpose: to help families of alcoholics. We do this by practicing the Twelve Steps of AA *ourselves*, by encouraging and understanding our alcoholic relatives, and by welcoming and giving comfort to families of alcoholics.
6. Our Al-Anon Family Groups ought never endorse, finance, or lend our name to any outside enterprise, lest problems of money, property, and prestige divert us from our primary spiritual aim. Although a separate entity, we should always cooperate with Alcoholics Anonymous.
7. Every group ought to be fully self-supporting, declining outside contributions.
8. Al-Anon Twelve-Step work should remain forever non-professional, but our service centers may employ special workers.

9. Our groups, as such, ought never be organized; but we may create service boards or committees directly responsible to those they serve.
10. The Al-Anon Family Groups have no opinion on outside issues; hence our name ought never be drawn into public controversy.
11. Our public relations policy is based on attraction rather than promotion; we need always maintain personal anonymity at the level of press, radio, TV, and films. We need guard with special care the anonymity of all AA members.
12. Anonymity is the spiritual foundation of all our Traditions, ever reminding us to place principles above personalities.

The Twelve Traditions safeguard the health of self-help meetings by keeping participants united in their purpose. They encourage a continuous turnover in leadership to avoid allowing any individual to dominate the group. Decisions about group issues are always made by group consensus, with the only authority being a loving God, as each member understands Him, and the Twelve Traditions. Self-help fellowships never accept donations or amass property and wealth, lest this divert attention from the primary spiritual purpose. They have absolutely no affiliation with other groups and express no opinions on outside issues. Hence, self-help fellowships never enter into controversy. Within meetings, controversy is avoided by prohibiting cross-talk (commenting on, questioning, or directing other members), and by placing the principles of the program above personalities. The prolonged airing of personal grievances is discouraged as unlikely to lead to a beneficial exchange of ideas.

Two Traditions deserve special emphasis and clarification. First, self-help fellowships are anonymous for two reasons. By using no last names, and by reminding members to safeguard whatever they hear in a meeting, these fellowships create an important sense of safety. Beginners are assured of a haven where their problems will not be complicated by becoming public knowledge. The second reason for anonymity is less obvious (which is probably why it is spelled out in the Twelve Traditions): to keep principles above personalities. By maintaining personal anonymity at the level of the public media, no individual member becomes identified with the program. This prevents possible damage to the fellowship by a member with a high public profile whose conduct may inadvertently reflect poorly on the program. It also prevents individuals from being tempted to seek profit from their participation in the program.

Finally, there is the Tradition of working by attraction rather than promotion. Much of the wisdom of Twelve Step recovery programs lies in recognizing that personal freedom and integrity come from a rigorously accurate assessment of what we can and can't control. It is not within anyone's ability to control whether another person is willing to enter into recovery or not. The only way one person will ever be influenced by another's recovery is if he or she is hurting enough to search for new ways to live, and can see that recovery has brought peace to someone else.

Evaluating a client's recovery includes not only exploring his understanding of and current relationship to the Twelve Steps, but also observing the way he uses the recovering fellowship and integrates the Twelve Traditions. Failure to enter into the fellowship can be a sign of a person's discomfort with dependence needs, an unwillingness to relinquish the omnipotent illusion of being able to gain control by oneself, a rigid misunderstanding of the program's relationship to spirituality, fear of emotional expression, and fear of rejection, to name a few prominent reasons. The inability to accept and integrate the Twelve Traditions governing group behavior may indicate difficulty in clarifying and sustaining boundaries. Any and all information of this nature can provide valuable guidance to the course of psychotherapy.

PSYCHOTHERAPY HISTORY

It is quite common to encounter ACAs who have attempted psychotherapy before, more or less successfully. A significant percentage will characterize their past therapists as lacking awareness of ACA issues. This stance must be carefully explored, and requesting a release of information to speak directly to previous therapists is highly recommended.

Whether a client's previous therapist(s) did or did not lack an understanding of the effect of parental alcoholism on developing children, the client is declaring an unmet need. She expects you to address this need, and usually to meet it. It is important both to honor this need and to be wary of it. In many cases, it heralds a tender moment in a client's life, a time when she is experiencing her first real willingness to share a painful past with a stranger. She needs you to validate the importance (and even the reality) of her parent's alcoholism and the depth of her pain. Failure to provide such validation may reenact the trauma of a family's denial.

At the same time, your response to the client's unmet need may be a litmus test for whether you are skilled or caring enough to help her. She may be transferring issues not only from her family of origin, but also from her previous therapist. You may be dealing with a client who has discontinued therapy without going through the termination process, or whose primary way of relating to people is through making them feel special.

Previous therapy experiences can distort your efforts to treat the client. To keep this from getting out of hand, it's best to address this issue at the start (although you will probably return to it later as well, once the therapeutic alliance can better contain it). An open discussion about the content and process of the earlier therapy can be diagnostically useful. In addition, it may predict the future course of your own therapeutic efforts with the client.

In all cases, it is a mistake to assume that you have special skills to meet a client's special needs, even if you have considerable training and experience in working with ACAs. While there may be a mote of truth to this view, it often fails to recognize that 1) many other therapists possess the same special skills as you, and 2) while special training in treating ACAs has value, it is largely limited to facilitating a client's entry into, and sustenance of, a strong therapeutic alliance. Once you and the client have entered this alliance, the psychodynamics and transferences encountered demand the same depth of skills required of any competent psychotherapist.

CONCLUSION

Clients with similar character structures and issues may still differ significantly along the recovery axis, a continuum which presents a predictable series of tasks. Therapeutic approaches which are effective at earlier points along the continuum become less effective later, while others become more effective. At Genesis, we use a continuum of therapeutic modalities, as described in *Volume Two: Treatment*. The decision about which therapeutic strategies to employ always rests on our diagnostic assessment of the individual client.

At least three facets of recovery can be evaluated. The central issues in a client's life can be staged—from denial, to willpower, to integrity. The activation of natural healing forces (honesty, feelings, and community) can be observed. And the involvement of a client in working the Twelve Steps and entering the recovering community can be explored. The investigation of these three facets holds great diagnostic value in and of itself.

8

THE EVALUATION
INTERVIEW

Theory building is similar to architecture in that both produce blueprints. But nobody lives in a blueprint, and no client is healed by a theoretical framework. As the architect depends on the contractor to interpret the prints accurately and give them concrete, nuts-and-bolts form in the real world, psychological theory depends on the therapist to translate abstract frameworks into therapeutic relationships with clients.

This chapter is like the "specifications sheet" the architect gives the contractor as a guide to choosing materials for constructing the actual building. It summarizes many of the nuts and bolts that go into constructing diagnostic interviews at Genesis.

GOALS OF THE
DIAGNOSTIC INTERVIEW

Diagnostic interviews have specific goals. The clearer the therapist is about them, the lighter the touch he can use in guiding the interview. We consider the following three goals paramount for the initial evaluation.

Assessing Symptoms and
Character Structure

Diagnostic interviews represent the therapist's best efforts to assess a client's strengths and needs before initiating a treatment plan. In addition to screening for evidence of alcohol and other drug abuse, PTSD, co-dependence, underlearning, and severe psychopathology, and estimating the extent of recovery, it is also useful to assess the client's primary defense mechanisms, her willingness and ability to be introspective, whether she has any inappropriate expectations for therapy, and the intangible sense of "fit" between you and the client.

Developing an Individualized Treatment Plan

Throughout the diagnostic interview, you will make decisions based on what you learn from the client. By the end of the session, you should be prepared to take one of three courses:

• *Defer formulating the treatment plan.* Further assessment is often necessary, and may take the form of contact with previous therapists, additional meetings with the client, or consultation with colleagues and supervisors to help organize the data before you. Your strategy for continuing the evaluation should be developed by the end of the session.

• *Defer implementing the treatment plan.* Often, referrals must be arranged before it makes sense to point a client in a given direction. This avoids sending people down blind alleys.

• *Discuss the recommended treatment plan with the client.* You may be able to formulate your therapeutic strategy during the course of the diagnostic interview. How you choose to discuss this with the client depends on whether you will be making a referral or accepting the client into your own practice. This brings us to the third goal of the initial evaluation.

Initiating the Therapeutic Alliance

Whether you refer the client elsewhere or keep seeing him yourself, a therapeutic alliance must be nurtured. In situations where you will be referring the client, it is important to develop a specialized alliance—usually more authoritative and less empathic—designed to help the client accept the referral. Excessive promotion of a therapeutic alliance between yourself and the client could interfere with the next therapist's ability to develop an effective connection.

For example, if you stimulate more catharsis during the evaluation than is appropriate at the beginning of therapy, and then refer the client to another therapist, the effects could be far-reaching. Some clients may feel abandoned by your referral and see it as confirming their distrust of therapists. Others may feel less accepted by the next therapist because further catharsis is not immediately facilitated.

I tend to remain more reserved and conservative in my approach to clients whom I am likely to be referring elsewhere. This is both a courtesy to the next therapist, and an aid to the client's efforts to connect with whomever ultimately becomes his therapist.

In cases where the client ends up entering individual therapy with me, I tend to separate the evaluation process from the initiation of therapy by announcing my recommendation, and then asking the client to sit with it for a couple of days before making a decision. This permits me to describe the course of therapy more directly than I might be willing to do once therapy has commenced. If a client wants to commit to therapy with me, she should call to schedule an appointment.

In reality, it is impossible to completely separate evaluation from treatment. A real person sits before you (or calls you on the telephone), looking for help from the moment contact is established. Initiation of the therapeutic alliance cannot be postponed until after the assessment is complete without greatly affecting the quality of the connection between client and therapist. A balance must be struck between the client's need to be met with a therapeutic stance, and the therapist's need to take an initial history. As a result, no evaluation process is free from therapeutic maneuvers, and no treatment process is free from assessment.

THE STRUCTURE OF THE
EVALUATION INTERVIEW

The "ideal" interview is rarely achieved. The purpose of the following outline is to guide you, not to control or regiment you. For my part, I find that having a framework for evaluation interviews is valuable for two reasons: It promotes thoroughness, and it provides a benchmark for comparing how different clients respond to a similar situation.

It is often diagnostically significant when I find myself deviating significantly from the interview structure. I must determine whether that particular client is resistant to being led, too disorganized to be contained, in sufficient crisis that thorough evaluation must be postponed temporarily, or unable to follow the structure for some other reason. There is also the possibility that I have deviated from the interview structure because of my own countertransference—the activation of my own personal issues in response to the client. This is discussed in more detail in Chapter 8 of *Volume Two: Treatment*.

The following interview structure is used by therapists at Genesis. The times indicate a chronological sequence for a 50-minute session.

Greeting
(minutes 0-5)

ACAs often enter the evaluation interview with intense feelings bubbling just below the surface. Many have had two or three days of mounting anxiety, disrupted sleep, vivid dreams, and difficulty focusing attention at work. Other ACAs may have none of this emotional prelude, yet find themselves suddenly filled with feeling upon entering the therapist's office. For many, entering therapy represents a momentous break with family rules, the culmination of extensive, hard-won change.

It is often helpful to chat momentarily with the client, rather than entering directly into the formal evaluation. An effective opening might be a comment on the long journey which usually precedes a person's getting into your office. This can validate the client's experience even before he tells you about it. The purpose of this initial greeting is to establish that your office is a safe place, and to take an active role in managing the client's anxiety.

In the background, you should be doing an informal mental status examination of the client as the interview progresses. Has the client tracked your comments? Was the abstractness of your comment about a "long journey" translated into an appropriate response? Does the client's anxiety respond to your management?

The first moments of contact with a new client are precious. It is important not to exert too great an influence on what the client is internally moved to do. In those cases where ACAs enter the evaluation interview and hit the ground running, I make no effort to stop them in order to "chat." I simply skip the greeting and move directly into the next part of the evaluation.

Determining the Presenting Problems
(minutes 5-15)

Your goal here is to work toward a concrete picture of the client's current emotional and behavioral dysfunction. Ask the client to describe the problems she is experiencing. Ask for specific examples of problems which are only vaguely described.

It is useful to explore the presenting problems on two levels. On the first level, try to develop a picture of the client's current problems. On the second, try to find out which ones the client thinks can be improved by therapy. It often helps to ask the client how she thinks her life would be different if therapy "worked."

Once the client has attempted to outline the presenting problem, and you have pushed her to be as concrete as possible, restate her concerns precisely, as well as in slightly different, clarifying terms. This clarification provides you with an opportunity to see how the client reacts to such an intervention. Meanwhile, you will be forming your first impressions of the client's expectations, capacity to be introspective, ability to organize material, and response to clarifying restatements.

Family History
(minutes 15-25)

Instruct the client to take ten minutes to "draw a verbal picture" of the family he comes from, including grandparents, how his parents met, ethnic, religious, and geographical background, siblings, and so on. Then become less active. Watch to see whether the client is able to organize this sweeping material into a limited presentation. Do details distract and get him off track? Can he prioritize events, objectively or subjectively, according to their significance? Are there large memory gaps? It is often useful to focus some attention on the events surrounding the client's separation from family. What were the circumstances of his leaving home? The family's dysfunctions, the client's defenses, and unresolved issues are often illustrated by the circumstances of a client's leaving home.

At some point during this part of the interview, be sure to ask specifically about any history of physical or sexual abuse. Pursue vague or affirmative answers enough to develop an initial picture of the concrete details of the abuse.

The family history is important in terms of both process and content. It is your only chance to observe how the client performs in a less structured situation. It also gives you the opportunity to record biographical data as it is being related. Possessing this information is critical to appropriate treatment, but most therapists are loathe to take notes during a session once psychotherapy has begun in earnest.

Focus on Parental Alcoholism
(minutes 25-30)

Ask for more details about the client's parents' drinking. Your goal is to get a concrete picture of specific drinking episodes, with emphasis on your client's childhood experiences of them.

This is frequently a time when feelings become more present. Comment on each feeling in turn and see how the client responds. Can a particular feeling be deepened by letting the client know that you have noticed it, and allowing time for it to be present? Or does the client resist this? Is there any evidence of the client's being overwhelmed by her feelings, or does psychic numbing supervene and eliminate them? This part of the evaluation interview gives you valuable information on two matters: the client's access to memories of the past, and his relationship to his feelings.

The client's underlying attitudes and beliefs about chemical dependence can often be fruitfully explored at this point. Direct questions about what the client sees as the cause of his parent's drinking should be careful to explore both the perspective held as a child, in the midst of the active alcoholism or other drug addiction, and the viewpoint he holds today.

Current Life Situation
(minutes 30-35)

The specifics of a client's current life situation (employment status, marital status, living arrangements, circle of friends, relationship with surviving family members, financial resources, physical health, and so on) are useful both diagnostically and practically. Are the client's presenting problems sufficiently severe that they have begun to lead to objective dysfunction socially, financially, medically . . . ? Or are they still restricted primarily to the client's perception of the quality of his life? By comparing factual information about the client's current life situation with the initial description of his problems, you can begin to develop a wider context for understanding the client.

One rationale for including this topic at this point in the interview—just slightly past the midpoint—stems from the need to evaluate the client's ability to contain affect once it has been mobilized. Switching the focus to factual information helps clients obtain some distance from their feelings. If containment cannot be accomplished, this may have diagnostic implications. For the purposes of furthering the interview, such containment is desirable.

A second rationale is purely practical: This gives you the chance to assess whether you will be able to conclude the evaluation interview within the 50-minute time frame. There is still a lot of information that needs to be transmitted, from the client to you and vice versa. How the client responds to your requests for factual information helps you decide whether you can finish the interview today, or whether you should start assuming that a second session will be necessary to obtain enough data to develop an informed treatment plan.

Focus on the Client's Own Relationship to Alcohol and Other Drugs (minutes 35-40)

Since ACAs are at higher risk than the general public of alcohol and other drug dependence, it behooves you to inquire directly about the client's own relationship to mind-altering chemicals. I find that this inquiry yields the most useful information if it is preceded by the exploration of parental chemical dependence, and then by the segment concerning a client's current life situation. This structure can create what I call a "Columbo effect." (You may recall that the TV detective played by Peter Falk disarmed his interviewees by seeming to discontinue a particular line of inquiry, only to return to it unexpectedly at a later moment.) In cases where a client is suppressing or minimizing information, structuring the interview in this way tends to lower her guard.

If this part of the interview begins to uncover even the possibility of a problematic relationship between the client and alcohol or other drugs, it is likely that a second interview will be needed to explore the topic more thoroughly. It is often useful to let the client know this immediately, and to take the rest of the time to discuss how the client might profitably explore the question.

You may want to suggest that the client read specific materials about chemical dependence, or attend an AA or NA (Narcotics Anonymous) meeting before the second interview. As is the case when exploring any client's relationship to alcohol or other drugs, the client's willingness—or resistance—to enter into such an inquiry may be the most important information to pay attention to.

Assessing Recovery
(minutes 40-45)

Turn the focus of the interview to a review of the client's participation in Twelve Step programs. If there is no history, explore the specific reasons why—ignorance of the programs' existence? fear of vulnerability? dislike of specific aspects of meetings, or of the Steps? This exploration frequently reveals a host of misconceptions and distortions, much as a Rorschach inkblot serves as a stimulus for clients' projections.

In cases where the client has been involved in Twelve Step programs, you should be familiar enough with the program to enter into a brief discussion of which steps are being worked and which tools are being used. The sophistication of the client's response is often a clear indication of how actively he is involved in recovery. Efforts to appear more deeply involved than one is are diagnostic of the client's continued devotion to life behind a facade, the need to manage other people's impressions, and a distorted relationship to willpower.

Focus also on previous therapy, with emphasis on the circum- stances of termination. Ask the client why she entered previous therapy, how long it lasted, what techniques were used, how the therapy affected her life, and what kind of relationship she had with the therapist. Gather evidence as to whether that relationship ended with the process of termination. If it didn't, then it is almost certain to contaminate the relationship you are establishing with the client.

In cases where the client has only recently terminated previous therapy, or is still seeing a therapist while interviewing with you, be especially careful that any actions you take are in the client's best interests. Every relationship has two sides— especially marriage and therapy. No matter what the client tells you about her recent or current therapy, it is absolutely essential for you to speak directly to the other therapist. There is no short-term gain (financial or professional esteem) that outweighs the costs (loss of integrity, enmeshment in unresolvable transference/countertransference) of wresting a client away from another therapist.

The proper procedure is to ask the client to sign a Release of Information form so you can freely contact the other therapist. At Genesis, we have these at hand whenever we do evaluations. If the client refuses to sign, it may not be possible to begin therapy. As a matter of course, I assume that the evaluation is incomplete and a treatment plan cannot be formulated until I have spoken with the therapist in question. In most cases, I also recommend that the client discuss her contact with me with the other therapist, along with any dissatisfactions she has about the therapy. If the therapy ended without proper termination, this may mean that the client must return to a therapist she has chosen to avoid. Encouraging the client to take this action occasionally leads to salvaging a previous therapy. More often, it sets the tone for openness and honesty in your own relationship with the client.

Discussing the Treatment Plan
(minutes 45-50)

The evaluation interview concludes either with concrete recommendations for therapy, or with arranging the next steps required to complete the evaluation. I also use this time to process the session briefly by asking how the interview has felt to the client, and whether he has any further questions.

It takes considerable discipline to complete an evaluation in 50 minutes. Since I know that I am capable of completing the task within that time, I must always explain to myself what happened when I fail to do so. The most common reason for going beyond 50 minutes is because I will be referring the client on to another person, and wish to complete the evaluation without needing a second full appointment. In all cases, I either finish the interview on time, or note clearly that the interview has gone over the usual time limit. This helps to maintain the sense of temporal boundaries, which is important for any client-therapist relationship.

THE TONE OF THE INTERVIEW

It is difficult to generalize about this, since every interview takes on its own specific tone. I have found that it's best to develop facility in a variety of tones, from empathic to confrontive and authoritative. A single tone may be appropriate to your own specific style of therapy, but it will render you less effective in the evaluation and referral process. Because the treatment plan may include anything from admission to a chemical dependence unit, to referral to a Twelve Step program, to educational, supportive, or interactional group therapy, to a variety of individual or family therapies, it's important to stay flexible in the tone you set.

Referrals are best accepted when delivered in an assured tone of authority. Many clients are comforted by a level of authority in a referring therapist that they would find unacceptable in someone with whom they were considering entering into therapy. Once I know that I will be referring a client elsewhere, I tend to become a bit more authoritative and removed. Within the client's mind, this minimizes the "competition" between me and the as yet unknown therapist. On the other hand, once I know that I will be recommending that the client enter into therapy with me, I immediately slide into a tone which is consistent with the style of therapy I will be performing with that particular client.

TECHNIQUES FOR OBTAINING
SPECIFIC DATA

There are certain kinds of information you will want to be sure to obtain during the evaluation interview—information that is essential to developing an individualized treatment plan. Specifically, you will want to find out about the client's chemical dependence, trauma, co-dependence, borderline disturbances, and stage of recovery. The following sections describe some useful tools for obtaining this information. They are not intended as an exhaustive review of interviewing skills.

Obtaining Data on Chemical Dependence

Evaluating chemical dependence is an art, an integration of intuition and discipline. The old ways of documenting signs and symptoms of physical addiction, and assessing quantity and frequency of alcohol and other drug use, have only limited usefulness. Occasionally the amount of usage, or overt signs of physical addiction, cement a diagnosis. More often, it is necessary to ferret out earlier signs of chemical dependence.

Techniques for evaluating early problems involve exploring a client's experience with mind-altering chemicals and his prevailing relationship to willpower, while monitoring his willingness to participate in such exploration. At the same time, the discipline behind this art involves recognizing a client's resistance to such participation, exploring this resistance, and not being sidetracked from correctly and persistently interpreting it as resistance, despite the client's rationalizations, intellectualizations, denial, bullying, or subtle manipulations.

In practice, even though it is often impossible to achieve certainty about the role of alcohol or other drugs in a particular client's life, it may be quite easy to conclude that open questions abound. Within the parameters of an evaluation interview, this is an appropriate end point. Before dynamic, or even supportive, psychotherapy can be initiated, a forum must be developed for addressing these open questions. The client's relationship to alcohol or other drugs must be clarified, usually through a combination of education, exposure to Twelve Step meetings (AA or NA, specifically), and individual work with a therapist trained in chemical dependence.

This process of clarification is extremely valuable for ACAs, whether they prove to be chemically dependent themselves or not. In the event that chemical dependence does exist, it will be directly addressed at the outset. This will set the stage for a more successful outcome to later psychotherapy. In the event that chemical dependence does not exist and the open questions are resolved, the ACA will have received important education regarding the illness which destroyed the relationship between him and a parent. Such education helps break down denial about past realities.

There is a simple test that can reveal the presence of open questions about a client's alcohol or other drug use: Before assessing alcohol and drug use, ask clients personal questions in other areas. The "test" involves assessing the quality of the client's answer, then comparing this to the quality of answers given to inquiries about alcohol or other drug use.

Because I'm a physician, I call this the "Bowel Movement" test. Every physician is accustomed to asking people during physical exams how many bowel movements they have each day. Some clients answer "One a day," without embarrassment or strain in their voices. But when asked equally direct questions about drinking, they may respond, "I drink socially," or "Just one drink a day," with an edge of nervousness in their voices. By comparing the directness of the two answers, and by being aware of the change in the tone of voice and the onset of nervousness, it is easy to notice an emotional charge connected to the issue of alcohol or other drug use—feelings that must be fully explored.

Obviously, psychotherapists will want to develop their own test, and leave the bowel movement example to physicians. The principle is the same. Ask about sex, financial status, or some other personal area, then ask about alcohol or other drug use, and watch for evidence of an emotional charge attached to the latter issue. This will usually be embedded in subtle changes in the quality of information offered, and in the client's interactions with you. Explore the details of this emotional charge, including the client's awareness of it and his sense of why it is present. Observe the client's willingness to participate in this exploration. When this approach leads to more and more unanswered questions, it must become the central theme of your contact with the client until resolution is achieved.

Obtaining Data on Trauma

A client's perception of being traumatized (or not) must always be taken seriously. But therapists also have a responsibility to look beyond the surface—to explore the details of the abuse, watch for objective evidence of stress-related symptoms, and remain suspicious when such symptoms exist in clients who deny that abuse occurred. Within the confines of an evaluation interview, this process can only be started, not completed.

When a client responds affirmatively to questions about abuse, it is important to assess the specificity and clarity of those memories. I have found it helpful to ask questions like these:

- Were you a direct victim of abuse, or did you see someone else being abused? (NOTE: In general, witnesses experience less amnesia than victims.[1])
- Do memories of specific abuse episodes return in response to specific smells, tastes, sights, sounds, etc.? (This is discussed in detail in Chapter 2 of *Volume Two: Treatment*.)
- Was the abuse physical? If so, were you (or the other person) hit with objects, or with the abuser's hand (closed or open)?
- What injuries ensued? Was medical care required?
- Do you remember what your feelings were at the time of the abuse, or shortly afterward? Do you have any feelings while discussing the abuse?
- Did you have anyone you could talk to openly about the abuse at the time?
- What were the circumstances of your first remembering the abuse?
- Was the abuse sexual? If so, what sexual acts occurred? Did you derive any excitement or pleasure from these acts?
- If the abuse was not overtly sexual, did you fear that it would become that way?
- Was there emotional abuse? What form did it take? What did the abusing adult say?
- In what situations did the physical, sexual, or emotional abuse occur?

- What role did intoxication play in the adult's abusive behavior?
- What were other family members doing during the abuse episodes?

These questions aid in the assessment at two different levels. First, the client's current relationship to her trauma story can indicate how much direct work on abuse issues remains to be done. Second, the questions serve to test the client's underlying character structure.

Trauma and the Borderline Client

In my own work, I try to discover as quickly as possible those borderline clients for whom abuse issues have become vehicles for what James Masterson calls the "talionic impulse."[2] Expressed Biblically as "an eye for an eye and a tooth for a tooth," the talionic impulse is one of revenge, seeking satisfaction by inflicting on others the pain one has suffered.

Masterson writes, "The borderline child experiences the parents' exploitation of his dependency and helplessness as the grossest form of cruelty and torture."[3] This often leads to behavior which is more intent on revenge than on healing—on "getting back" instead of getting better. Such a client may have a history of feeling abused by previous therapists. And such a client will have a tendency to interpret any perceived slight on your part as abusive, thereby justifying his own vengeful response toward you.

In a climate where abuse issues can be discussed openly, such as the therapeutic setting, borderline clients may feel encouraged (and entitled) to continue focusing directly on past episodes of abuse. Unless you can help the client move beyond the impulse to seek revenge, no resolution is possible. For this reason, it is of paramount importance to recognize the borderline aspect to such clients' abuse issues, and tailor your therapy accordingly.

Trauma and the
Non-Borderline Client

Exploring the details of abuse in non-borderline clients is your best opportunity to look for symptoms of post-traumatic stress disorder (PTSD). Memories of the trauma can often trigger the defenses used to tolerate the abuse, with results you can observe and assess.

For example, does the client flip into a reportorial style of talking, with little feeling connected to the contents of what she is relating? These are signs of psychic numbing. Does the client's sympathetic nervous system become activated—e.g., does she flush, perspire, have a pounding heart, or show other signs of anxiety? Since the definition of trauma involves exposure "to an overwhelming event resulting in helplessness in the face of intolerable danger, anxiety, and instinctual arousal,"[4] these reactions can be interpreted as smoke confirming the existence of fire. Does the client start denying the existence or severity of the abuse as soon as you begin talking about it? Or does she quickly begin excusing the parent, perhaps by switching the focus to the parent's own pain and abuse?

Finally, does the client begin to get overwhelmed and lost in her feelings, switching from recalling memories to re-experiencing the trauma? If this should happen, you may need to take an active and direct role in helping the client contain her feelings before the interview can proceed. This is in marked contrast to clients who are able to pull back from the feelings on their own when the therapist indicates that it's time to shift topics.

During the evaluation interview, a significant number of ACAs will be out of touch with the fact that they suffered emotional, physical, or sexual abuse. They will answer negatively to direct questions about abuse. Only time will tell what really happened. For the purposes of the evaluation, it is only necessary to note whether the primary symptoms of PTSD are present. If they are, without explanation for their origin, this fact may affect the treatment plan. These stress-related symptoms will need to be at least partially resolved before characterological change is possible through dynamic psychotherapy, whether individual or group. Otherwise, the anxiety spurring clients on toward characterological change will either be overwhelming or numbed out.

One last point: It is often useful to inquire about abuse which the client has perpetrated on others. This often opens an entirely new and important facet of the client's behavior and experience. It also may provide an independent window on what the client perceives to be abuse, as well as on the harshness with which the client has come to judge her own behavior.

Obtaining Data on
Co-Dependence

In an effort to put into operation the criteria for co-dependence advanced in *Diagnosing and Treating Co-dependence*,[5] I developed a Structured Interview for Adult Co-dependence (see Appendix III, pages 239-49). While this has yet to be tested for validity and reliability, it nonetheless provides clinical direction for interviewers attempting to elicit evidence for the different criteria I have proposed.

The questions and score sheet on pages 216-22 have been abstracted from the structured interview. They are designed to clarify how each criterion is to be applied to real clients in an interview setting. It isn't necessary to ask the questions in any programmed manner; in fact, since many of the answers will have been given spontaneously during the course of the evaluation interview outlined above, you may be able to skip some of the questions.

CO-DEPENDENCE QUESTIONNAIRE

1. Do you ever worry excessively about any members of your family?

2. Are you ever embarrassed by another family member's behavior?

3. Do you feel personally less worthwhile because of another family member's behavior?

4. Are you often perfectionistic about yourself?

5. Have you tried to control family members?

6. Do you take pride in your own self-control?

7. Do you often feel personally inadequate?

8. Do you feel guilty or responsible for someone else's behavior?

9. Have you taken over family responsibilities which you do not believe should be yours?

10. Have you ever lied to cover up someone else's misbehavior?

11. Do you often meet other people's needs while you neglect your own?

12. Do you lack self-confidence in intimate situations?

13. Are you afraid that others will leave you?

14. Are you often unaware of what you are feeling?

15. Does it feel like you start to get smothered or overwhelmed by people close to you?

16. Do you tend to see things as either black or white?

17. Do your emotions get into a roller-coaster, with quick ups and downs?

18. Do you feel complete only when you are in a relationship, or lose your own identity in relationships?

19. Do you often rescue or punish other people?

20. Are you afraid to let your feelings come out freely?

21. Do you have dramatic emotional outbursts?

22. Are you often depressed?

23. Have you been suicidal?

24. Is it hard to let down your guard without feeling that a catastrophe might happen?

25. Do you have compulsions (such as eating, TV, work, sex . . .)?

26. Do you often feel anxious?

27. Have you tried to ignore problems, hoping they will get better on their own?

28. Have you been a victim of physical or sexual abuse as an adult?

29. Do you suffer from stress-related medical illnesses?

30. Are you chemically dependent yourself?

31. Have you been in a committed relationship with someone who is actively chemically dependent for two years without seeking outside support?

SCORE SHEET

The numbers in parentheses refer to the questions in the questionnaire.

1. Willpower Score

Criterion A: Continued investment of self-esteem in the ability to control both oneself and others in the face of serious adverse consequences.

Which willpower traits are demonstrated?

_____ Worry (1)

_____ Embarrassment/Shame (2)

_____ Personal inadequacy (3, 7)

_____ Perfectionism (4)

_____ Efforts to control others (5)

_____ Pride in self-control (6)

_____ Guilt/responsibility (8)

2. Lack of Entitlement Score

Criterion B: Assumption of responsibility for meeting others' needs, to the exclusion of acknowledging one's own needs.

Which traits are demonstrated?

_____ Taking over responsibilities (9)

_____ Covering up (needs others to look okay) (10)

_____ Neglects own needs (11)

_____ Lack of self-confidence (12)

_____ Fear of being abandoned (13)

3. Borderline Score

Criterion C: Anxiety and boundary distortions around intimacy and separation.

Which borderline traits are demonstrated?

_____ Patterns of unstable and intense relationships (taken from more extensive psychosocial history)

_____ Often unaware of feelings (14)

_____ Feels smothered or overwhelmed by others (15)

_____ Black-and-white thinking (16)

_____ Wide swings in emotion (17)

_____ Enmeshment of identity in relationships (18)

_____ Thoughts of suicide (23)

4. Interpersonal Compulsions Score

Criterion D: Enmeshment in relationships with personality disordered, chemically dependent, and impulse disordered individuals.

Which interpersonal compulsions are demonstrated?

_____ Loyalty to, or repeated relationships with, people with personality, substance abuse, or impulse disorders (taken from psychosocial history)

_____ Rescuing/punishing (19)

5. Associated Symptoms Score

Criterion E: Exhibits at least three of the following: 1) excessive reliance on denial, 2) constriction of emotions (with or without dramatic outbursts), 3) depression, 4) hypervigilance, 5) compulsions, 6) anxiety, 7) alcohol or other drug abuse, 8) recurrent victim of physical or sexual abuse, 9) stress-related medical illnesses, 10) has remained in a primary relationship with an active alcoholic or other drug addict for at least two years without seeking outside support.

Which of the following associated symptoms are demonstrated?

_____ Constriction of emotions (20), with or without outbursts (21)

_____ Depression (22)

_____ Hypervigilance (24)

_____ Compulsions (25)

_____ Anxiety (26)

_____ Denial (27)

_____ Alcohol or other drug abuse (30)

_____ Recurrent victim of physical/sexual abuse (28)

_____ Stress-related medical illnesses (29)

_____ Two years without seeking help (31)

Obtaining Data on
Borderline Disturbances

Otto Kernberg's sequenced interventions, described in Chapter 6, provide a valuable tool for unveiling a client's borderline pathology. It is useful to briefly reiterate those here, with special emphasis on their role in the evaluation interview.

• *Clarification.* Kernberg's first level of intervention—"the exploration, with the patient, of all the elements in the information he has provided that are vague, unclear, puzzling, contradictory, or incomplete"[6]—is often useful, if not necessary, during the interview's initial efforts to outline the concrete details of the presenting problem. Including it at this early point helps you to quickly discover the most severe borderline pathology before proceeding with the evaluation.

• *Confrontation.* Kernberg's second level of intervention is the nonjudgmental presentation to the client of areas of information that seem contradictory or incongruous. There are often incongruities between the client's feelings and the material being presented during the family history segment of the evaluation interview. You can note these in gentle comments about feelings that exist just below the surface of how a client is presenting himself. When the client uses this confrontation as an invitation to express these feelings a bit more, it is clear evidence that he is reacting with trust, rather than mistrust, to your intervention.

• *Interpretation.* Kernberg's third level of intervention involves suggesting unconscious forces which may possibly explain the incongruities.

• *Transference interpretation.* This most powerful intervention involves the relationship between client and therapist in an interpretation.

By the end of the evaluation, you may be able to point out how the client's presenting problem has actually happened within the interview. For example, when the presenting problem includes difficulty with intimacy, it is especially useful to note how this difficulty was experienced in the interactions which have just transpired between yourself and the client. This is a particularly powerful way of activating subtle borderline characteristics, which can help you to judge whether the client is capable of embarking on a course of introspective psychotherapy.

Obtaining Data on Recovery

An excellent way to explore the concrete recovery work a client has done is to focus attention on some aspect of her compulsive behavior. A direct question about compulsions often reveals whether the client has even begun to apply the concept of recovery to this aspect of her behavior. It's remarkable to see how often ACAs have enough understanding of the CD model to label their compulsive eating, work activity, sexual behavior, etc. as an "addiction," but have not begun to take seriously the discipline of working the Twelve Steps.

When you focus attention on a compulsion, you attempt to move the client beyond a discussion of the target of her compulsive behavior. For example, instead of discussing the kind of food a compulsive overeater uses, or the types of sexual experiences the "sex addict" seeks, it is important to explore the *experience* of being compelled, without regard to the specific behaviors which resolve this feeling for the client. I have found it helpful to ask questions like these:

- Under what circumstances is the compulsion most likely to appear?
- What is your very first indication that the compulsion has begun?
- What internal sensations start to mount as you resist giving in to the compulsion?
- How do these feelings change once you have decided to give in to the compulsion, but before you have begun any compulsive behavior? (For example, on the way to the refrigerator, but before any food has been consumed.)
- What happens on a feeling level after the compulsive behavior begins?
- What happens on the feeling level after the compulsion has ebbed?

Also try to find out whether the client's reaction to the compulsion demonstrates a distorted relationship to willpower. You might ask questions like these:

- What strategies do you use for trying to free yourself from the compulsion, or to abstain from the compulsive behavior?
- What are you powerless over?
- When you fight the compulsion, what do you actually do inside?
- Why do you feel shame about having the compulsion (as opposed to feeling shame only upon acting on the compulsion)?
- Why do you think your willpower has *not* worked? What seems weak or broken in you?

When you ask this array of questions, you are not only evaluating whether the client has any answers, but also the degree to which these questions make sense to her. Many ACAs who have abstractly accepted the Twelve Step perspective are completely unwilling to integrate this framework into concrete action in their own personal lives. Exploring how they use recovery principles to counter an active compulsion is an excellent way to evaluate their stage of recovery.

ORGANIZING THE DATA

The last step before formulating the individualized treatment plan is to organize the data obtained from the evaluation interview. There are three reasons for using a standardized structure to record this information: 1) it acts as a final safeguard to guarantee the completeness of the data collected, 2) it facilitates the rational development of a treatment plan, and 3) it creates a valuable record which can be transmitted to subsequent therapists if the client is referred.

At Genesis, we use an evaluation form which organizes the data as follows:

1. *Identifying information* (name, address, phone, interviewer, date of interview)
2. *Presentation*

    a. current problems (concrete examples)
    b. reasons for seeking therapy (goals and expectations)
3. *History*
    a. family (including a genogram)
    b. personal (including the circumstances of leaving the family, up to the present time)
    c. chemical dependence history (including treatment, recovery, and current use)
      — family
      — personal
4. *Medical history* (including any current illnesses and medications being taken)
5. *Psychiatric history* (including hospitalizations, use of psychopharmacology, suicide attempts, previous therapy and diagnoses)
6. *Assessment of trauma*
    a. events (victim, observer, perpetrator, emotional, physical, sexual)
    b. effects on current life
      — re-experiencing the trauma
      — psychic numbing
      — hypervigilance/anxiety
      — survivor guilt/depression
7. *Co-dependence*
      — self-esteem based on willpower, denial, and control
      — excessively responsible
      — boundary distortions
      — relationship history (pattern of choices, enmeshment, and failure to seek outside help)
      — compulsive behavior (type, how disruptive, strategies for combating)
8. *MSE (Mental Status Exam)*, when appropriate
9. *Primary coping mechanisms*
10. *Highest level of functioning* (DSM-III-R)
11. *Recovery*
    a. history
    b. current support network

   c. stage
      — survival
      — without emerging awareness
      — with emerging awareness
      — reidentification
      — core issues
      — integration
12. *Impressions*
   a. DSM-III-R diagnosis
      — Axis I (symptom diagnosis)
      — Axis II (characterological diagnosis)
   b. Comments
13. *Recommendations*
   a. further evaluation (include previous therapists to be contacted)
   b. treatment plan (include referral, when appropriate)

FORMULATING
THE TREATMENT PLAN

The evaluation process concludes with formulating an individualized treatment plan and discussing it with the client, thereby initiating the plan. The range of possible recommendations is extremely wide: from no therapy required, to referral to Twelve Step programs, medical evaluation, education (reading, video, lectures, conferences), workshops or discussion groups to help personalize and integrate the education, supportive counseling (group or individual), couples or family therapy, behavior modification, experiential therapy (through workshops, retreats, gestalt/psychodrama groups, or Reichian therapy and other body work modalities) to increase access to feelings, pharmocotherapy, dynamic psychotherapy (group or individual) geared toward characterological change, or immediate hospitalization. Many of these modalities are not mutually exclusive and should be recommended in tandem, or in sequence.

The evaluation methods outlined in this book will enable you to gather enough information to move into treating the client.

However, it is not yet possible to discuss the process of formulating treatment plans. The final formulation of any treatment plan depends on a firm grasp of the powers and limitations of different treatment modalities. Volume two of *Evaluating and Treating Adult Children of Alcoholics* concentrates on appropriate treatment of the specific characteristics found in ACAs.

Appendix I

DRIVE THEORY
VERSUS TRAUMA THEORY

Psychological theories alert us to patterns in human behavior, but they also begin to *determine* what behavior we notice. This confuses many of the debates between competing theories of human psychopathology. Recent work with ACAs has contributed to a fruitful reopening of one such debate: that between drive theory and trauma theory.

Sigmund Freud defined many of the parameters for this debate. His initial work on the unconscious was undertaken primarily with hysterical patients, whose frequent reports of having been sexually molested as children led him to propose that their symptoms resulted from repressing memories of early sexual traumas. When he explored their stories further, however, he found that some patients were relating screen memories, not memories of actual events from their lives. Their unconscious had constructed memories which had *emotional* validity, but the events had never happened.

Screen memories interested Freud enough that he attempted to explain how and why the human mind would produce them. An answer seemed to lie in his new theories of childhood sexuality. Attributing sexual passions to children gave him a way to explain both the production of screen memories and later hysterical symptoms. The origins of both, he concluded, could be found in the strength of children's sexual drives (the Id), not in sexual traumas. Most of Freud's work emphasizes the role instinctual drives play in producing internal conflicts (neuroses) and personality styles (anal, oral, and phallic). Drive theory today continues to hold that the development of personality and human relationships is motivated and shaped by an interplay between the expression, and the defenses against expression, of innate drives.

For decades, Freud paid scant further attention to those hysterical patients who had experienced real sexual trauma. Not until 1920, with the publication of *Beyond the Pleasure Principle*, did he again see trauma as a major source of psychopathology. After the concept of neurosis (which specifically refers to the symptomatic results of internal conflict with one's drives) had become firmly entrenched, a debate developed regarding whether "traumatic neuroses" exist. In this debate, Freud believed that the damage done by trauma results primarily from the failure to dissipate the emotional reaction to it. Social situations may make the expression of this emotion impossible. Or the trauma may have concerned something so personally painful that it was volitionally repressed. Unfortunately, these formulations left lingering confusion regarding the relative roles played by an individual's unique disposition and the severity of the trauma.

The unresolved debate between drive and trauma theories has often lurked in the background of other debates in psychology. Most recently, the works of Kernberg and Kohut on narcissism and borderline personalities have embodied the same debate. Kernberg posits that these personality disorders form at a developmental stage before neuroses can develop, stemming from the failure to resolve conflicts between starkly elemental *drives*, and from the use of primitive defenses to cope with such conflicts. Kohut, on the other hand, argues that the emerging Self is a mental apparatus over and above traditionally recognized mental structures, such as id, ego, and superego, and *trauma* is primarily responsible for interrupting development of the Self. Psychopathology results when personality development must take place around these traumatic deficits. Again, the debate between the relative contributions of drive/conflict and trauma/deficit to personality pathology is unresolved. Kernberg and Kohut demonstrate the significantly different directions that can result on the basis of which side of the debate you incorporate into your overall psychological theories.

More recently, Alice Miller's[1] description of the long-term effects of growing up with narcissistically wounded parents has brought renewed attention to Freud's initial abandonment of the finding that many of his patients suffered actual sexual traumas during childhood. She argues that the practice of psychoanalysis has been too narrowly guided by drive theory, which has placed excessive emphasis on the internal impulses of a patient and often underestimated the degree of trauma suffered. Such an attitude runs the risk of inadvertently enhancing the effects of that trauma by perpetuating the family's failure to recognize its existence. Miller believes that by focusing attention during therapy on the details of the traumas, including the feelings it engendered, therapists offer clients the long needed opportunity to communicate their feelings, often for the first time, to a person who will respect and validate them.

As in any dialectic, the "truth" lies in a synthesis of both points of view. Our view must become more balanced. While instinctual feelings *drive* us through the maturation process, our developing Self *pulls* us along as well. When traumatic events, such as parental alcoholism, disrupt the development of this Self, our drives must interact with a false self built around deficits. Psychopathology stems both from deficits in the Self and from conflicts between drives that have come under the control of a false self. Both the drive theory and the trauma theory describe real phenomena, and our understanding of each unique individual patient will be enhanced by filtering their story through each of these lenses.

Perhaps much of the debate between these two theoretical perspectives can be circumvented by recognizing that individual clients defend against being overwhelmed in two general ways: repression/suppression, and dissociation. In his study of "Dissociation and Hypnotizability in PTSD," David Spiegel[2] suggests that repression/suppression defend against *painful memories*, while dissociation defends against *painful experiences*. He states that spontaneous reliving in post-traumatic stress disorder, rather than simply remembering a traumatic event, "owes some of its hypnotic-like . . . intensity to the fact that the patient was in a dissociated state during the trauma and is thus in a similar mental state while reliving it."[3]

Repression tends to occur when our experience of the actual world conflicts with our idealized image of how things should be. When no dissociation occurs during the unpleasant experience, repression provides some distance by creating an impermeable boundary between our unconscious and conscious worlds. Painful memories, and their associated feelings, become unavailable to our awareness; and this process itself lies outside our awareness. Repression creates a horizontal split within ourselves, prohibiting uncomfortable material from rising into consciousness. Suppression, on the other hand, is an imitation of repression. It stems from our conscious efforts to divert attention from painful material. Although we may be unaware that we are preventing attention from focusing on a particular topic, we do not lose awareness that the topic exists. An example of how suppression is experienced would be feeling sad, but having a clutching in the throat, and an inability to cry despite a professed desire to release the feeling.

Dissociation is a vertical split, dividing our experience into different "states of mind," and dividing our very sense of Self. In its most blatant forms, it contributes to multiple personalities. According to Spiegel, dissociation defends consciousness from the immediate experience of painful events, but "the process of dividing one's self becomes part of one's identity. . . ."[4] As dissociation becomes a more pervasively employed defense, people lose emotional attachment to facets of their Self. Portions of their own deep experience, which is the basis of any true autonomy and of critical importance to the life of one's true Self, are no longer identified with.

As stated earlier, such a split will not heal with time alone. To the extent that COAs dissociate during childhood in order to avoid being overwhelmed, they will probably continue using dissociation during adulthood. They will continue to go into a fog whenever they feel threatened. They will continue to take their identity from only a portion of who they are (e.g., the caretaker identity may result when an ACA has renounced his own normal need to be taken care of). The portion with which they fail to fully identify will be driven, harnessed, used, abused, and buffeted about by their "willpower run rampant." This can be done because the price being paid by the dissociated aspects of themselves is not fully felt.

Trauma tends to generate dissociation. Conflicting drives tend to generate repression/suppression. These different defenses need to be worked with differently. The relative balance between these two categories of defenses in an individual client is a rough estimate of the balance between the direct effects of trauma and the existence of drive conflict in that client.

Appendix II

DIFFERENTIATING CO-DEPENDENCE FROM SELF-DEFEATING PERSONALITY DISORDER

An appendix to DSM-III-R presents three diagnoses, including self-defeating personality disorder, to "facilitate further systematic clinical study and research." For coding purposes, self-defeating personality disorder is recorded under Personality Disorder Not Otherwise Specified (Self-Defeating Personality Disorder).

"The essential feature of this disorder is a pervasive pattern of self-defeating behavior,"[1] as indicated by at least five of the following:

1) chooses people and situations that lead to disappointment, failure, or mistreatment even when better options are clearly available

2) rejects or renders ineffective the attempts of others to help him or her

3) following positive personal events (e.g., new achievement), responds with depression, guilt, or behavior that produces pain (e.g., an accident)

4) incites angry or rejecting responses from others and then feels hurt, defeated, or humiliated (e.g., makes fun of spouse in public, provoking an angry retort, then feels devastated)

5) rejects opportunities for pleasure, or is reluctant to acknowledge enjoying himself or herself (despite having adequate social skills and the capacity for pleasure)

6) fails to accomplish tasks crucial to his or her personal objectives despite demonstrated ability to do so (e.g., helps fellow students write papers, but is unable to write his or her own)

7) is uninterested in or rejects people who consistently treat him or her well (e.g., is unattracted to caring sexual partners)

8) engages in excessive self-sacrifice that is unsolicited by the intended recipients of the sacrifice.[2]

These criteria have enough in common with the criteria presented for co-dependence (see Chapter 4) that it is legitimate to ask whether the concept of co-dependence might not be handled best by subsuming it under the diagnosis of self-defeating personality disorder. The argument in favor of this is strengthened by three points self-defeating personality disorder has in common with co-dependence: (1) People are predisposed to both co-dependence and self-defeating personality disorder by "having been physically, sexually, or psychologically abused as a child or having been in a family in which there was abuse of a spouse."[3] (2) Dysthymia (i.e., low-grade, chronic depression) and suicide are complications of both. And (3) both are described as being one of the more common personality disorders.

My reluctance to place co-dependence under the category of self-defeating personality disorder is because, first, I object to the name itself. But, on a much deeper level, it is the underlying implications of this name which feel alien to the concept of co-dependence, as I understand it. DSM-III-R acknowledges that the traditional concept of masochism is the source for self-defeating personality disorder, but states that the name change was made specifically to "avoid the historic association of the term 'masochism' with older psychoanalytic views of female sexuality and the implication that a person with the disorder derives unconscious pleasure from suffering."[4] Perhaps they have avoided this historical association, but I do not believe that the criteria have significantly moved beyond the assumption that the actual underlying *motivation* within people is to prolong their painful sense of defeat and failure.

Imputing the motive of defeating one's efforts to achieve a more fulfilling life misses a central point contained in the diagnosis of co-dependence, as I have defined it. The motive of a co-dependent is to force strategies based on a distorted relationship to willpower to be successful. The pain and defeat are not the goal; they are the byproduct of being devoted to a flawed strategy. The devotion to such a strategy comes from a sincere effort to redeem oneself in the noblest way possible (i.e., through self-control). This underlying and central dynamic is very different from the motives which I believe are still contained in self-defeating personality disorder, despite the abandoning of "masochism" as the name for this disorder.

Appendix III

STRUCTURED INTERVIEW FOR ADULT CO-DEPENDENCE

I. Patient Identification

Mr., Mrs., Miss, Ms.: _____ Home Phone:_____

Address: _____ Work Phone:_____

Age:_____ Birth Date:_____ Place of Birth:_____

II. Current Family Information

Current status: Never married___Separated ___Widowed ___

Currently married ___Divorced ___Live-in _____

No. of marriages:_____

Explain circumstances leading to end of marriage:_____

_____

_____

Children:

_____   _____   _____
Name   Age

_____   _____   _____

_____   _____   _____

_____   _____   _____

Describe current living constellation:_____

_____

_____

_____

III. Educational Background

Highest grade completed:_____

Any problems in school?_____

IV. Religious Background

Religious affiliations: _____

How active? _____

V. Employment & Military

Occupation at present time: _____ Dates:_____

Other employment (past 10 yrs.)   Dates   Reasons for leaving

_____   _____   _____

_____   _____   _____

_____   _____   _____

Military service: _____ Dates: _____

   Branch: _____ Disabilities: _____

Any current work-related problems? _____

VI. Economic Information

Level of income (including spouse): $10,000—$20,000

No. of cars owned: _____ $20,000—$40,000

Own or rent home? _____ $40,000—$60,000

                                      Above $60,000

Major outstanding debts: _____

_____

Bankruptcies or loss of credit: _____

_____

VII. Medical Information

Serious or long-term childhood illnesses: _____

_____

Serious or long-term adulthood illnesses: _____

_____

Surgery: _____

Current medical problems:

_____

Medications: _____

Name	Dose	Frequency
_____	_____	_____
_____	_____	_____
_____	_____	_____

History of the following:

_____ High blood pressure   _____ Migraines

_____ Stroke   _____ Heart attack

_____ Peptic ulcers   _____ Gastritis

_____ Colitis   _____ Indigestion, diarrhea, constipation

_____ Asthma   _____ Hyperventilation

_____ Cancer   _____ Rheumatoid arthritis

_____ Allergies   _____ Dermatitis

_____ Insomnia   _____ Eating disorder

_____ Menstrual irregularities   _____ Psychiatric illnesses

VIII. **Family History**

Mother's name:_____ Age:_____

Major illnesses: _____

_____

Describe:_____

Father's name:_____ Age:_____

Major illnesses: _____

_____

Describe:_____

Describe their relationship:_____

_____

Brothers and sisters (Place self below, as well)

_____ Age:_____

_____ Age:_____

_____ Age:_____

_____ Age:_____

_____ Age:_____

The major problems in my family were:_____

_____

_____

_____

_____

Evidence of psychiatric illnesses:_____

_____

_____

Evidence of child abuse:_____

Evidence of sexual abuse:_____

IX. Co-Dependence

1. Do you worry excessively about any member of your

   family?_____

   Why?_____

2. Are you ever embarrassed by another family member's

   behavior?_____

   _____

3. Do you feel personally less worthwhile because of

   another family member's behavior? _____

   _____

4. Are you perfectionist about yourself?_____

_____

5. Have you tried to control family members?_____

_____

6. Do you take pride in your self-control?_____

_____

7. Do you often feel personally inadequate?_____

_____

8. Do you feel guilty or responsible for someone else's

   behavior?_____

_____

9. Have you taken over family responsibilities which you

   do not believe should be yours?_____

_____

10. Have you ever lied to cover up someone else's

    misbehavior?_____

_____

    Or covered up?_____

_____

11. Do you often meet other people's needs while you

neglect your own?_____

_____

12. Do you feel self-confident in intimate situations?_____

_____

13. Are you afraid that others might leave you?_____

_____

14. Are you often unaware of what you are feeling?_____

_____

15. Does it feel like you start to get smothered or

overwhelmed by people close to you?_____

_____

16. Do you tend to see things as either black or white?_____

_____

17. Do your emotions get onto a roller coaster, with quick

ups and downs?_____

_____

18. Do you only feel complete when you are in a

relationship/or lose your identity in relationships?_____

_____

19. Do you often rescue or punish other people?_____

_____

20. Are you often afraid to let your feelings come out freely?

_____

21. Do you have dramatic emotional outbursts?_____

_____

22. Are you often depressed?_____

_____

23. Have you been suicidal?_____

_____

24. Is it hard to let down your guard without feeling a

catastrophe might happen?_____

_____

25. Do you have any compulsions? (Eating, work, TV, sex) ____

_____

26. Do you often feel anxious? _____

_____

27. Have you tried to ignore problems, hoping they will get

better on their own?_____

_____

28. Have you been a victim of physical or sexual abuse as

    an adult?_____

    _____

29. Have you ever thought of going to Al Anon/AA?_____

    _____

30. Have you ever gone? _____

    _____

31. Has anyone in your family ever been in treatment for

    alcohol or other drug dependence?_____

    Explain:_____

    _____

    _____

X. **Family Alcohol/Drug History**

What were your family of origin's general attitudes about

drinking and other drug use? _____

_____

Did any of your grandparents abuse alcohol/drugs?_____

_____

What was your father's alcohol/drug use? _____

_____

Your mother's?_____

_____

Your brothers' and sisters'?_____

_____

Did any distant relatives abuse alcohol/drugs?_____

_____

What is your spouse's alcohol/drug use like?_____

_____

Your children's alcohol/drug use like? _____

_____

Describe your own alcohol/drug use: _____

_____

Do you ever worry that your use might be excessive?

Yes _____ No _____

Explain:_____

REFERENCES

INTRODUCTION

1. Hindman, M. "Children of Alcoholic Parents," *Alcohol, Health and Reasearch World NIAAA*, 1975-6: 2-6. NIAAA's estimate is fifteen years old, and therefore almost certainly low. Nevertheless, 28 million people is already a huge number, capable of forming an unbroken line from New York City, to Seattle, to Los Angeles, and back to New York City. A more accurate assessment of the number of COAs today is clearly needed.

CHAPTER 1

1. Theodore Millon, *Disorders of Personality: DSM-III, Axis II* (New York: John Wiley and Sons, Inc., 1981), p. 93.
2. *Diagnostic and Statistical Manual of Mental Disorders*, Third Edition, Revised (Washington, D.C.: American Psychiatric Association, 1987). Referred to as DSM-III-R.

CHAPTER 2

1. N.S. Cotton, "The Familial Incidence of Alcoholism: A Review," *Journal of Studies in Alcoholism* 40:89-116, 1979.
2. Lennart Kaij, *Alcoholism in Twins. Studies on the Etiology and Sequels of Abuse of Alcohol* (Stockholm: Alonquist and Winkell Publishers, 1960).
3. Marc Schuckit, "Twin Studies on substance abuse: An overview," in Gedda, Parisi and Nance, eds., *Twin Research: 3. Epidemiological and Clinical Studies* (New York: Alan R. Liss, Inc., 1981).

4. Donald Goodwin, *Is Alcoholism Hereditary?* (New York: Oxford University Press, 1976).

5. Ting-Kai Li *et al.*, "Progress toward a voluntary oral consumption model of alcoholism," *Drug and Alcohol Dependence* 4(1-2):45-60, 1979; and Ting-Kai Li, *Alcohol and Alcoholism*, supplement 1:91-96, 1987.

6. Marc Schuckit, "Genetics and the Risk for Alcoholism," *Journal of the American Medical Association*, Vol. 254, No. 18:2614-2617, November 8, 1985.

7. Henri Begleiter, "Event-related brain potentials in boys at risk for alcoholism," *Science*, 225:1493-1496, 1984.

8. Blum, *et al.*, "Allelic Association of Human Dopamine D2 Receptor Gene in Alcoholism," *Journal of the American Medical Association*, Vol. 263, No. 15:2055-2060, April 18, 1990.

9. The speed with which blackouts begin and end is comparable to events in the brain such as the beginning and ending of REM sleep, which depends on the switching on and off of brain impulses from a single body of nerve cells. Research might do best to focus on the relationship of the anterior septal nuclei, which are responsible for creating rhythmic (beta) electrical waves in the hippocampus. Without the organizing influence of beta waves, the hippocampus becomes ineffective in boosting immediate experience into the realm of memory [Richard Thompson *et al.*, "Hippocampal Substrate of Classical Conditioning," *Physiological Psychology*, Vol. 8, No. 2:262-279]. Such a mechanism for blackouts amounts to the existence of a functional, reversible Korsakoff's syndrome. When the pathways providing beta waves to the hippocampus are destroyed, as the midline infarcts of Korsakoff's would do, the blackout becomes permanent.

10. Isabel Birnbaum, "Study links women's social drinking with sober-state mood disturbances," *Medical World News—Psychiatry Edition*, p. 6, May 31, 1984.

11. E. M. Jellinek, "Phases of Alcohol Addiction," *Quarterly Journal of Studies on Alcoholism*, Vol. 13, No. 4:673-684, December 1952.

12. Jerome D. Levin, *Treatment of Alcoholism and Other Addictions: A Self-Psychology Approach* (Northvale, NJ: Jason Aronson Inc., 1987), p. 62.

13. George Vaillant, *Adaptation to Life* (Boston: Little, Brown and Company, 1977), p. 83.

14. Levin, pp. 50-60.

15. *Alcoholics Anonymous*, Third Edition (Alcoholics Anonymous World Services, Inc., 1976), p. 62.

16. Gregory Bateson, "The Cybernetics of `Self': A Theory of Alcoholism," *Psychiatry*, Vol. 34, No. 1:1-18, 1971.

17. Bateson, p. 8.

18. Levin, p. 229.

19. Levin, p. 4.

20. Levin, p. 5.

21. Sigmund Freud, "On Narcissism: An Introduction (1914)," *General Psychological Theory* (New York: Collier Books, 1963), p. 70.

22. Levin, p. 63.

23. Sharon Wegscheider, *Another Chance* (Palo Alto, CA: Science and Behavior Books, 1981), pp. 84-88.

24. Claudia Black, *It Will Never Happen To Me,* (Denver: M.A.C, 1981), pp. 53-64.

25. The table and descriptions are modified from Timmen L. Cermak, M.D., *A Time to Heal* (Los Angeles: Jeremy P. Tarcher, Inc., 1988).

26. Bruno Bettelheim, "Punishment versus Discipline," *The Atlantic Monthly,* pp. 51-59, November 1985.

27. Peter Steinglass, *et al., The Alcoholic Family* (New York: Basic Books, Inc., 1987).

28. Steinglass, p. 9.

29. Whereas many authors speak of the chaos and uncertainty within alcoholic homes, Steinglass is struck by the remarkable intolerance for uncertainty and the stereotyped nature of behavior during the intoxicated state. His view may stem in part from the fact that more unstable, chaotic families are unlikely to become effective research subjects. The discrepancy may also stem from the difference between behavioral and subjective perspectives. The card-sorting experiment reveals how the family system generated stereotyped behavior among individual members during the second sorting trial, when everyone was in communication. Uncertainty was decreased by conforming. However, the behavioral response creating more certainty may well have been motivated by an underlying subjective sense of how close family life was to flying out of control. People's subjective experience (e.g., feelings of chaos) can differ from their overt behavior (e.g., stereotypic and predictable, in an effort to contain the inner sense of chaos).

30. Steinglass, p. 223.

31. Steinglass, p. 226.

32. *Alcoholics Anonymous,* pp. 122-134.

33. Stephanie Brown, *Treating The Alcoholic: A Developmental Model of Recovery* (New York: John Wiley and Sons, Inc., 1985), pp. 32-37.

34. Brown, p. 35.

35. Brown, p. 37.

36. Levin, p. 1.

CHAPTER 3

1. Mardi Horowitz, M.D., *Stress Response Syndromes* (Northvale, NJ: Jason Aronson Inc., 1976), p. 56.

2. Horowitz, pp. 1-5.

3. George Vaillant, *The Natural History of Alcoholism* (Cambridge, MA: Harvard University Press, 1983), p. 20. I feel comfortable substituting the word "stress" for "sadism" because I am relatively sure that Vaillant doesn't mean to imply that alcoholics obtain sexual pleasure from inflicting suffering—the classic meaning of "sadism."

4. *Diagnostic and Statistical Manual of Mental Disorders* [DSM-III-R], Third Edition, Revised (Washington, D.C.: American Psychiatric Association, 1987), p. 11.

5. NACoA's charter statement has since been revised to read: "We define children of alcoholics as those people who have been impacted by the alcoholism or other drug dependence of a parent, or another adult filling the parental role. This results in a recognizable, diagnosable and treatable condition which can be passed from one generation to the next."

6. C.B. Scrignar, M.D., "Post-Traumatic Stress Disorder," *The Psychiatric Times*, p. 8, July 1987.

7. DSM-III-R, p. 247.

8. DSM-III-R, p. 250.

9. Harry A. Wilmer, M.D., Ph.D., "Post-Traumatic Stress Disorder," *Psychiatric Annals*, Vol. 12, Number 11, November 1982, pp. 995-1003.

10. DSM-III-R, p. 250.

11. DSM-III-R, p. 250.

12. Lenore Terr, M.D., "Chowchilla Revisited: The Effects of Psychic Trauma Four Years After a School-Bus Kidnapping," *Am. J. Psychiatry*, Vol. 140, No. 12:1543-1550, December 1983.

13. Terr, p. 1547.

14. Bessel van der Kolk, M.D., "Trauma and Psychiatric Illness," *The Psychiatric Times*, p. 6, July 1987.

15. Spencer Eth and Robert Pynoos, *Post-Traumatic Stress Disorder in Children* (Washington, D.C.: American Psychiatric Press, Inc., 1985), p. 24.

16. National Committee for the Prevention of Child Abuse Factsheet.

17. James Garbarino, Edna Guttman, and Janis Wilson Seeley, *The Psychologically Battered Child* (San Francisco: Jossey-Bass Publishers, 1986), p. 8.

18. Garbarino, pp. 57-59.

19. Garbarino, pp. 11-12.

CHAPTER 4

1. James Masterson, M.D., *The Narcissistic and Borderline Disorders: An Integrated Developmental Approach* (New York: Brunner/Mazel, Inc., 1981), p. 7.

2. Timmen L. Cermak, M.D., *Diagnosing and Treating Co-dependence* (Minneapolis: Johnson Institute, 1986), pp. 2-4.

3. Charles Alexander, "The Definition of Co-dependence," panel at the San Francisco Conference on Children of Alcoholics, The National Association for Children of Alcoholics, July 11, 1985.

4. See Leonard Horowitz, "Projective Identification in Dyads and Groups," *International Journal of Group Psychotherapy* 33:259-279, 1983.

5. "Diagnostic Criteria for Codependency," *Journal of Psychoactive Drugs*, Vol. 18, No. 1:15-20, January-March 1986, and Cermak, *Diagnosing and Treating Co-dependence*, p. 11.

6. Sigmund Freud, "On Narcissism: An Introduction (1914)," *General Psychological Theory* (New York: Collier Books, 1963), p. 70.

7. Freud, p. 72.

8. Alice Miller, *The Drama of the Gifted Child* (New York: Basic Books, Inc./Harper Colophon Books, 1979). Despite its inattention to questions of alcoholism, this book remains one of the most valuable for anyone treating ACAs.

9. *Alcoholics Anonymous*, Third Edition (Alcoholics Anonymous World Services, Inc., 1976), p. 62.

10. Vernon Johnson, *I'll Quit Tomorrow* (New York: Harper and Row, 1973), p. 30.

11. *Diagnostic and Statistical Manual of Mental Disorders* [DSM-III-R], Third Edition, Revised (Washington, D.C.: American Psychiatric Association, 1987), p. 305.

12. DSM-III-R, p. 305.

13. Cermak, *Diagnosing and Treating Co-dependence*, pp. 11-35.

14. DSM-III-R, p. 337.

15. An argument could be made that co-dependence corresponds to Meissner's description of the "needy, clinging and demanding" variety of narcissism, quoted by James Masterson, from a presentation at American Psychiatric Association, May 1979; see James Masterson, *The Narcissistic and Borderline Disorders: An Integrated Developmental Approach* (New York: Brunner/Mazel Publishers, 1981), p. 8.

16. Jael Greenleaf, "Co-alcoholic: Para-alcoholic," Los Angeles: The 361 Foundation, 1981.

17. Terrance Gorski (personal communication).

18. Masterson, *The Narcissistic and Borderline Disorders*.

19. Masterson, p. 7.

20. Masterson, pp. 13, 22-23.

21. Heinz Kohut, *The Analysis of the Self* (Madison, CT: International Universities Press, 1971), pp. 25-28.

22. Miller, pp. 34-35.

23. Masterson states that the child's autonomy does not resonate "with the projections the mother had placed on the child in order to shape him

or her for use as an object essential to maintain her own intrapsychic equilibrium." See Masterson, pp. 22-23.

24. Miller, p. 85.

25. Kohut, p. 27.

26. Phillip S. Freeman and John G. Gunderson, "Treatment of Personality Disorders," *Psychiatric Annals*, Vol. 19, Number 3:150, March 1989.

27. Kohut, p. 28.

28. Margaret Mahler, Fred Pine, and Anni Bergman, *The Psychological Birth of the Human Infant* (New York: Basic Books, 1975), pp. 43-64.

29. It is perhaps symptomatic of Western society's narrow focus on individualism as the ultimate goal that we have been more cognizant of the line of development, both in its healthy and pathologic manifestations, stemming from narcissistic needs. This is supported by the work of Takeo Doi, who has explored the Japanese comfort with dependence and the desire to be passively loved *(amae)*, which is seen as a basic human need long neglected in the Western World. See Takeo Doi, *The Anatomy of Dependence* (Tokyo: Kodansha International Ltd., through New York: Harper and Row, 1973), p. 29. The affirmative attitude toward dependence in Japan diffuses these feelings throughout adult life, shaping individuals' perceptions of reality. Clearly, if self-reliance were not accepted so unthinkingly as the goal of maturation (and of therapy) in our society, many of our reactions to the basic echoistic impulse would be different. Such cross-cultural considerations lie outside the scope of this book, but are ultimately important to consider.

30. Sheldon Cashdan, *Object Relations Therapy* (New York: W.W. Norton & Company, 1988), pp. 10-11.

31. Daniel Stern, *The Interpersonal World of the Infant* (New York: Basic Books, 1985), pp. 138-161.

32. Stern makes a valuable distinction between attuning to "categorical" and "vitality" affects. Categorical affects are those emotions for which we have simple words (e.g., sadness, joy, anger), and which can be identified on the faces of other mammals. Vitality affects are the energetic, kinetic aspects of our feeling experience (e.g., surging, fading, bursting). Focused attention involves being attuned to both, which makes successful interaction difficult, if not impossible, for parents to simulate cognitively (i.e., paying enough attention to merely label a child's feelings verbally).

33. Paul Ekman *et al.*, "Smiles When Lying," *Journal of Personality and Social Psychology*, Vol. 54, No. 3:414-420.

34. Kohut, p. 26.

35. George Vaillant, *Adaptation to Life* (Boston: Little, Brown and Company, 1977), p. 83.

36. Vaillant, p. 160.

37. Cermak, *Diagnosing and Treating Co-dependence*, p. 11.

38. Timmen Cermak, *A Time to Heal* (Los Angeles: Jeremy P. Tarcher, Inc., 1988), pp. 115-119.

39. Kohut, p. 26.

CHAPTER 5

1. Peter Steinglass, *et al.*, *The Alcoholic Family* (New York: Basic Books, 1987).

2. Stephanie Brown, *Treating the Alcoholic* (New York: John Wiley and Sons, Inc., 1985), pp. 83-88.

3. Alice Miller, *The Drama of the Gifted Child* (New York: Basic Books, Inc./Harper Colophon Books, 1979), p. 17.

4. Miller, p. 10.

5. Franz Alexander introduced this concept in 1946 when he stated that the basic principle of treatment is "to expose the patient, under more favorable circumstances, to emotional situations which he could not handle in the past. The patient, in order to be helped, must undergo a corrective emotional experience suitable to repair the traumatic influence of previous experience." See F. Alexander and T. French, *Psychoanalytic Therapy: Principles and Application* (New York: Ronald Press, 1946), p. 66.

6. Irvin Yalom, *The Theory and Practice of Group Psychotherapy* (New York: Basic Books, Inc., 1975), p. 28.

7. Madeleine Davis and David Wallbridge, *Boundary and Space: An Introduction to the Work of D.W. Winnicott* (London: H. Karnac Ltd., 1981), pp. 24 and 38.

8. Barbara L. Wood, *Children of Alcoholism: The Struggle for Self and Intimacy in Adult Life* (New York: New York University Press, 1987), p. 41.

9. Wood, p. 33.

10. Heinz Kohut, as quoted in Wood, p. 33.

11. Heinz Kohut, *How Does Analysis Cure?* (Chicago: The University of Chicago Press, 1984), p. 24.

CHAPTER 6

1. Theodore Millon, *Disorders of Personality (DSM-III: Axis II)* (New York: John Wiley and Sons, Inc., 1981), p. 331.

2. Otto Kernberg, *Severe Personality Disorders* (New Haven, CT: Yale University Press, 1984), p. 5.

3. Millon, p. 347.

4. Summarized in Millon, p. 347. See also John Gunderson, "Characteristics of Borderlines," in Peter Hartcollis (ed.), *Borderline Personality Disorders* (New York: International Universities Press, 1977), pp. 173-192;

and John Gunderson and Margaret Singer, "Defining Borderline Patients: An Overview," *American Journal of Psychiatry*, 132:1-10, 1975.

5. *Diagnostic and Statistical Manual of Mental Disorders* [DSM-III-R], Third Edition, Revised (Washington, D.C.: American Psychiatric Association, 1987), p. 347.

6. Kernberg, p. 251.

7. Margaret Mahler, Fred Pine, and Anni Bergman, *The Psychological Birth of the Human Infant* (New York: Basic Books, 1975), p. 229.

8. Judith Herman and Bessel van der Kolk, "Traumatic Antecedents of Borderline Personality Disorder," in Bessel van der Kold, *Psychological Trauma* (Washington, D.C.: American Psychiatric Press, Inc., 1987).

9. Masterson, p. 132.

10. Masterson, p. 151.

11. Kernberg, pp. 3-51.

12. Kernberg, p. 8.

13. Kernberg, p. 8

14. Kernberg, pp. 8-9.

15. Kernberg, p. 9.

16. Kernberg, p. 9.

17. Kernberg, p. 9.

CHAPTER 7

1. *Alcoholics Anonymous*, Third Edition (Alcoholics Anonymous World Services, Inc., 1976), p. xiii.

2. E. M. Jellinek, "Phases of Alcohol Addiction," *Quarterly Journal of Studies on Alcohol*, Vol. 13, No. 4:673-684, December 1952.

3. Stephanie Brown, *Treating the Alcoholic* (New York: John Wiley and Sons, Inc., 1985), pp. 55-72.

4. Brown, p. 62.

5. Gregory Bateson, "The Cybernetics of `Self': A Theory of Alcoholism," *Psychiatry*, Vol. 34, No. 1:1-18, 1971.

6. Bateson, p. 321.

7. Brown, p. 37.

8. Herb Gravitz and Julie Bowden, *Guide to Recovery* (Holmes Beach, FL: Learning Publications, Inc., 1985), reprinted as *Recovery: A Guide for Children of Alcoholics* (New York: Simon and Schuster, 1987).

9. Stephanie Brown, *Treating Adult Children of Alcoholics* (New York: John Wiley and Sons, Inc., 1988), pp. 210-212.

10. The discussion of the Twelve Steps and Twelve Traditions is taken from Marc Galanter, ed., *Recent Developments in Alcoholism*, Volume 7 (New York: Plenum Publishing Corp., 1989), "Alanon and Recovery," pp. 91-104.

11. For a complete discussion of this topic, see Ernest Kurtz, *Not-God: A History of Alcoholics Anonymous* (Center City, MN: Hazelden, 1979).

CHAPTER 8

1. Spencer Eth and Robert Pynoos (eds.), *Post-Traumatic Stress Disorder in Children* (Washington, D.C.: American Psychiatric Press, Inc.. 1985), pp. 23-24.
2. James Masterson, M.D., *The Narcissistic and Borderline Disorders: An Integrated Developmental Approach* (New York: Brunner/Mazel, Inc., 1981), pp. 182-193.
3. Masterson, p. 187.
4. Eth and Pynoos, p. 173.
5. Timmen L. Cermak, M.D., *Diagnosing and Treating Co-dependence* (Minneapolis: Johnson Institute, 1986), p. 11.
6. Otto Kernberg, *Severe Personality Disorders* (New Haven, CT: Yale University Press, 1984), p. 8.

APPENDIX I

1. Alice Miller, *The Drama of the Gifted Child* (New York: Basic Books, Inc./Harper Colophon Books, 1979).
2. David Spiegel, Thurman Hunt, and Harvey Dondershine, "Dissociation and Hypnotizability in Posttraumatic Stress Disorder," *American Journal of Psychiatry*, Vol. 145. No. 3:301-305, March 1988.
3. Spiegel, p. 301.
4. Spiegel, p. 304.

APPENDIX II

1. *Diagnostic and Statistical Manual of Mental Disorders* [DSM-III-R], Third Edition, Revised (Washington, D.C.: American Psychiatric Association, 1987), p. 371.
2. DSM-III-R, pp. 373-374.
3. DSM-III-R, p. 373.
4. DSM-III-R, p. 371.

BIBLIOGRAPHY

BOOKS—PROFESSIONAL

———— *Alcoholics Anonymous* (New York: Alcoholics Anonymous World Services, Inc., 1976).

Brown, Stephanie, *Treating the Alcoholic* (New York: John Wiley and Sons, Inc., 1985).

Brown, Stephanie, *Treating Adult Children of Alcoholics* (New York: John Wiley and Sons, Inc., 1988).

Cermak, Timmen, *Diagnosing and Treating Co-dependence* (Minneapolis: Johnson Institute, 1986).

Cashdan, Sheldon, *Object Relations Therapy* (New York: W.W. Norton & Company, 1988).

Cork, Margaret, *The Forgotten Children* (Ontario, Canada: General Publishing Company, 1969).

———— *Diagnostic and Statistical Manual of Mental Disorders* [DSM-III-R] (Washington, D.C.: American Psychiatric Association, 1987).

Doi, Takeo, *The Anatomy of Dependence* (Tokyo: Kodansha International Ltd., 1971, distributed by New York: Harper and Row).

Eth, Spencer and Robert Pynoos, *Post-Traumatic Stress Disorder in Children* (Washington, D.C.: American Psychiatric Press, Inc., 1985).

Garbarino, James, Edna Guttman, and Janis Wilson Seeley, *The Psychologically Battered Child* (San Francisco: Jossey-Bass Publishers, 1986).

Horowitz, Mardi, *Stress Response Syndromes* (Northvale, NJ: Jason Aronson Inc., 1976).

Johnson, Vernon, *Intervention: How to Help Someone Who Doesn't Want Help* (Minneapolis: Johnson Institute, 1986).

Kohut, Heinz, *The Analysis of the Self* (Madison, CT: International Universities Press, 1971).

Levin, Jerome, *Treatment of Alcoholism and Other Addictions: A Self-Psychology Approach* (Northvale, NJ: Jason Aronson Inc., 1987).

261

Mahler, Margaret, Fred Pine, and Anni Bergman, *The Psychological Birth of the Human Infant* (New York: Basic Books, 1975).

Masterson, James, *The Narcissistic and Borderline Disorders: An Integrated Developmental Approach* (New York: Brunner/Mazel, Inc., 1981).

Miller, Alice, *The Drama of the Gifted Child* (New York: Basic Books, Inc./ Harper Colophon Books, 1979).

Millon, Theodore, *Disorders of Personality: DSM-III, Axis II* (New York: John Wiley and Sons, Inc., 1981).

Reich, Wilhelm, *Character Analysis* (New York: Farrar, Straus & Giroux, 1949).

Schwartz, Harvey, ed., *Psychotherapy of the Combat Veteran* (New York: Spectrum Publications, 1984).

Steinglass, Peter, *et al.*, *The Alcoholic Family* (New York: Basic Books, Inc., 1987).

Stern, Daniel, *The Interpersonal World of the Infant* (New York: Basic Books, 1985).

Vaillant, George, *Adaptation to Life* (Boston: Little, Brown and Company, 1977).

Vaillant, George, *The Natural History of Alcoholism* (Cambridge, MA: Harvard University Press, 1983).

van der Kolk, Bessel, *Psychological Trauma* (Washington, D.C.: American Psychiatric Press, 1987).

Vannicelli, Marsha, *Group Psychotherapy with Adult Children of Alcoholics* (New York: Guilford Press, 1989).

Wood, Barbara, *Children of Alcoholism: The Struggle for Self and Intimacy in Adult Life* (New York: New York University Press, 1987).

Yalom, Irvin, *The Theory and Practice of Group Psychotherapy* (New York: Basic Books, Inc., 1975).

BOOKS—GENERAL PUBLIC

Black, Claudia, *It Will Never Happen To Me* (New York: Ballantine, 1987).

Bowden, Julie and Herb Gravitz, *Genesis: Spirituality in Recovery from Childhood Traumas* (Pompano Beach, FL: Health Communications, 1988).

Cermak, Timmen, *A Primer on Adult Children of Alcoholics* (Pompano Beach, FL: Health Communications, 1985).

Cermak, Timmen, *A Time to Heal* (Los Angeles: Jeremy P. Tarcher, Inc., 1988).

Gravitz, Herb and Julie Bowden, *Recovery: A Guide for Children of Alcoholics* (New York: Simon and Schuster, 1987).

Johnson, Vernon, *I'll Quit Tomorrow* (New York: Harper and Row, 1973).

Mellody, Pia, *Facing Co-dependency* (New York: Harper and Row, 1989).

Wegscheider, Sharon, *Another Chance: Hope and Health for the Alcoholic Family* (Palo Alto, CA: Science and Behavior Books, 1981).

INDEX

When the Johnson Institute first opened its doors in 1966, few people knew or believed that alcoholism was a disease. Fewer still thought that anything could be done to help the chemically dependent person other than wait for him or her to "hit bottom" and then pick up the pieces.

We've spent over twenty years spreading the good news that chemical dependence is a *treatable* disease. Through our publications, films, video and audio cassettes, and our training and consultation services, we've given hope and help to hundreds of thousands of people across the country and around the world. The intervention and treatment methods we've pioneered have restored shattered careers, healed relationships with co-workers and friends, saved lives, and brought families back together.

Today the Johnson Institute is an internationally recognized leader in the field of chemical dependence intervention, treatment, and recovery. Individuals, organizations, and businesses, large and small, rely on us to provide them with the tools they need. Schools, universities, hospitals, treatment centers, and other health care agencies look to us for experience, expertise, innovation, and results. With care, compassion, and commitment, we will continue to reach out to chemically dependent persons, their families, and the professionals who serve them.

To find out more about us, write or call:

The Johnson Institute
7151 Metro Boulevard
Minneapolis, MN 55439-2122
1-800-231-5165
In MN: 1-800-247-0484
or (612) 944-0511
In CAN: 1-800-447-6660

Need a copy for a friend? You may order directly.

EVALUATING AND TREATING
ADULT CHILDREN OF ALCOHOLICS
Volume One: EVALUATION
Volume Two: TREATMENT
Timmen L. Cermak, M.D.
A Johnson Institute Professional Series Book
$21.95 each volume; $37.95 set

Order Form

Please send ___ copy (copies) of **VOLUME ONE: EVALUATION** and/or ___ copy (copies) of **VOLUME TWO: TREATMENT**. Price $21.95 each or $37.95 set. Please add $3.00 shipping for the first book and $1.25 for each additional copy.

Name (please print)

Address

City/State/Zip

Attention

Please note that orders under $75.00 must be prepaid.

If paying by credit card, please complete the following:

☐ Bill the full payment to my credit card.

☐ VISA ☐ MasterCard ☐ American Express

Credit card number: _____

For MASTERCARD
Write the 4 digits below the account number: _____

Expiration date: _____

Signature on card: _____

For faster service, call our Order Department TOLL-FREE:
1-800-231-5165
In Minnesota call:
1-800-247-0484
or **(612) 944-0511**
In Canada call:
1-800-447-6660

Return this order form to:
The Johnson Institute
7151 Metro Boulevard
Minneapolis, MN 55439-2122
Ship to (if different from above):

Name (please print)

Address

City/State/Zip